THE BRIARPATCH BOOK

THE BRIARPATCH BOOK

experiences in right livelihood and simple living

from the Briarpatch Community

A NEW GLIDE/REED BOOK

San Francisco   *Los Angeles*

Copyright ©1978 by Briarpatch. All rights reserved.

First printing: July 1978

Library of Congress Cataloging in Publication Data

Main entry under title:

The Briarpatch book.

A collection of 1st 8 issues of the Briarpatch review.
1. Small business—Management—Addresses, essays, lectures.
HD69.S6B73   658'.022   78-5990
ISBN 0-912078-63-4
ISBN 0-912078-60-X pbk.

New Glide Publications participates in the Cataloging in Publication Program of the Library of Congress. However, in our opinion, the data provided us for this book by CIP does not adequately nor accurately reflect its scope and content. Therefore, we are offering our librarian/users the choice between LC's treatment and an Alternative CIP prepared by Sanford Berman, Head Cataloger at Hennepin County Library, Edina, Minnesota.

Alternative Cataloging-In-Publication

The Briarpatch book. New Glide Publications; Reed Books, 1978.

Reprint of Briarpatch review: a journal of right livelihood & simple living, issues 1-8, Spring 1975-Autumn 1977.

1. Briarpatch Network. 2. Small business. 3. Skill-sharing. 4. Alternative economics. 5. Alternative life-styles. 6. Appropriate technology. I. New Glide Publications. II. Reed Books. III. Title: Briarpatch review book. IV. Title: Right livelihood book. V. Title: Simple living book.
658.022

Published by New Glide Publications, Inc. in association with Reed Books, Inc., a subsidiary of Addison House, Inc.

Reed Books: Publishing office, 9155 West Sunset Boulevard, Los Angeles, Ca. 90069. Marketing c/o Addison House, Morgan's Run, Danbury, N.H. 03230

New Glide Publications: 330 Ellis Street, San Francisco, Ca. 94102

Production by David Charlsen & Others/Linda Gunnarson

Printed in the United States of America

Contents

Introduction

The Briarpatch Book is a flag we are holding in the air to find people like ourselves. "Briarpatch" is a word that conveys a set of values: openness, sharing, and serving people through business. The Briarpatch consists of several thousand people throughout America who recognize and have found each other through shared interests. What we have in common are our business values and the joy and excitement we feel about our work. Many hundreds of us in the San Francisco Bay Area already know each other on a face-to-face basis through the Briarpatch Network, and our community is growing exuberantly.

This book is a collection of our first eight *Briarpatch Reviews,* which have given the members of the network and our friends a glimpse into the lives and businesses of other Briars. These articles reveal how a Briar's life is an expression of his or her personal values and include much of what we have learned in running our businesses—our successes and failures, how we got started, and how we are growing. We have included countless examples of the ingredients that have made our lives happy and our businesses fun.

Our concern as Briars is the celebration of life and business. We find joy in business, and our businesses are gems radiating the excitement of our lives. The Briarpatch is a network of small-business people who have three values in common: we are in business because we love it; we find our reward in serving people rather than in amassing large sums of money; and we share our resources with each other as much as we can, especially our knowledge of business. We share management and marketing information, legal and technical knowhow, names of suppliers, and what general practices work and do not work. We are committed to keeping our books and financial records open. Our customers, employees, friends, and relatives know how much we earn, how much our supplies cost, and anything else they want to know about the financial workings of our businesses.

We share naturally because we love what we are doing, and we are open because our practices are honest. If you share these values, then you, too, are a Briar. Welcome. This book is for you. We have reprinted these first eight issues of the *Briarpatch Review* because of growing national interest in the Briarpatch and because the *Review*, even with its faults, gives the most accurate picture of who we are.

A History of the Briarpatch

Dick Raymond is the father of the Briarpatch concept which emerged in early 1973. Dick also is founder of the Portola Institute, which has been the catalyst for several community-based groups and publisher of the revolutionary *Whole Earth Catalog.* Interestingly, a book called *The Brier-Patch Philosophy* had been published in 1906; it presented a nineteenth-century naturalistic/religious view of the rabbit world in which everything worked out for the best in the long run. Dick did not know of that book, and ironically his idea grew out of a much different experience. He and many others in the early 1970s were disturbed with the endless Viet Nam War and high inflation rates. Many within Portola were predicting an apocalypse, with the economy falling in shambles around our feet. In this milieu, Stewart Brand was examining the tools for post-apocalyptic survival and planning in his new *CoEvolution Quarterly.*

Dick's Briarpatch idea grew out of his image of a dinosaur-like demise of existing large businesses. In his first visions of the Briarpatch he saw the giant corporate dinosaurs unable to find food for their enormous profit appetites. He visualized a business apocalypse, using such terms as "living with joy in the cracks" to describe the new subsociety in which "the cracks" referred to his apocalyptic earthquake image. The Briarpatch was to be the social system for survival, with Briars using the tools of living on less, sharing with each other, and learning through new small businesses. To this, Dick added the positive value of doing it all with joy. In his vision, Briars were to be doing what they loved most, secure from the ravages of the crumbling culture around them. Their lack of material possessions and small-scale living would appear to others like real briarpatches—thorny places so unappealing to the greedy people around them that, like rabbits, Briars would be safe.

Dick and I were close friends and worked together on various Portola projects. Although I personally didn't believe in an apocalypse, I loved his Briarpatch idea for its joy and wisdom and quoted Dick's definition of the Briarpatch in *The Seven Laws of Money,* which Rasberry and I were writing.

Dick lived south of San Francisco in suburban Menlo Park, where the Portola Institute is located and where the very first Briarpatch journal was compiled by Gurney Norman. Gurney edited and published this first journal called the *Briarpatch Review* and sent it free to a select mailing list of friends and users of the Whole Earth Truck Store. Gurney is one of our spiritual heroes and the author of *Divine Right's Trip,* a novel first published in the *Last Whole Earth Catalog.* His *Briarpatch Review* described the new Briarpatch Auto Coop, which had started that summer in Menlo Park, the Zen Center in San Francisco, and various Portola projects. The journal had a subdued but glossy layout in tablet format and was published in November 1973. *The Seven Laws of Money* was nearly ready for the printer by that time, and we encouraged subscriptions to the new journal in the last page of the book. However, Gurney moved on, and there was no community in Menlo Park to put out a second issue.

A sustained *Briarpatch Review* needed a real Briarpatch network to nourish it, and San Francisco was the ideal community in which such a network could be created. The two principals in that venture were Andy Alpine, a former lawyer and researcher, and me. We both lived in San Francisco and had met while working on another project. We got along wonderfully, and I hired Andy to do some work for me in sex research and to search for a waterfront office where I could offer small-business counseling. Andy finished the research and found the office by May 1974, and I opened the office in June.

Three months later I found that I needed help. I had been giving free advice to small-business people and potential Briars once a week, helping many to start their own businesses. They would get their advice on Wednesday and start following it. By the next Monday they needed a truck, by Tuesday they wanted a bookkeeper, and I wasn't around to help them with the necessary follow-through. Andy was the perfect person to help out, and he was willing to do it. He needed $250 a month, which we initially raised with six-month pledges of support of $50 to $100 from Lew Durham; Dick Raymond; Elliot Buckdrucker, a CPA friend; Werner Hebenstreit, an insurance broker; Tom Silk, a lawyer; Ron Wilton, a film producer; and me. My free business consultation and Andy's follow-up grew into the Briarpatch Network, a community which agreed to support Andy after our six-month pledges had run out.

Lew Durham, who was a founder of Glide Memorial United Methodist Church's radical 1960s social-change programs, played a role twice in 1974. He was one of the founding contributors who supported Andy's work, and in July he helped put on a conference concerning right livelihood and business. The conference was held at a camp eighty miles south of San Francisco, with twenty-five to thirty people attending. We all had great fun, and many of those people became part of the Briarpatch Network.

Although an actual Briarpatch community existed by the end of 1974, the original *Briarpatch Review* of Menlo Park had been defunct for twelve months, and letters were piling up from readers of *The Seven Laws* requesting information and subscriptions. Dick Raymond was encouraging anyone who was interested to take responsibility for the long-overdue next issue. Annie Styron and I had dinner with Dick and his wife one evening in November 1974 and left that night committed to doing the *Briarpatch Review* together. Annie had worked on the *Whole Earth Catalog* and on Ram Dass' *Be Here Now*, published while she was living at the Lama Foundation in New Mexico. She was excited, skilled, and energetic, and we worked wonderfully well together.

Our eight-page sample *Review* was distributed for comments at a Briarpatch Network garage sale, and by April 1975 we had the first issue published, with much help from Judi Johnston and other friends. Everyone came to that first issue-collation event, which turned into a party and thereafter a tradition. The people who help put together the *Review* are mentioned in each issue, and they all are wonderful and essential.

Since our first issue, several changes have taken place that should be noted here. Kris Anundsen became a major contributor, typist, and editor from the second issue onward. Andy Alpine took the name Bahauddin in late 1976 after study and initiation in a Sufi order and was joined by Charles Albert Parsons as co-coordinator of the Briarpatch Network. Annie Styron worked with Kris and me on the six issues up to Summer 1976 and then moved on to other projects. Recently we received a vital injection of new help and support when Tom Hargadon joined the staff. He is a lawyer, bar owner, and former urban planner who took over subscriptions, accounting, and mail and distribution tasks. Deon Kaner joined us on the Fall 1976 issue, helping us on layouts. I worked hard on the seventh issue to provide a smooth transition among the staff and felt comfortable leaving the eighth issue to the new crew of Tom, Deon, and the replacement for Kris—Aryae Coopersmith, our new editor.

Few projects have been so rewarding in our lives. We feel that the enormous efforts involved are worth it when the love and appreciation of our readers come through via the mail and when new people have arrived to carry on the *Review.*

With All Our Blemishes and Freckles

In this compilation of the first eight *Briarpatch Reviews* published in San Francisco, we didn't edit our mistakes or leave out calendar events that have long passed. They are part of our history.

When Annie and I and our friends were designing the *Briarpatch Review,* it was important to us to reflect the spirit of the newly emerging Briarpatch Network and to encourage others to create a similar kind of journal for themselves. To us, high-gloss perfection was not necessary; in fact, it was undesirable.

The design that you see here evolved from our having made a series of careful choices to impart a warm and exciting down-home quality to the *Review.* For instance, the page size is obtained by folding a standard 8½" by 14" sheet in half. We decided to print the first issue of our *Review* on heavy, rough paper because we liked the texture and because the paper was relatively inexpensive. We chose the mimeograph process since we felt that most people have access to a mimeo machine should they want to do their own "Review." Annie and I felt that color was vital to expressing the joy and excitement of the Briarpatch and that with mimeo we could afford the luxury of going beyond black and white printing. We had been impressed with some beautiful color mimeograph flyers we had seen posted throughout San Francisco that had been created by the Neighborhood Arts Council, a marvelous group dedicated to stimulating indigenous art within neighborhoods. Like homebaked cookies, each poster was unique. We got in touch with Arlene Goldbard, the woman who had designed the flyers, and she generously helped us print the first *Review.* In our second and third issues we combined color mimeograph with offset printing. In our later issues we moved totally to offset printing as the mimeograph process had been taking too much time. Annie and I found a friend who would print the *Review* at a very low rate and who also was willing to learn to use color on her offset machine.

In this book we have limited ourselves to two colors, which helps keep the sales price low while still giving us the warmth color provides. We also have changed a few graphics in cases where our original experiments resulted in unreadable pages. Because the Briarpatch is so much about learning for each of us, the blemishes and freckles in our work are part of what we gladly share with you.

The Publishing Deal

The publishing of *The Briarpatch Book* is the result of natural alliances. New Glide Publications originally was the publishing arm of Glide Church, which helped with printing many issues of the *Review* and where I am employed as business manager. Rasberry is a partner in New Glide, and Ruth Gottstein, another of the principals in the company, and her husband are members of the Briarpatch Network.

This book is co-published by New Glide and Reed Books, the newly formed West Coast subsidiary of Addison House. Our publishing contract is unique. Instead of a standard royalty arrangement, we share with the publishers in the profits of the book once all production and marketing expenses have been paid.

Pricing Our Books

Why price our books at exactly $8.00 (softcover) and $15.00 (hardcover)? Traditionally, publishers and booksellers would recommend prices of $7.95 and $14.95 so that the books would appear to be in the cheaper $7 and $14 price ranges. Based on this kind of thinking, products sold in our culture are priced at $3.99, $6.98, etc.; so why aren't we doing it?

It is important to Briars that the integrity of our lives carry over into our businesses. Following the example of Stewart Brand's *Whole Earth Catalog,* we are open and accessible in every way. The openness in business that so clearly joins us together extends to our pricing. Cutting one cent off a price to make something appear less expensive is part of a deceptive game that many business people play and that we in the Briarpatch discourage. In our culture, we don't use deceptive pricing in "professional" relationships between client and supplier. For example, there is never a $19.95 charge for a visit to a dentist or veterinarian. We would be embarrassed by such phoniness. In Japan, a culture noted for its honesty, all prices are in round numbers; so we know this could be a business reality in our country.

We have raised our flag. If you are an alternative business person and are committed to service through creative labor, we welcome your support, articles, and comments. Join us, please, and subscribe if you want to become more directly involved.

Michael Phillips with Rasberry
San Francisco, 1978

BRIARPATCH REVIEW

This is the second edition of the Briarpatch Review. The
first review came out in November 1973, 5,000 copies, 21
pages edited by Gurney Norman. We did it as an effort to
help the folks in Briarpatch County (which already exists)
develop a self-awareness. Since the first review, the
group has been growing steadily to where we now have a network of Briarpatch enterprises and people all over the
United States and Canada who consider themselves briars.

As Dick Raymond seems to have phrased it, "Briarpatch
Society" consists of people learning to live with joy in
the cracks. And especially, if you see yourself as part
of a group that is more committed to "learning how the
world works" than to acquiring possessions and status,
then you must be a Briar.

We aren't too hot for new ideas, schemes, or ideologies.
We want reports from people on real attempts, real failures and the joys of shareable experiences that worked and
are working. The main criteria is helpfullness and fun.
We aren't big readers so there are lots of pictures and
short paragraphs. Generally the information and feedback
we would like would be concerned with the following subjects:
1. Living on less.
2. Giving, sharing and exchange of skills and services in
    business.
3. Humanistic management methods and unusual organization
    solutions.
4. RIGHT LIVELIHOOD.
5. City and country survival.
6. Better practices and traditions for those who have tools
    and work to do.

CONTENTS

This issue was put together by:

Michael Phillips   Annie Helmuth
Judi Johnston   Jim Morgan

with thanks to:

Richard Raymond   Gurney Norman
Ritchie Gordon   Fran Bennett
Salli Rasberry

Cover: Jim Wintersteen

Printing: Arlene Goldbard, San Francisco

© 1975 Portola Institute Menlo Park California

Messages from the Briarpatch

The Briarpatch Review is one of the workings of the Briarpatch network and we want to encourage an exchange of information with our readers. In a sense, this is a membership magazine--a publication which links up the people who practice Right Livelihood with the philosophy, experience and tools of the New Age trade. Consider yourself a member. And let us hear from you. Since the first Review was published way back in 1973, we've received responses in the form of exuberant praise, scepticism and thoughtful advice...

As far as living joyfully in the cracks, may I suggest being a volunteer in medical research? I have been getting $25 a month for more than a year so far, testing a male birth control pill. Not only is this promoting some needed social change, it would probably cover much of the money needs of a true briar.

Bob Wallace
New World Computer Services
P.O. Box 5415
Seattle, Washington 98105

Well, I'm sure you have heard the story about the man who was offered a pill guaranteed to make him smarter. When he remarked, on biting into it, that it was a sheep's pill, he was told, "See, you're getting smarter already." Ha-Ha. I feel a little like that man. I paid $25 for a lifetime subscription to a magazine that purported to be able to teach me about economics, and sure enough, I learned something about economics. But I have lately gotten over my initial amusement and have begun to wonder about just what did happen to my 25 bucks. If you really are going to put out a magazine, I won't begrudge you the cash. Anyway, please fill me in, a postcard will be fine.

Dan Barton
91 Red River
Austin, Texas

I suggest that you think about the idea of articles on briar games. I'm super-interested in the direction Stewart Brand has been taking in the fields of recreation, relaxation, excitement and challenge. I personally am enamored of the game of basketball and plan on submitting articles that would get more briars dribbling.

Mike Crone
544 W. Clover Dr.
Memphis, TN 38117

On a personal level I would very much like to find out if there is anything that Briarpatch and I can do for each other. Af far as skills other than writing, I am a pasta chef of some local renown, making both fettuccine and ravioli on my own machine. I know celestial navigation and engineering, though to date I have not put it to any more telling use than inventing a better mousetrap which releases the mouse unharmed. I do competent carpentry and masonry work and I have some skill as a sheet metal worker and used to install gas and oil furnaces. What I would really like to do is work with someone in steam engines, solar heating, wind power or whatever.

I love writing and intend to do it all my life but I have come to the conclusion that one has to do more than merely write--it simply makes your life too one-sided. So I'll be looking forward to your next edition of Briarpatch Review and your next open meeting. In the meanwhile if you can point any other members of Briarpatch in my direction I would be most grateful, or suggest some people who might have some ideas.

Paul Ciotti
1756 Marin Ave.
Berkeley, CA 94707

I was indeed surprised and pleased to get the first copy of the Review. The accounts of activities are interesting, but more importantly they are inspirational. Reading about real people pursuing right livelihood in various enterprises is encouraging to me. It is a bolster to my confidence to witness others "getting on with it."

Jeff Adams
482-19th Ave.
San Francisco, CA 94121

Well yes it's May 9th and the garden's only just plowed. Well, it's tough to live together yessir --especially if you're a bunch of anarchistic hung-up middle-class dropouts with big ideas yessir. Hard to stay up front while maintaining that nothing is necessarily "right" or "wrong". We got burned out of our house Dec. 7th. Don't never trust no wood stove. Always respect your tools. Well here's yr letter.
            Scott Robinson
            Patti Huels
            Rt 307 W.
            Jefferson, O. 44047

P.S. We're gettin married on the farm June 22nd.

editorial postscript

The first issue of Briarpatch Review had many more reasons to fail than to succeed. It was pretty thin on content. And some of the content was soon to be proven utterly dumb. (Freelandia). It was nowhere explained why a journal about alternative economics, directed to people who identify with the notion of "Briarpatch" life and work, should cost a whole dollar.

There are families interested in Briarpatch ideas who can feed themselves for a day on what a dollar can buy.

Briarpatch Review #1 was a walking contradiction of itself.

But at least we got it out! Before, there was no Review. Afterwards, there was one. We mailed copies to 5,000 people, free of charge. About 1,000 people responded with letters and money. Many people sent in more than the requested dollar. We received about $800 in all, enough to encourage Issue #2, if not in fact to pay for it. A mailing list was created. After a year, new energies have gathered, mainly in the form of present editors Annie, Michael, and Judi.

Clearly, the reason for the survival of Briarpatch Review through at least this second issue is simply the power of the Briarpatch concept itself. That concept has still not been completely defined. New pieces of the definition continue to come in, to add to the original notions set forth last issue by Dick Raymond, Michael Phillips, and other writers in other publications. The idea has something to do with the

growing refusal of increasing
numbers of people to let all
power over their lives, and
livelihoods, pass into the
hands of the government and
other large corporations.
Ingenuity is bustin' out all
over, in response to a real
cultural need, and this Review is only one of the places
where the people's ingenuity
is being described.

The present editors have
asked me to correct my ommis-
sion in Issue #1 and insert
a note of explanation about
the $1.00 price tag for a
copy of this little journal.
Obviously, the money that
readers send is in the nature
of a gift, an investment in
a worthy idea that is even
now finding concrete expression in the lives of thousands
of people all over the country. The idea will survive
without your dollar, so don't
feel guilty if you don't send
one in. But the point is to
help the network, to encourage
the inter-connectedness of
us all, to help the rose bloom
upon the briars as a source
of inspiration to people who
are trying hard, as well as
a source of practical information and general help.

                Peace,

                Gurney Norman

membership

You know whether you are a
Briar or not. The Briarpatch
Review is intended to be the
membership magazine of the
Briarpatch. There are no membership dues. If you wish to
make a gift, to tithe, or
share and help in any way,
that's wonderful--we need to
hear from you! To be on the
membership mailing lists and
get future issues of The
Briarpatch Review, write us
at 330 Ellis Street, San
Francisco, CA 94102. If you
would like to help cover the
cost of The Briarpatch Review,
we estimate it at $5.00 a year.

FARM CHARTER

The Farm Charter has its roots in a small diverse group of people attempting to buy land in the Santa Cruz mountains; and to somehow turn their endeavor into a means of livelihood. After three years of shoestring budgets, hard work, and emotional conflicts some people left, others joined, and some remained through it all. Together, they slowly worked out an agreement by which all eight people living on a paying for this land could live realistically and ethically together or part ways with proper recompense and justice.

This is a brief abstract of the legal document which emerged from so much patient struggle, presented here as a "Briarpatch" method of land ownership/ stewardship. The rest of the Farm Charter details the technical aspects of buying and selling partnership interests, death of a partner, attorney's fees, service of notices, and voluntary dissolution of the entire partnership.

As a useful model we are offering complete copies of the Farm Charter Partnership Agreement for those of you who wish detailed information on its legal construction. Send $1.00 to cover printing and mailing costs to The Briarpatch Review, 330 Ellis Street, San Francisco 94102.

THE FARM CHARTER PARTNERSHIP AGREEMENT

1) Statement of Purpose: to purchase and support one 120-acre homestead; to live, work, and build in a manner harmonious with nature and the people involved, which makes this venture non-speculative; and to engage in incidental activities to such purpose.

2) The Partnership commences upon execution of this Agreement and dissolves by mutual agreement of the parties or as otherwise designated.

3) Financial Aspects: each partner agrees to purchase one share of the land the value of that share being 1/8 the purchase price of the land; each partner must contribute $125 a month as his/her share of principal due on loans and/or deeds of trust and of property taxes.

4) Each partner must contribute an equal pro rata share toward operating expenses which include food, fuel, garden supplies, livestock, tools, construction, etc.

5) No partner is required to contribute more money to the capital of the partnership and no partner is allowed to make voluntary contributions to the capital without the written consent of all the partners.

6) No portion of the capital of the partnership may be withdrawn without written consent of all partners.

7) No partner is entitled to interest on his/her contributions.

8) No partner may loan or advance money to the partnership without written consent of a majority of the partners.

9) Accounting transactions of the partnership shall be kept in proper books and each partner is responsible to see that his/her partnership transactions are recorded. The books are kept on a cash basis. Each partner shall have an individual capital account and an individual operating expense account.

10) Each partner must live on the land and must devote a pre-determined amount of effort toward maintaining and improving the partnership.

11) Guest numbers and length of stay are restricted and any variation must be agreed to by unanimous vote.

12) New partners will be determined by unanimous vote.

13) No partner is entitled to salary or compensation for services.

14) Each partner has the authority to bind the partnership in making contracts and/or incurring liabilities up to $250. Any greater amount must have the consent of the other partners. Any violators will be held individually liable.

15) Each partner must discharge all his/her obligations as they come due and protect the partnership from all costs, claims, and demands.

16) No partner shall, without written consent of all the other partners; loan partnership funds; extend partnership credit to a previously determined untrustworthy person; incur any obligations for the partnership except in the ordinary course of partnership business; become bail, surety, or indorser for any other person.

17) Decisions concerning sale of the land is based on ownership interest of each partner; in all other decisions each partner has one vote - major operating decisions require unanimous approval (large debts, etc.), all other decisions require 2/3 approval.

18) No partner may assign his/her interest in the partnership; however, partnership interest may be passed on the heirs.

19) A partner may be expelled from the partnership for a willful breach of this agreement and other certain acts by service on him/her of a written notice

signed by each of the other partners, stating the date of expulsion and the cause. The expelled partner is entitled to receive his/her ownership interest as reflected in his/her adjusted capital account, and reimbursement for a private dwelling at the price determined at the time of construction. Any partner may voluntarily withdraw from the partnership by giving all other partners 90 days notice.

Jim Morgan's SUGGESTION FOR FARM CHARTERS

The farm charter should have an earth awareness article tailored to the needs and ideals of the community to preserve the aesthetics that brought people to the place and the productivity that allows them to live there. Ecological changes have a tendency to happen so slowly that those of us living closest to them are the last to perceive them. Definition of those qualities you wish to preserve in your land can act as a reference point to help you be aware of, and to shape, your own impact on the place you love.

It's been my observation that people drawing up land charters or covenants overlook the intimate relationships between economics and biology. Economic problems are most immediate and usually get the most attention. Biological problems are less visible, less immediate, but not less important because the soil, trees, shrubs, grasses, streams, etc., all influence the social, spiritual, aesthetic and economic value of land. If these are abused, changed, or destroyed they can alter the land's productivity, spirituality or desirability as a home.

A good way to approach an earth awareness article is to give the soil legal status as a living, breathing entity which must be covered in winter, fed, and protected from trampling, overgrazing and erosion. A stream should also be considered a living being whose bank vegetation, natural courses, water clarity and living creatures are protected. Vegetative cover on the land should be given status according to the community's needs in compatibility with the soil.

FORBES, FEBRUARY 1, 1975

Hello, Sucker!

Here's your chance to be the first on your block to get in on the latest scare craze.

How about investing in dehydrated food? Although food storage ideas have been with the Mormons for 15 years, it was a relatively dormant business until mid-1973 when the nation was hit by gasoline and food shortages. But already the business supports 20 to 30 little companies and should produce some $30 million in revenues this year.

According to one story, basketball player Jerry Lucas even went out and bought a two-year supply of food for 12 people, and Clyde Juchau, owner of Neo-Life Co., tells of a fellow who invested $25,000 in his food plan instead of buying stocks, gold or silver.

"It's catastrophy buying", says Juchau. The competitors are pushing a "food plan" costing between $414 and $749 with enough dehydrated food to feed an individual from 3 months to a year. One company states in its propaganda that a food shortage is predicted by an official of the U.S. Department of Agriculture, while others claim

their food plans are "real life insurance you can eat."

Suppose the inevitable arrives and you have to eat the stuff: could you? "I wouldn't feed some of the items in my line to a dog" admits John Ballard of Houston's INSTA-FOODS. "I got one I thought would go over great. That's peanut butter mix. I mixed some up and put it on a cracker. I chewed and chewed and chewed and just couldn't swallow it."

Judith Johnston, who's been living in the Rocky Mountains and thinking about the problem for five years, says:

We store food and I believe that a form of disaster or collapse is in our immediate future. But I do not believe that some pre-planned, pre-packaged "food plan" will solve anyone's problems: except for a false sense of peace-of-mind. I question the quality of the food (chemical content, vitamin losses due to

11

processing, failure of packages to seal completely, and so forth), and I question its applicability to each individual's needs.

My suggestions for food storage is do-it-yourself. Water tight and air tight plastic buckets, canisters, and barrel drums of different sizes are available at fairly low cost. Examine the food before you store it and check for cleanliness, overall quality, and quantity. Think it through carefully: do you need salt, or clean water, or powdered milk? Do you have a vitamin or mineral deficiency that needs special attention? Tailor your food storage to your own personal needs and to the needs of your physical surroundings (mountain meadows or innercity?) What about medical supplies, tools, or a means to make a fire?

Food storage is not a joke nor should it be a get-rich-quick scheme. It is an important aspect of your possible future.

FREE CPA Advice:

Elliot is a CPA (certified public accountant) who is a friend of Briarpatch businesses. We asked what he looks at in guessing whether a business is sound. His list:

Just Checking Around:

1. Takes business seriously. A Proprietor takes a real interest in "business" as a place to learn how the world works and has an understanding that this is done by openness, study, curiosity, care and common sense. There's plenty of room for fun and humor with Elliot, but the person who says "I can never learn how to read a financial report", or"I'm a designer, I can't bother with petty negotiations" won't survive in business.

2. Organized. There is a certain aura that lets you know that the way everything is done is well thought out, that there is care given to details. This is true even when much appears piled-up and left out on the table. Elliot remembers a man who died young of a heart attack after running a poor business. Elliot said, "I can understand why; when he got up in the morning he was going to

work to either do last year's paperwork or put out today's fire."

Looking at Statements:

3. The Current Ratio. He looks at the Balance Sheet on the financial statement (if they don't have one he knows what bad shape they're in). Under Assets he takes the total of Cash, Accounts Receivable and Inventory and he compares this to the total of Taxes that are due, Accounts Payable and Notes or Contracts due in the next 12 months. If the ratio is 1½ to 1 or 2 to 1 things are probably OK. If they are worse that means he must look much deeper for potential trouble because the business doesn't have much in the way of "survival resources".

Example:

Assets

Cash	$ 300
Accts.Recvble	700
Inventory	2,000
	$3,000

Liability

Accts.Payable	$1,200
Taxes due	300
Notes	500
	$2,000

4. Positive Cash Flow. This may be funny but a lot of businesses actually spend more than is coming in by using the capital they had to start the business or being overdrawn at the bank. Elliot compares: all cash receipts to all cash disbursements that have been paid on an operating basis (he usually goes back a few months) if the first is lower, stand back!

Making Improvements: These are the things he would like to see in a business:

1. Monthly list of accounts payable and accounts receivable showing their age. This is essential to understand the cash flow and control inventory.

Example:

Receivables

Customer	Amount	Age 1-30	30-60
Macy's	$ 500	$500	
Army	1,200		$1,200
Shell	150	150	
County	200		200
Library	80		80

Payables

Descript.	Amount	1-30	30-60
Utilities	$120	$120	
Rent	180	180	
Table	55		55

2. Elliot would like to see small businesses have financial statements (preferably on an accrual basis) prepared by the business if they don't have the capability of an accountant. This doesn't cost too much if the business records are kept up-to-date. These are essential in order to detect if some basic business flaw has developed and cannot be recognized on a day-to-day basis.

3. When he looks at a business's books and make judgements or recommendations these are the key things he looks at:

a) Journals. These are the check registers and cash receipt entries that are the core data of accounting. Is the posting up to date or are they weeks behind? Are their totals accurate?

b) Ledgers. These are the summary entries used to summarize assets, costs, liabilities, revenues and expenses. Do they balance?

c) Chart of Accounts. These are the coded account titles (or separate pages) in the ledgers where specific details are clustered together. The checks for garbage, gas, electricity, would all be under utilities. Are the categories too large and important details being overlooked? Are they too small and time is being wasted on insignificant information?

How to Start Your
Own Craft Business
Herb Genfan and
Lyn Taetzsch
1974; 203pp.
$7.95 postpaid

BOOK

The CoEvolution Quarterly

Remarkably clear, comprehensive book. By simply stating how to do it, why, and including a copy of the completed form, it leads you painlessly through the paperwork of getting licensed, financed, legally-covered, and taxed. Equally fine sections demonstrate streamlined systems for bookkeeping, inventorying, shipping, using the U.P.S., selling an area (wholesale, consignment, direct), doing fairs and shows, collecting bills, and once launched, how to analyze your progress, and where to expand or cut. To echo those who know, "Wish I'd read it when I started!"

—Diana Sloat

If you are selling to retail stores who like the way your work sells, their customers expect a ready supply of your work. Store owners, you'll find, want your goods on their shelves within a week or two after they order. Your success at this stage depends almost entirely on how quickly you deliver.

Production and inventory systems are well worth the time in planning and in keeping them up to date. If you've heard of a business failing because of "poor management," lack of organization is one of the factors that cause such failure. With other craftspeople competing for customers you can, by using control systems, be the one that makes it and stays in business.

•

Your own business, as you can see, will be quite a challenge. It lives, and you live with it; in a fairly short time you can see the results of actions, your decisions. If you buy a new tool either it works or it doesn't. If you design a new vase, it sells or it doesn't. In any case, you learn something, you change and grow.

If you want to expand and take out a loan, you work it out on paper, scrape together as many numbers and quantifiable facts as possible, throw in a dash of pure intuition and hope, and plunge ahead. What you accomplish lifts you right off the ground. And your failures provide useful feedback for the next decision, the next risk.

Living Poor with Style

Ernest Callenbach
1972; 176 pages

$1.95 postpaid

from:
Bantam Books, Inc.
666 Fifth Ave.
New York, N.Y. 10019
or Whole Earth

*Chick Callenbach is a godfather
of the Briarpatch so we called
him in Berkeley to ask what
he's been doing and thinking
about lately.*

mussels

Michael: What would you add
to Living Poor With Style in
today's world?

Chick: My ideas have changed
about certain kinds of things
so that for instance I'm sitting here wearing a pair of·
pants that I got down at the
Value Village the other night
for 65¢, but I notice little
by little the prices in the
used clothing places have
been creeping up to the point
where they're only marginally
lower than Sears or Penney's.
And used furniture has gotten
to be outrageously expensive.
It seems to me if I were doing the part on furniture
again I would talk a lot about
building your own. People
need to get with building and
scrounging and transforming
things.

Michael: Have you looked at
wealthy suburban second-hand
stores? I suspect maybe the
thing to do is try in upper
middle class areas outside
the big cities.

Chick: Oh, one thing I would
put in now in the section on
plants is that there are so
many plants around now that
you can take cuttings from,
it's almost never necessary
to go buy a plant. You can

almost always find a friend
who'll give you a cutting and
things grow quite rapidly.
Besides, it isn't the size of
the plant that matters anyway,
it's whether you love it.
Even a little plant has a lot
to say for itself.

Something I discovered recent-
ly--it's about eating seaweed.
I was up along the coast of
Mendocino; we had a little
fire on the beach and there
was a lot of seaweed lying
around. The way we discovered this, we tried getting
the fire going and it would-
n't burn well. We put the
seaweed on it, and it didn't
actually burn, it just sort
of got toasted, and I said to
myself, you know, that looks
good (my father used to eat
it for his digestion). So we
sat there toasting seaweed
and had a very nice snack.
It tasted like those thin,
salty crackers they serve at
cocktail parties.

Michael: What impresses me
about the story is your attitude. It's there, maybe it's
edible.

Chick: Yes, and of course
there's another connected
thing--mussels cooked over a
fire with butter, wine and le-
mon. They're really good.

Michael: In the responses
readers made to Living Poor,

were there specific areas
that were commented on most
often?

Chick: Nothing special, no
consistency. It was more an
attitudinal thing. A way of
looking at your life and trying to take control of it.

-anyone tried it?

Three Bowls

I showed my children (age 5, 7 and 11) the way food is eaten in some Buddhist monasteries. They now eat just what they take, and clean everything themselves. Meals are quieter and.... The oldest, Cynthia, describes it. Mike Phillips.

JAPANESE BOWLS

Using Japanese bowls is a very ingenious way of eating. The bowls come in all different colors. They can be very beautiful.

To use Japanese bowls, you must have 3 bowls, a napkin, and some chopsticks. You always put the eating part of the chopsticks off the table. Whoever is serving the meal goes around to everyone to serve them their food. When they come to you, if you want some of what they are serving you rub your hands together and they put the food in your bowl. When you don't want any more, you lift up your right hand and push it up in an upright position. If you don't want any food whatsoever, you put your head down.

Before you eat you put a little of your food into a bowl which is fed to the universe. This bowl after everyone has put some thing in it is put outside for the birds.

When you eat you may only eat one type of food at a time.

When you are finished, you are given some tea in one of your dirty bowls. You wash the bowl out with your finger and pour it into the next bowl. You do the same thing to all the bowls. With the tea in the last bowl you have cleaned out you wash your chopsticks and drink the tea you have washed the bowls with. You use a small towel to dry the bowls.

To put the bowls away you pile them one on top of the other on top of a square piece of cloth. You put the towel inside the top bowl. Put two of the corners of the cloth over the bowls, put the chopsticks on top, fold over the other two corners, and put the napkin on top.

I like to eat this way.

by Cynthia Phillips.

17

from cradle to grave-

At one of the Briarpatch network meetings at Pier 40, we talked about incorporating the Briarpatch so that we could get group medical insurance. In discussing the details of how to do it through Portola or the various kinds of group insurance plans, Eleanor McCauley asked the right question: "Why do we want to go to some outside group to buy insurance? The Briarpatch is all about finding new ways to take care of ourselves." Michael Phillips remembered reading an article in the Wall Street Journal about a doctor in Denver who set up his own system and facilities for his patients. This is the report based on a telephone interview with Dr. Sam (who prefers to remain anonymous), a talk he gave, and the Wall Street Journal story:

Dr. Sam practiced among poor whites, blacks, and Mexicans in a low-income neighborhood of Denver, Colorado. In 1970 he grossed about $130,000, with $73,000 of that money coming from Medicare and Medicaid. But in February 1971, he initiated a "total health-care" package which plummeted his medical income to zero. The plan provided (for $20 to $40 a month) unrestricted visits to or from the doctor, and free hospital and dental care.

Competitors and regulatory officials took a dim view of Dr. Sam's plan. Although no one questioned Dr. Sam's abilities as a physician, and his ethics appeared above suspicion, the Colorado Insurance Commission hauled the doctor into court during April 1971 charging that his plan was fiscally unsound and dangerous to the public. After several sessions in court (which included a large showing of support by his patients) the doctor was fined $2,000 for not obeying the court injunction to drop the health plan and he was sternly lectured on the penalities of continuing the health package.

Dr. Sam contended that his

in one box

critics overlooked several cost-saving innovations of his plan, including elimination of paper work to the point where his patients had no contracts and paid monthly "on faith." He did not bill Blue Shield or Medicare-Medicaid for his fees because of legal complexities. (The absence of monthly bills made it difficult for the state to prove its contention that Dr. Sam was running an illegal insurance plan.)

Costly illnesses did occur, however, and one patient's plan paid $3,500 in hospital bills for heart surgery and $700 in surgeon's fees. Because much of the current costliness of modern medical care occurs at the hospital level, Dr. Sam constructed a six-bed modular facility to house his patients, himself and his wife, and six children. To elude all the state and federal regulations covering hospitals, he labeled his facility a "home-pital."

STATISTICS OF DR. SAM'S PROGRAM

In the middle of the 3½ year program there were 809 regular paying members of the community, with another 100 irregular fringe members who were not included in the following statistics:

Medicare-Medicaid -	347
Blue Cross/Blue Shield -	345
No insurance -	17
	809

Patients under 10 yrs. -	157
10 to 19 yrs. -	127
20 to 39 yrs. -	162
40 to 59 yrs. -	150
60 and over -	213
	809

Revenue from everyone was based on a scale of fees from $10 for some couples to a high of $40 for a family; the total averaged $4,500 or about $5.50 a month per person.

The work load was:

25-30 patients in the office daily

3 hospital calls per day
3 house calls per day

Expenses (approx.):

Specialists	$ 540
Pathology-Lab	130
Hospitalization	1,460
Office; medicines & blood tests	2,210
Total per month	$4,340

The expenses were less than the revenues by $160 ($4,500-$4,340) but this did not cover Dr. Sam's personal and family costs of $550. per month. To do so would have required more like $6.50 per person or reduced costs in some categories.

When asked four years later in a telephone interview why his patients had rejected his plan, Dr. Sam replied that, "...we had developed the program to a point where we just didn't need any more money. We were providing a health care program that offered my services and facilities on an exchange basis. It was effective in providing me and my family with a way to survive, but it was too progressive for the times. I feel that people are too involved with money to accept another way of doing something like this."

Dr. Sam dissolved his health plan because he didn't want to get involved in any more legalities. He wasn't trying to commit suicide, but rather to introduce a reform concept which turned out to be unacceptable to society. He felt that his philosophy and program were too radical and threatening to people, especially when he went off money entirely during the last five months of the program. To continue he felt would have been foolhardy.

Dr. Sam applied applied three basic guidelines to his concept. They are:

1. There is a creative control in our lives over which we have no sayso--we cannot con-trol our destiny.

2. You have to be willing to share in all things, just like you share in the things that are offered you.

3. There is no greater or lesser value of anything that you're dealing with. All things have an equal value, whether it's an ant, a horse, or a human being.

After dissolving his program, Dr. Sam went into retreat to develop his philosophy. He returned a year later to cancer research and education where he hopes to apply these guidelines.

Question: Do you think he dreamed the impossible dream?

AUTOMATIC

A portable job where you can go to work stoned, work where you want, and set your own hours. All you need is an Automatic Human Jukebox like the one operated in New York, San Francisco and Europe by Grimes Poznikov. Grimes has been doing this for 3 years and earns between $3 and $6 an hour. So far he doesn't know anyone else doing it. The Jukebox is built out of cardboard Grimes found in a trash bin on 43rd and Broadway in New York City. The music is usually a trumpet, occasionally a kazoo, operated by "any amount" of money put in with a special 25¢ charge for photographers. According to Grimes, a 5 to 45 second raucous laughter follows most AHJ selections. He says there is little need for "uniformed officers" in the area of AHJ operation as "motivations (i.e. greed, anxiety, frustration) to commit serious crime are dispersed."

HUMAN

JUKEBOX

A three-page pamphlet by Grimes on his views of the world, with emphasis on his livelihood and how to make your own Automatic Human Jukebox is available from The Briarpatch Review for 50¢.

Over the past six months we've been conducting an experiment. It's a support network of people in business in the Greater Bay Area who share similar values. One basic value is that we are in business not only for the economic return, but to learn about ourselves and the world through business. Our position is that greed is not necessary and that a simple lifestyle permits us to approach our businesses, our employees, our customers, and our lives with joy and honesty. If we are not in business for a large return, then our prices don't have to be as high, our employees can be treated more humanly, and our customers are not looked upon as dollar bills.

The Network has been fostering ownership participation, humanistic management, cooperative decisionmaking and publicly visible accounting. We daily experience the concept of Right Livelihood as a realization of self and a honing of the individual's talents through his/her work.

The Briarpatch Network grew out of a conference last summer called by Dick Raymond of Portola Institute and Louie Durham, formerly of San Francisco's Glide Church. At that time 25 folks representing as many businesses, came together at a camp in the Santa Cruz mountains to discuss what we had in common. The conference was of great value in that the participants realized that there were others who supported their ideas. At the end of the conference, the concensus was for a continuing involvement.

As it now stands, the Briarpatch Network consists of lawyers, accountants, bankers, management, marketing and financial consultants together with jugglers, bakers, carpenters, veterinarians and insurance experts (to name just a few) offering each other their specific knowledge of the business world.

During the first six months, membership was an intuitive understanding among the participants. Operational expenses were handled by twenty Briars making contributions of from $5 to $50 a month, averaging about $300 for me and $50 for expenses. Our future plan is to have each Briar contribute the amount of ongoing support that he/she feels appropriate.

The network provides a way for individual members to get together for help, advice and support on fantasies and ongoing projects that they'd like fulfilled or problems they'd like solved. Through the Briarpatch coordinator, these needs are dealt with and directed to a Briar who can help. Weekly pre-arranged consulting sessions and workshops on tax, accounting, legal and insurance problems have been going on for the past six months. And joyous celebrations like Ground Hog Day and Sunday evening pot-luck meals are some of the Briarpatch activities which bring us closer together for sharing and learning.

Other projects we are planning are: smaller workshops concerned with topics like competition and property, alterna-tives to group health insurance, a fund for short-term cash flow loans, and establishing closer ties with businesses and individuals in the city and rural Northern California. We are also experimenting with a quarterly newsletter stating each member's needs, abilities and surpluses, so that Briars will know what's going on with everyone else.

It's been fun and it looks like we'll be playing together for a while. The Briarpatch Network offers Briars the opportunity to give time, labor, love, energy, materials, skills, and money to other Briars and, of course, to receive. It works.

-Andy Alpine

BRIAR NETWORKING

-The newly opened Sacred Grounds Coffee Home in San Francisco was able to take over the lease on the Espresso machine from Pood's Foods, a delicatessen in Sausalito. Fred Pood didn't need it any-more and the women did; saving $1,000.

-Sunshine Appleby's Body Center had massage workshops at Wilbur Hot Springs, where Richard and Kathleen have gotten new clients and Sunshine paid for using the spectacular mineral hot baths by doing massages.

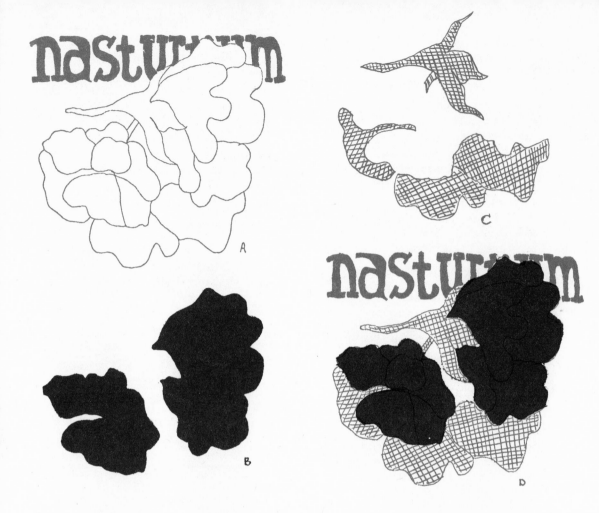

The Briarpatch Review is printed on a Gestetner Duplicator, a machine similar to the standard mimeograph. The Duplicator has a companion machine called the Gestefax which electronically cuts stencils from anything prepared in black and white. This printing process is comparatively inexpensive and with the correct preparation can produce clean, colorful fliers and newsletters.

The image that you put on the Gestefax is called the "original." It is the original drawing, paste-up, photograph or written copy.

In order to print a 3-color poster (we have simulated the third color—indicated by green crosshatching—for the nasturtium on this page), you need to make 3 separate stencils for the 3 colors...in this case, green, brown, and the crosshatching.

Begin with a clean white piece of paper, either 8½ x 14 or 8½ x 11. Do not use cardboard since the original must be pliable enough to go around the Gestefax drum. Tape the paper to your drawing surface so it doesn't move around. For the first color separation (green), draw your basic design, as shown in drawing A. The original drawing usually is done in black. Do the initial sketch with a light lead pencil that can be erased or a non-photo blue pencil which the Gestefax won't pick up. Leave a margin of at least ½ inch around the paper since the Duplicator doesn't print clearly on the edges.

Now you have a black and white drawing of the nasturtium. It is your first separation and will print, in this case, in green.

Next, take a piece of tracing paper or acetate exactly the size of your first piece of paper and tape it over the original so that all the edges match. On this, in black ink, fill in everything that you want to be in your second color. In drawing B, it is shown in brown, but remember that your original must be in black ink.

For the third color separation, take another piece of tracing paper and follow the same procedure and end up with an image like drawing C, which is the third color (here shown as crosshatching).

These 3 separations are placed, in turn, on the Gestefax to produce 3 stencils. Then each stencil, in turn, is run on the Duplicator with the desired color of ink, processing one stack of paper 3 times. The result is a duplication of the multi-color composite nasturtium you desire (drawing D).

For more information, contact Arlene Goldbard, 350 Pacific, San Francisco, CA 94111. Phone: 415-397-7878.

Open Credit Bureau

We checked this out in San Francisco and found that it worked "fine". They were very cooperative.

Have you ever been denied credit and suspected it was because of an error in your file? Thanks to the 1971 Fair Credit Reporting Act, you now have the right to know the "nature and substance" of everything in your file. And the chances of finding something amiss are high enough to warrant taking a look. The Federal Trade Commission has thousands of consumer complaints on file, and in a recent survey Business Week correspondents around the country often found their own files incomplete and out of date.

To find out who to contact about your record, call the Better Business Bureau or use the yellow pages of the phone book to locate your local credit agency. You can walk into most bureaus unannounced, fill out a form, and see an interviewer. If you'd rather discuss your file over the phone, you will have to fill out and return the form then wait for the agency to contact you.

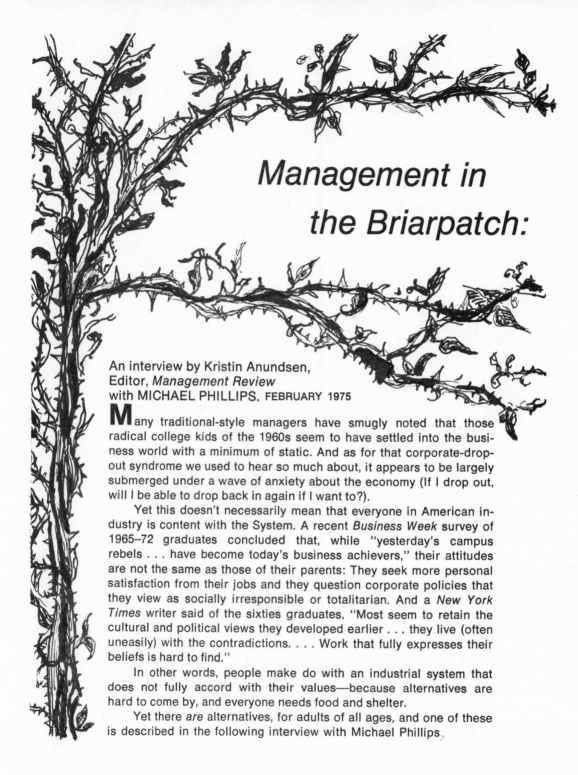

Management in the Briarpatch:

An interview by Kristin Anundsen,
Editor, *Management Review*
with MICHAEL PHILLIPS, FEBRUARY 1975

Many traditional-style managers have smugly noted that those radical college kids of the 1960s seem to have settled into the business world with a minimum of static. And as for that corporate-dropout syndrome we used to hear so much about, it appears to be largely submerged under a wave of anxiety about the economy (If I drop out, will I be able to drop back in again if I want to?).

Yet this doesn't necessarily mean that everyone in American industry is content with the System. A recent *Business Week* survey of 1965–72 graduates concluded that, while "yesterday's campus rebels . . . have become today's business achievers," their attitudes are not the same as those of their parents: They seek more personal satisfaction from their jobs and they question corporate policies that they view as socially irresponsible or totalitarian. And a *New York Times* writer said of the sixties graduates, "Most seem to retain the cultural and political views they developed earlier . . . they live (often uneasily) with the contradictions. . . . Work that fully expresses their beliefs is hard to find."

In other words, people make do with an industrial system that does not fully accord with their values—because alternatives are hard to come by, and everyone needs food and shelter.

Yet there *are* alternatives, for adults of all ages, and one of these is described in the following interview with Michael Phillips.

26

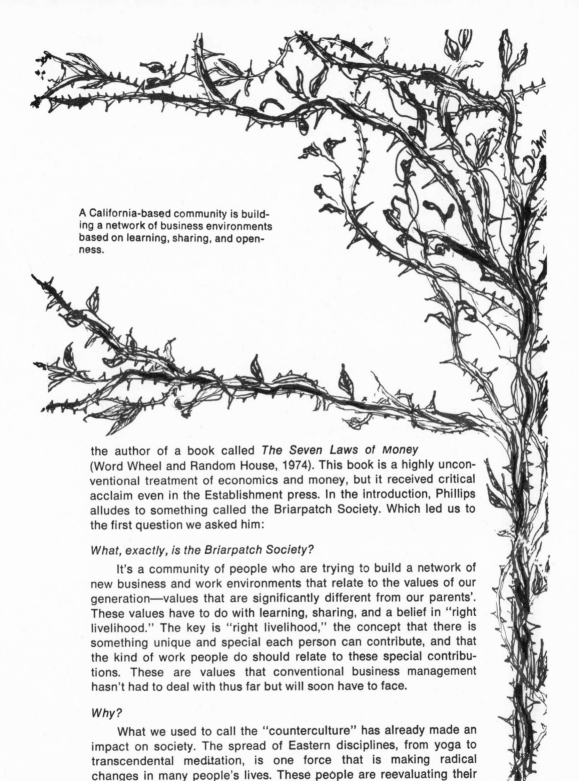

A California-based community is building a network of business environments based on learning, sharing, and openness.

the author of a book called *The Seven Laws of Money* (Word Wheel and Random House, 1974). This book is a highly unconventional treatment of economics and money, but it received critical acclaim even in the Establishment press. In the introduction, Phillips alludes to something called the Briarpatch Society. Which led us to the first question we asked him:

What, exactly, is the Briarpatch Society?

It's a community of people who are trying to build a network of new business and work environments that relate to the values of our generation—values that are significantly different from our parents'. These values have to do with learning, sharing, and a belief in "right livelihood." The key is "right livelihood," the concept that there is something unique and special each person can contribute, and that the kind of work people do should relate to these special contributions. These are values that conventional business management hasn't had to deal with thus far but will soon have to face.

Why?

What we used to call the "counterculture" has already made an impact on society. The spread of Eastern disciplines, from yoga to transcendental meditation, is one force that is making radical changes in many people's lives. These people are reevaluating their personal goals and ways of living, and they will want new ways of working.

How do new values relate to new ways of working, and to the Briar-patch in particular?

In the Briarpatch, we're experimenting with new management styles. So far, management in the Briarpatch is based on three principles: failing young, learning how the world works, and learning to share. Underlying all three of these is the value of openness. *The Seven Laws of Money* deals with how to be more open about money. Now we're evolving a kind of management that deals with how to be more honest and open with each other.

Public financial statements

How is this openness expressed?

Well, for example, the auto repair shops we run have their financial statements posted on the wall, right next to the cost of parts and supplies. Also, the wages of everyone in Briarpatch organizations are public information—in fact, all the information about our corporations is available to all the members and all the customers. We feel we have to be able to justify the wage structure and resource allocation of the companies to anyone who asks.

Our assumption is that everyone can learn managerial skills if they have enough information and experience. So we freely give each other all the information we can. Since our accounting is posted and open to everyone, the person who makes out a sales receipt, and the customer also, can see how that receipt relates to the final balance sheet.

Let's discuss those three basic principles, beginning with "failing young."

We start with the assumption that failure is desirable, since it's a learning experience. For every "success" in life there are 10 failures—and that means 10 times as many opportunities to learn. If failure is accepted, people are more willing to try. And if they try and fail, they evaluate the consequences of their own behavior more effectively and they understand responsibility better. Of course, when you have the attitude that failure is acceptable—even desirable—fewer things become "failure."

What about "learning how the world works"?

People who are open and growing are looking at all parts of their lives, including work, as a chance to learn about the world around them. Day-to-day business decision making is a great chance to learn, because the consequences of decisions are often very tangible.

To us, the best decision makers are not the ones who come up with the most brilliant, rational solutions, but the ones who are able to look at the alternatives and then make *nonrational* judgments, incorporating an understanding that isn't inherent in the situation or the information at hand. The realm of logic and rational thought comprises only 2 percent of "how the world works." If someone makes a successful decision, it's not because he got the 2 percent right, but because he was making some accurate judgment in the remaining 98 percent.

And how do you get to the stage of using that 98 percent effectively?

By sharing—which is the third principle. To share, you have to accept what other people offer you, in the broad sense. When you have really been able to open youself to other people's experiences and perceptions, you're sharing. It takes time to learn to trust other people's experiences, but when you can, you can make better decisions. Take an example: The board of Point Foundation, which is part of the Briarpatch, has six regular directors plus a seventh who is a different guest each meeting. A new person brings a unique experience and the others share it. Consequently, the Point board meetings are more fun—there's always something unexpected, and the decisions are much better, going beyond the regular boundaries of decision making. This is "open" in a mathematical sense too: We always have one element that's new.

What kinds of organizations, besides foundations, are part of the Briarpatch?

We have maybe 20 businesses—a wide cross section, including a bakery, a bookstore, auto repair shops, an ice cream store, a wholesale food distributor, and a publishing firm. Mostly, these companies were started by people who just wanted to fulfill their own desires to do the things they like doing. The bakery was started by a few people who wanted to bake their own bread, and found that others liked what they baked.

A different lifestyle

Is Briarpatch an organized group?

It's really a matter of self-definition: If you say you're a Briar, then you are. Since the book came out, people have come to us and said, "I feel 'good' about the Seven Laws of Money and I want to be part of the Briarpatch." So they are. They know that means they are willing to live a little differently from the traditional business person. The first question they have to answer for themselves is, "What's the minimum I need to live on?" We feel that sharing more and consuming less are important contributions we can make to the world.

As a consequence, we prefer to be as labor-intensive as possible, to employ as many people as possible. It's better to have six people working irregular hours earning $2.50 an hour, if they can all live on and enjoy that, than to have three people working steadily at $5 an hour.

What other differences are there between Briarpatch and other businesses?

Our total intent is to understand and enjoy what we're doing. To an outsider that might appear inefficient. We'll stop and talk to a customer who says, "This is too expensive." We can probably learn from that person, and the customer can learn what our business is about. In a case like this, an alliance is formed—the customer makes a personal and emotional investment in our business.

In a way, we probably use our resources more effectively than many other businesses. We have a sort of "family alliance" in which information and resources are shared and valuable experiences are passed on as soon as possible. Surplus operating cash from one business can be used to make loans to other businesses. When we found an insurance agent who understood what we're doing, we shared that agent with the others—immediately—and all got lower rates.

Is there a central clearing house through which you all keep in contact?

We hired a coordinator last year. Twelve of us chip in $25 a month each toward his salary. His job is to make us all aware of what the others are doing and to make sure that resources are shared. This strong communication network extends only through northern California, although Briarpatch businesses are all over the country.

What are the other Briarpatch jobs like?

We design jobs so that people can go from one company to another, from the profit-making realm to the foundation realm, from gardener to shop supervisor. Wherever curiosity leads Briars, they're encouraged to go: up or down or horizontal. We operate on the assumption that wages don't determine how valuable a person is. An economist who is a good typist may be termed more "valuable" as an economist than as a secretary, but if he gets great satisfaction out of doing what secretaries do, he should do that. Actually, we try to avoid having the position of "secretary"; we've found that as few people want to be secretaries as want to be presidents.

Not too many people realize that management can be rewarding and exciting. By sharing experiences, we're trying to show that management *can* be, in itself, a right livelihood for the appropriate people.

How do you define "management"?

It's a set of experiences that allow one person to help other people be more effective. A good manager can help people realize their own qualities and make the best use of them—and then go on to be independent. A manager and the person being managed are like teacher and student; the good teacher often is the student of the person he's teaching.

Can large organizations be run in the same way as Briarpatch ones?

I don't see why not. The largest business we now have has only 30 employees, but when the opportunity comes along to try a business that can offer real economies of scale, we'll try it. So far the Briarpatch is only a couple of years old.

How well are the companies doing?

They're healthy in the sense that people are learning and having fun. Some of the businesses have changed from what they were originally, and some have closed. But the community is growing and the people are excited; their needs are being met.

Outside the larger industrial culture

Are some of the Briars corporate dropouts?

Yes, some. And several are Harvard MBAs. One of them had been part of the top management of a national accounting firm; now he's the office manager of a Briarpatch publishing venture. Our coordinator has a law degree and a doctorate in international relations, and he worked for a multinational corporation for six years. And a third Briar ran one of the largest endowed churches on the West Coast and has had staffs of up to 200 people; now he organizes communal housing in the Briarpatch network.

Communal housing?

Yes—since being in the Briarpatch involves being able to live more joyously with less money, we encourage communal groups. These aren't "communes" in the 1960s sense. Most people, even if they drop out of business, retain some of their middle-class values. Although they want a sense of community, they still want privacy for themselves and their families. So we help and encourage groups of eight to 14 people to get together in a dwelling that's large enough for each person or family to have enough private space. They may share some bathrooms and a kitchen as well as expenses. The legal forms for these groupings vary: In some cases they're condominiums, in others they're co-ops or partnerships. The houses are bought, rented, or leased. This kind of living, incidentally, is ideal for divorced people with children.

A lot of administrative time is necessary to make this kind of living arrangement work well. Each person should expect to spend eight to 10 hours a week just talking with other people in the community. That's what keeps the community together.

This sense of community is at the center of what Briarpatch is all about. Group support can generate the kind of success that money can't. If you have enough people committed to an idea, you should have more than adequate resources to accomplish whatever the group wishes to do.

In the introduction to your book, you mentioned that the Briarpatch Society consists of people learning to live in the cracks. What does that mean?

A briarpatch is a group of thorny bushes that grow in inhospitable places, use little water or soil, and are very successful at surviving without being bulky. "Live in the cracks" comes from a metaphor we use: The larger industrial culture, with its monolithic pyramidal structures, is going to find itself in the middle of an earthquake— cracking when it becomes too much out of tune with people's values. These will be difficult times. Those who survive will be the ones who can live in the cracks that open up. Weeds survive in the cracks; as concrete breaks apart, here comes that weed, or briar bush, which can survive on much less. In the Briarpatch, we can survive on much less and enjoy life much more.

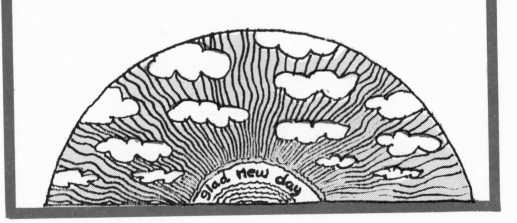

EGGS & PEANUT BUTTER

David Weitzman
1974; 176 pages $5.95 postpaid
from:

World Wheel Books
Post Office Box 441
Menlo Park, Ca 94025

Eggs & Peanut Butter is a book
I wish I had written--rather,
<u>could</u> have. It shows the hu-
manist/teacher at work in the
classroom, one who likes kids,
respects them as persons, is
aware of their feelings, does-
n't upset them with aimless
group "dynamics", and makes
classes stimulating and worthwhile to them. We all of us
can learn from the book's
bubbling ideas--every teacher
and teacher-to-be will be better for having read it.

For all its light-hearted,
free-wheeling, sometimes slap-
bang style, it is basically a
serious plea for a looser,
freer, more honest interplay
of shared thoughts and feelings between teacher and pupil.
It is a treasure of imagina-
tive presentation, a grab-bag
of pleasant surprises--in short,
great fun to read.

It should be every student
teacher's bedside book, and it
would have to jolt even the
experienced teacher into productive self-awareness. I cannot imagine anyone interested
in education who could pick it
up, read it, and put it down
unaffected.

                    -T. Robert Basset
                     Professor of Education
                     Bloomfield College

WILL

At Portola Institute, education is defined as "learning how the world works." and one of the major premises of Briarpatch economics is that working and learning can be nearly synonomous.

In recent months, more and more business groups have become allied with the briarpatch (more than 75 groups in the San Francisco area are now supporting a Briarpatch circuit-rider -- see "Creating a Briarpatch network.")

Simultaneously, within recent months news stories have appeared that point to the crumbling myth of the financial benefits of a college education. Prof. Dale Jorgenson, in a recent interview with Stewart Brand in the Winter issue of "Co-Evolution Quarterly," stated, "As you know, there's been practically a collapse in the market for college education, equal to or greater than the collapse that has occurred in the stock market. Rates of return on college education have dropped from large, positive numbers like 10% (which is what the stock market used to earn in the good old days) to numbers like 0%. College

graduates are not all that much better off than people who started working right after high school, ending up with slightly less income than the college graduate after graduation."

In an article entitled " "School is Bad: Work is Worse" published by the University of Chicago, a group from Portola Institute proposes that educational reform has not been especially effective or popular, despite some apparent public clamor, because our culture is still predominantly sympathetic to our industrial, profit seeking traditions. If educational reform is to occur, they argue, it will be necessary to start with the reformation of our industrial culture rather than directly assault our public schools.

Does this mean that Harvard's days are numbered? Probably not, but more importantly, that's still not the best question. A better question might be "How can anyone defend our American educational system?"

The answer to this, which sounds quite contradictory, is that the American system of education is very defensible, because it does exactly what it was designed to do: it produces a society of competitive, acquisitive, regimented individuals who can read well, write properly, and calculate competently while fitting into a society that allows the strong to lead the weak.

Perhaps one of the big things going for the Briarpatch society is that it represents potentially a valid reformation of traditional business-based society. Just look at the premises we start from: cooperation, non-acquisitiveness, individual uniqueness (right livelihood), as examples.

A briar may want (probably will always want) a public school system for reading, writing, and calculating. And let's face it, a business establishment isn't always ideally suited to offer the best grounding in physics, chemistry, and lots of other subjects. But who needs an educational system encouraging acquisitiveness, expansionism, and conformity?

Here at Portola Institute, as we work actively with other Briarpatch enterprises, we are learning plenty of planning, politics, human behavior, law, and even chemistry, physics, and athletics. But most importantly, without

attending any "formal" classes, we are part of a society learning to share, discipline itself, open up, and inquire.

We're glad to be a part of it.
                                    -Michael Joan Vetch

Buying a New Business

Sunshine bought a business in downtown San Francisco with her small savings. He Here she tells the story of what happened. Sunshine is joyful, energetic and supportive. Her bountiful energy has been very important in the total Briarpatch network.

This is a real life story from me a real woman person who made a real attempt at running a business in downtown San Francisco, beginning a massage parlor and evolving into a growth center.

What worked was the learning process of being with other high energy people. What I learned is that I want to work with others in agreement. I do not want employees; I don't want to get involved in a pay-check relationship. Working things out by reaching a common decision makes much more sense to me than decisions handed down, which never get carried out exactly anyway.

What didn't work was going into heavy debt to buy the business, starting it alone, then trying to find people to join me, being run by my old movies of what it meant to be a success.

What I learned was that people energy can move mountains. At one point we were all thirteen of us dividing up evenly the monies we earned doing massage and workshops. That meant those who cleaned the floors and answered the phones got as much as those doing massage. That also meant we each valued the other's work as highly as our own. Perhaps that was too unwieldy an idea for that time and place. None of us were able to support ourselves, so we all took part-time jobs on the side.

Then we got into leadership problems. It was all my money and when I suggested we all begin putting part of our outside paychecks into the till, there was strong opposition. This sort of sharing was a brand new idea to most of us. I least of all was ready to let go of my fears about total economic loss

(which simply postponed what was already happening.). On the positive side, all thirteen of us were doing what we wanted to do. I define the project as a failure in the sense that it was not economically viable at that point. I have let go of the negative connotations of failure and consider it simply a start-ing point for something else.

What finally happened was that the original people left leav-ing me and some new people with less high energy, and I lost heart for continuing on that level. What I did was bring the business to a hibernation point. I took three months off to take stock, to reflect on what I had learned, and where I wanted to go from here. I am now moving into a collective to share childraising responsibil-ities and I am working towards creating cooperative working situations. I am resolved that I do not want to work in any other way, even tho I have no tradition encouraging me with that point of view.

The many lessons I learned and the insights into how I want to do business, what it means to be in business, were all extremely important data for any new pro-jects I undertake. Knowing there is a support system of other Briarpatchers struggling with similar issues is also very encouraging to me.

—Sunshine Appleby

```
Mimeograph printing  -$1,100.00
Mailing list work    -    390.00
Mailing costs        -     50.00
Supplies             -     75.00
Office expenses      -    100.00
```

All labor was donated.
Revenue: All previous revenue
was used to pay for the expenses of the first edition
in November 1973.
Borrowing:

$500 from Annie Helmuth;
$1,000 from Michael Phillips,
to be repaid out of The
Briarpatch Review sales and
member contributions.

price

The Briarpatch Review sells
for $1.00 retail, including
sales tax. We include tax because that is more truthful.
Most Briarpatch stores tell
us that they enter the "total"
sale price in their register
and then later look at their
total register receipts to
figure out how much they owe
in sales tax. So it's easy
and honest to just ring up the
$1.00. We charge the retailer
50¢ a copy.

distribution

5,000 copies of The Briarpatch
Review were printed in this
edition. 1,500 were mailed to
Briarpatch members and people
who asked for copies; 2,500
are for sale in Briarpatch and
book stores (if you want
copies to sell, please ask).
The balance, 1,000, are for
use as back issues.

articles-ideas

We would love some more Briarpatch writers. We suggest you
try to stay under 500 words
and try your talent at several
subjects. You know what the
Briarpatch is as well as anyone so go ahead and write what
you want. Try to talk about
real successes and failures
and what happened. The Review
is an information exchange to
keep the community growing together. We can't pay for
material yet--hopefully the
information you'll glean from
the Review will repay you for
your contribution.

"Didn't the fox never catch the rabbit, Uncle Remus?"

"He come might nigh it, honey, sho's you born--Brer Fox did. One day after Brer Rabbit fooled him with the calamus root, Brer Fox went to work en got him some tar, en mix it wid some turpentine, en fix up a contrap-shun what he call a Tar Baby, en he took dis here Tar Baby en he set him in de big road, en den he lay off in de bushes fer to see what de news wuz gonna be.

En he didn't hafta wait long, neither, cause by-n-by here come Brer Rabbit down de road--lippity clippity--jes as sassy as a jay-bird, til he spy Tar Baby. "Mawnin!" sez Brer Rabbit, "Nice wedder dis mawnin." Tar Baby, he ain't sayin' nothin', en Brer Fox he lay low. "How you come on, den? Is you deaf? You stuck up, dat's what you is," sez Brer Rabbit, "en if you don't take off dat hat en tell me howdy, I'm gonna bust you wide open." Tar Baby stay still en Brer Fox, he lay low.

Brer Rabbit keep on axin' him, en de Tar Baby, she keep on sayin' nothin' til presently Brer Rabbit draw back wid his fist, en blip he tuck em side er de head. His fist stuck, en he can't pull loose. "Ef you don't lemme loose, I'll knock you agin," en wid dat he fotch er a wipe wid de other hand, en dat stuck, too.

Den Brer Fox he stroll by: "Howdy, Brer Rabbit, you look sorter stuck up dis mawnin,"

BRER RABBIT

en den he roll on de ground, en laughed en laughed til he could n't laugh no mo. "Well, I speck I got you dis time, Brer Rabbit. Maybe I ain't, but I speck I is. You been runnin' round here sassin' me a mighty long time. En den you allers somewheres you ain't got no business. Who ask you to come en strike up a 'quaintance wid dis here Tar Baby? En who stuck you up dar whar you is? Nobody in de round worril. You jes took en jam yo-self on dat Tar Baby widout waitin' fer any invite," sez Brer Fox, "En dar you is, en dar you'll stay til I fixes up a brush-pile and fires her up, cause I'm gonna bobby-cue you dis day, sho," sez Brer Fox.

Den Brer Rabbit talk mighty humble. "I don't care what you do wid me, Brer Fox, jes so you don't fling me in dat briarpatch. Roast me, Brer Fox, but don't fling me in dat briarpatch." Brer Fox wanta hurt Brer Rabbit bad as he kin, so he cotch him by de hind legs en slung him right in de middle of de briar-patch.

By-m-by he hear somebody call him, en way up de hill he see Brer Rabbit settin' cross-legged on a log combin' de pitch outta his hair wid a chip. Den Brer Fox know dat he bin swop off mighty bad. Brer Rabbit wuz bleedzed fer to fling back some of his sass, en he holler out: "Bred en bawn in a briarpatch, Brer Fox--bred en bawn in a briarpatch!" en wid dat he skip out jes as lively as a cricket in de embers."

BRIARPATCH REVIEW

CONTENTS

This issue was put together by:

Kristin Anundsen   Annie Helmuth
Michael Phillips   Kathy Mayer

with thanks to:

Andy Alpine   Mary Jew
Judi Johnston   Arlene Goldbard

Cover and
special graphics: Jim Wintersteen

©1975 Portola Institute Menlo Park California

Messages from the Briarpatch

One of the most rewarding aspects of publishing the Briarpatch Review is getting letters from Briars. Our readers write to us like friends--telling us how they feel and what they're doing-- and the letters give such a warm feeling of community that reading one is like getting a hug. And of course, these Briars are talking to each other as well as to us, giving valuable information and support. That's what the Review

is all about: communication, communion....We need these responses to know whether we're meeting your needs and how we can make the Review truly relevant to Briarpatch living. The following are just a few of the many messages we've had since the publication of the last issue.

-people index

The Whole Earth Catalog provided access to tools and was very successful. Now picture this: a catalog, maybe as large as the Last Whole Earth, but with names, addresses, telephone numbers of people. Okay? A very special telephone and address book. A telephone and address book providing access to people, each with a bit, or several bits, of knowledge which could be shared for the price of a letter or phone call with someone needing that knowledge. Everything indexed into proper headings. Every person in the book because he or she wants to share his or her knowledge. Think of the possibilities.

For example, my father has been a buttermaker and creamery man for 35 years. Besides that he has a wonderful fund of knowledge about electrical wiring and refrigeration. Suppose we had a heading like "Dairy Products":

Dairy Products: Paul Gasche, 725 Daggett Ave., Napoleon, Ohio, 43545. Ph. 419-592-6192. Buttermaker, house wiring, refrigeration.

Cross index this under electricity or house wiring. Here is a wealth of knowledge that can be tapped for the price of a phone call or a letter. Suppose a commune wants to make a churn, or is having problems when they try to churn large amounts of butter. Or an individual using a fruit jar can't get butter from cream. A phone call and probably Dad could tell them what was wrong.

Do you see what I mean? It seems feasible to me. It seems practical. It seems worthwhile. It seems warm and friendly. It seems humane. It seems in keeping with the kind of lifestyle we'd like to see emerge. Indeed, the kind of lifestyle that is emerging.

So why don't I start such a catalog? I'll be happy to do the indexing and the typing if you can get 10,000 people to send me the information and will seriously consider the manuscript.

We all have skills, experiences, talents we could share if only we knew who wanted them and could reach these people at the time they needed the knowledge.

Delmer O. Gasche
RR # 1 Box 180
Morenci, Mich.
49256

-cerro gordo new town

A hit of happiness came my way the other day when a friend of mine lent me his copy of Briarpatch Review, Springtime, 1975. When I left Portola in February, it seemed that the Review had died an untimely and tragic death; now it's back!

After finishing the Energy Primer early this year, Dian and I moved to Cottage Grove, Oregon to work on the Cerro Gordo new town project. After the initial shock of moving from the Bay Area to a small town in Oregon, we find we really like it here.

We are buying an 80-year-old house and we hope to fix it up to something we really feel good about. It has good vibes now, even in its very rough state, and we hope we can rebuild without losing these feelings. I hope to use the old woodshed as a study, and Dian is planning a greenhouse just off the kitchen.

Cerro Gordo is progressing slowly. We hope to build a new town on 1,200 acres we own east of town. "We" are a group of some hundred families all up and down the West Coast who want to build a car-free, ecologically oriented new town. Our dreams include alternative energy sources to heat our homes, smaller than usual housing, and many cooperative, no/low-profit ventures.

In the last couple of weeks I have organized a cooperative tool shop. About 15 of us have agreed to pay $10 a month towards the rent of some 1,400 sq. ft. of warehouse space. We are setting up our table saws, radial arm saws, work benches, etc. there so that we might all have a well-equipped shop to work in. Ashes, the local food co-op, is locating its dried food storage and sales operation in the same place. In the next couple of months, I plan to organize a Community Development Corporation to help fund small businesses organized and staffed by Cerro Gordo Community Association members, as well as publish a crafts catalog for local craftspeople. Local talent can build you a stove, sew you a bike bag, weld you a sculpture, saw you a set of super-sturdy bunk beds, or fabricate super-sized wooden letters, among other things.

I was casting around for a name for my little "consulting" business the other day when my friend lent me the new Briarpatch Review. Flash, I had the name. I am now dba "Briarpatch Services." I guess that name will be subtitled "Economic Development, Facilities Planning, and Solar Technology." Econ. Dev. refers to developing new

43

jobs for the Cerro Gordo new town, Facilities Planning covers the engineering and construction management work I used to do in the dinosaur world (Briars need it too), and Solar Technology covers all those fun things the Energy Primer got me into.

If anyone "out there" is interested in hearing more about the Cerro Gordo new town project, write for more info.

Chuck Missar
704 Whiteaker St.
Cottage Grove, Ore.
97424

- livestock

When someone begins trying to support himself on a subsistence farm, his first impulse is to acquire livestock.

I believe that this is a mistake. Because as soon as you get the animal home you are immediately faced with the multiple problems of feed, feed storage, shelter, and control (that is, fences), all of which are mighty hard to come by when you're starting from scratch.

If I had it to do over
I would put all my efforts
into gardening until I was
providing myself with a
year-round supply of vegetables, grains, and legumes.

After you've gotten
this far you might decide
that you don't need as much
animal protein as you thought.

When you are ready for
livestock you might start
with something like bantam
chickens. They provide most
of their own food during
the summer. They require
a small shelter. They don't
have to be fenced. They
produce both eggs and meat
and you don't have the
problem of preserving the
meat without utilities
because you eat it all in
one sitting.

Don't go to the large
animals (goat, cow, horse)
until you have summer and
winter pasture and only
have to buy hay for bad
weather. Buying grain for
these animals is bad
enough but when you have
to buy enough hay to feed
all winter the hardship
is too great.

Art D. Smith
Rt. 2, Box 17
Dixon, Mo. 65459

- do it!

What you refer to as
Right Livelihood, I've called
a "heart-singing job." I
have one (for the last four
years).

I've had really horrible
times in my life when I've
worried about money almost
constantly and not had quite
enough. Other times I've
just gone ahead and done the
thing I felt was important
and the money has appeared.
Now I have less (money) than
I've ever had, and yet I've
plenty to do everything I
want. It is fantastic.
There are periods even now
when I get gripped by the
worries--and it does para-
lyze me for a few days. When
this happens, I've learned
(although it is very hard to
do when the paralysis occurs)
to do something positive.

Make some positive action--
write a letter to someone
who has done something nice,
send out some mailing pieces,
do some volunteer work. And
invariably something good
happens--hardly ever as a
direct result or response
to the positive action. An
old written-off customer
pays his bill, or a new
cash order comes in from
a brand new source, or
someone asks us out to
dinner. It hasn't failed yet.
The hard part is taking the
positive step when you feel
awful.

About us: Robert and
I started a small press in
the summer of 1971 with $300
in the bank for our summer
living money. We just decided to go ahead and do it
because it seemed right. I
believe it was, because we
are still going and 93% of
the time I look forward to
getting started in the morning. We started with a
little booklet on spinning
(which has now sold over
18,000 copies) and we've
gone on to put out other
people's works on yarns and
fibers that were considered

"too limited" by the large
publishers. We now have
eight titles and last year
we were able to quit our
moonlight jobs.

Christine Thresh
443 Sebastopol Ave.
Santa Rosa, Calif.
95401

P.S. It just happened
again. I've been typing this
letter, and when I typed the
part about things always
working out, I thought to
myself, "Yes they do, but
what about today? The rent
is due and we don't have
enough to cover it." A friend
just called (she has a small
magazine that we typeset on
our IBM composer) and she
said she was coming over and
bringing her money this
evening. It really does
work.

-more on money

Good day for reading
The Seven Laws of Money.
  /two hawks circling,
then hovering still against
the wind
The book was an abso-
lute delight, especially
when I was viewing it from
my role as an accountant.

On this planet, the way we handle our money says a lot about how we handle our global resources.

In my work with many small struggling enterprises, I've found that the words "debit" and "credit" can be explained much more readily by using the concept of yin and yang. From what little I know of Zen teachings, a Zen text of accounting, an approach from that perception, might be an efficient and graceful teaching device.

That accountants are the "high priests" of money may be only because they have learned the ritual of measuring its flow via a monetary shorthand. This ritual allows them to toy with the alternative futures of this flow via the macrame of financial projections. I sincerely wish that more people knew the relatively simple rules of double entry; they too could play with the macrame.

It scares me to think of all the people who are not doing what they want to do (and therefore being more productive) simply because our schools and our society have created this Puritan view of cash and currency. The prime example of this Puritan-spawned myopia is the fact that it has taken account-ants 40 years to publicly acknowledge the fact that the value of the dollar changes constantly. They have yet to agree on how to deal with this phenom-enon in a practical way.

There are alternative currencies, for alter-native purposes. How 'bout using a negative value currency? Now we give others money to take our trash away (or hide it, or deodorize it, or put it in the water or sky). We could achieve something completely different if we had to take trash or pollu-tion in order to get the goods we want.

One of the most useful of financial statements, more so than the balance sheet or the income state-ment, is the Statement of Changes in Financial Con-dition, for it tells you where the capital has been coming from and where it is going. This statement has many working variations, and is also commonly known as a funds flow statement.

So much for my ramb-lings; I'd like to hear yours. Sign me up for a subscription to the Briar-patch Review.

Stephen Johnson
P.O. Box 2401
Fort Collins, Co.

47

A Restaurant That Does Everything Wrong

by Michael Phillips

If a conventional restauranteur were to describe the Communion Restaurant in San Francisco, he or she would probably say in tones of incredulity: "This restaurant isn't to be believed; they've done every single thing wrong."

Like what? "First they opened it in the wino section of town; second, they have enough space to seat about 60 people but the tables are so far apart they only handle 40 people at a time; then there are all sorts of special oddities." Such as? "No smoking, no talking, no shoes in the part of the restaurant that's Japanese style, and no bus boys; when you're done eating you take your own dishes to the kitchen and put the cloth napkin in a bag. There are no paintings on the walls, no music, and most incredible of all, no cashier. The cash register is an open box where you make your own change."

That is incredible, and it's not all. The Communion serves Indian food--chapatis, curry, and such--changing only the vegetables, and you may eat as much as you need. The Briar restauranteurs originally charged 80 cents for all this, then when they made more money than they could use they dropped the price to 60 cents.

Still, Communion is a success-- especially in Briarpatch terms. A year and a half old now, it's a project of joy. Annie Helmuth and I visited the group to research the story of their experiment. (We had eaten there many times and been very touched by the experience each time; it reminded us of our Zen meditation retreats.) According to the group, it is the work that matters and not who does it, so they have asked us not to use their names in this article.

48

BUILDING

To open the restaurant, they saved $5,000, earned through construction jobs. Only restaurants in poor neighborhoods were available at this price. For $3,000 they bought a lease on a Folsom Street place which included a refrigerator, a steam table, a stove, and some formica tables. The monthly rent is $200. The rest of the $5,000 was added to hard work and scavenged lumber to remodel everything.

They cut the stove in half with an acetylene torch to make it more useful for the Indian food they serve, built their own chairs out of plywood and woven strings, and rebuilt the rectangular formica tables into square and round tables with wooden tops. (As they explain, "What side would you choose to sit on? If the table is rectangular you have a <u>pre-ference</u>, so you create comfort for one person and discomfort for another.") Everything that was bought or built was based on the number of diners who could be comfortably served by two people. Once that was decided, it determined the number of tables and chairs, the size of the pots, and the amount of kitchen area.

One of the founding members, a new arrival from India, found that "this country looks like a huge supermarket. You turn on any TV channel and most of what you see is about food. I spent my first three months learning about food. I asked the question, how do Americans know when they are really hungry? They are constantly being bombarded by food stimulation. When they eat in restaurants people are constantly distracted by music, talk, and visual stimulus; this way they are conditioned to forget what hunger really is." Communion was started to let people have a chance to learn how their bodies feel about food-- how to pay full attention to food and to their eating.

TAKE WHAT YOU NEED

Communion emphasizes, "Take only as much as you need. There is a difference between want and need. Want is all ideas and need is real." People who eat regularly at Communion don't eat as much as when they first started coming in--even the group members eat less than they used to.

More than 70% of Communion's customers are regulars eating there four or more days a week. The total leftover food that comes back on the plates is less than a five member family would leave, even with 160 meals a day. "Our customers realize that if they spoil food you have to cook more and they have to pay more," say the group members.

They learned cooking by doing it, observing each time the quality of the ingredients, taste, cooking time, and effects. They pay close attention to money as well as to the food consumed. A few months ago they noticed that the change box, where customers make their own change, had less money in it than it should. They put up a sign reading, "Do we need a cashier?" The next week the money in the box matched the number of meals served and the sign came down.

PRICES

The price of the meals has changed over the year and a half that Communion has been open. It started at 80 cents and after a month it was clear that this would bring in more than the group needed so the price was reduced to 75 cents per meal. After eight months the price was reduced again to 60 cents because the group did not want to make a profit. As they told us, "We didn't open this restaurant to make money," but since "food doesn't come from nowhere, we can't be a charity." Recently the price has gone up to $1.00 so they can save some money. They would like to sell the restaurant at the end of this year to someone who will run it the way they do, and then they will start a farm, preferably in the southern United States. They want to learn about producing food, just as they learned about cooking and serving it. They would welcome help in finding a 40-plus acre farm.

OPEN BOOKS

The Communion books are completely open to everyone, and they are neatly kept with a daily record of receipts and meals served. The hours have changed over the last year: They were 11 AM to 8 PM, with lunch and dinner six days a week; now they are 11 AM to 2 PM and 5-8 PM five days a week. Work starts at 6 AM, when shopping is done at the vegetable markets and cooking begins, it ends at 9 PM after cleaning up. Usually there are two volunteers learning and sharing in the work with the group members.

Communion Open Books

Month since opening	Number of people served	Money in the cash box	Price of meal	Number of days open per month	Rent	Other costs approx.	Net leftover for "take home" to pay workers' living expenses
1st	660	$ 525	80¢	20	$200	$870	–($555)
2nd	3,530	$2,500	75¢	25	$200	$1,800	$500
4th	4,030	$3,020	75¢	22	$200	$1,500	$1,330

Communion took a vacation to decrease the number of customers. They couldn't serve the way they wanted to if there were too many people in the restaurant.

7th	3,080	$2,300	75¢	20	$200	$1,200	$900

The price was dropped to 60¢ and a few weeks more vacation were taken to reduce customers.

10th	3,000	$1,900	60¢	20	$200	$1,100	$600
most recent	2,900	$2,900	$1.00	20	$200	$1,300	$1,400

* The above chart does not take inventory into account, and we do shop in bulk. For example, oil is purchased by the 55-gallon drum and lasts about 2 1/2 months, milk by the 200 lb. drum and once a month. What this means is that expenses for one month may seem less or more if you don't take the existing inventory into account.

* Besides food, other monthly expenses are: utilities - $90, supplies - $25, transportation - $50.

* The average price of food per person is 45¢. Thus to feed 3,000 people would cost about $1,350., which is a typical monthly figure.

* The total amount of income from the restaurant going towards the workers' subsistence was $4,566 in 1974, as per the IRS return. Basically four people were supported by this income and there was about $1,500 not spent and left in the restaurant account. Therefore personal living expenses for the group amounted to about $250 a month. This of course does not include food, since everyone eats at the restaurant.

Briarpatch Cooperative Market

by Annie Helmuth

If you don't raise your own, a direct-charge food co-op like the Briarpatch Cooperative Market in Palo Alto, California might be the best place to buy your food. Here, you have a chance to control the quality and price of what you eat.

Planning for the Briarpatch Co-op Market began in 1974 with a group who were disenchanted with a local co-op they felt had become too much like a big supermarket--with no real relationship to the customers, too much junk food, and a tendency to exploit everybody's secret cravings for things like Mars bars and potato chips. They wanted a place with more natural foods and they wanted involvement in the store's policies and environment--an opportunity to take control of an important aspect of their lives.

Bob Luft and Alice Newton, co-managers of the Market, explained to us how their co-op was different from co-ops that are open to the public. Food is sold to the members at cost, plus a very small markup to cover breakage and spoilage. In order to buy at the Market you must become a member by buying at least one $10 share and committing yourself to buying $100 worth within 18 months. Share investments cover stock and equipment and are refundable.

weighing organic food

52

The "direct charge system" means that overhead expenses are divided among members equally. Members pay a weekly fee of 50¢ for every person in the family over six years old. The fee pays for overhead costs like rent, salaries and utilities. According to Alice, "this means that we can sell what people want to buy rather than pushing high mark-up items. Paying a regular direct charge encourages people to be more concerned about the operations of the store. They can see that what they decide to do affects what they pay because overhead costs determine what the direct charge will be. For example, if the membership decides to have the store open more days, then overhead could go up and so could the charge, which is based on total overhead costs for a three-month period."

Each adult member must work two hours a month at the store. There is an annual meeting of the members and each household gets one vote. The board of directors meets once a week as do committees on areas like inventory, research and education, newsletter and management. The management committee considers efficiency problems such as the best hours to have the store open, improving procedures, etc. The Market is open eight hours a day, four days a week. Bob and Alice are the only paid people except for the person who buys the produce for them. Originally, Bob and Alice were going to split one full-time salary of $700 a month, but they decided to be more realistic about the amount of time they were putting in and how much they needed to live on, so each receives $500 a month to avoid any ex-

ploitation between them or in relation to their work.

We asked Bob and Alice to tell us how they felt about the positive and negative aspects of the enterprise. Alice, a registered nurse who had worked with several small food co-ops, told us: "I began working with the Market because I was interested in doing something related to food and nutrition as well as being involved in a community effort that I felt good about socially and politically. The Market has been and continues to be a very satisfying experience for me. I feel much closer to the community I'm living in. The store is a meeting place for friends, and a lot of energy flows through the Briarpatch. Many people have put in extra time because it feels so good to be a part of making it happen. There is definitely a feeling of collective effort and collective success at Briarpatch."

Bob learned about the Market from a community paper, Grapevine. Like Alice, he was looking for work that would include political involvement

"I dig working with people," he told us. "Through the Market I'm always meeting really fine people and it's rewarding to see them volunteer their time, contributing different skills towards improving the store, and just watching it grow. I worked for the state government as a research assistant when I got out of college, so I have direct experience with bureaucracies. I really notice the contrast in working at the Market. Here we just do what has to be done. There are no experts. We gain confidence from figuring out for

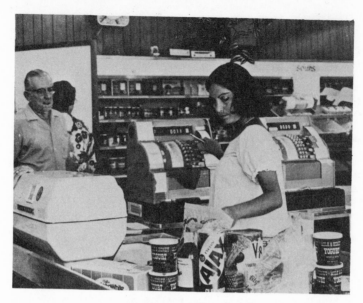

Briarpatch checkout counter

ourselves and we know the Market will be as good as we make it."

Of course, there are headaches involved in running a market like Briarpatch. Members have to decide what the store is going to carry and how it's going to be priced; they also have to depend on each other to stock shelves, take inventory, buy produce, run the cash register, and sweep up at night. There is a lot of work to be done all the time, and sometimes there haven't been enough people on hand to do it.

But there are many compensations: a warm, friendly work-and-shopping place with hanging plants, a quilt on the wall, a comfortable couch, books to browse in, and games for the kids; and shoppers who are friends and fellow workers,

sharing goals and ideals for the place. And it's not all work—there have been picnics and potlucks too. Finally, to some members the real payoff is in the savings; Bob and Alice report that Briarpatch members save 10 to 20% on their food bills. There are now about 420 member households involved in Briarpatch Market.

Dave Smith, one of the original members of the co-op, told us that it had originated through Morris Lippman, a seasoned co-oper who has been active in co-ops for forty years (yes, there were co-ops during the Depression) and Bill Duncan, who put together the Briarpatch Cooperative Auto Shop. During its beginning stages members held a meeting every two or three weeks. They discussed organizing a community around the Market, but the idea died down. They found that a co-op meets food needs in a particular, direct way and that politics and food don't seem to mix. However, the members are interested in educating their members by posting information about the contents, the nutritive value, and sometimes the political implications of the food. There is a committee on research and education which does things like put cards next to all items telling where the food comes from.

The Briarpatch Market members were lucky to find a 7-11 Food Store they could lease; this meant that little renovation was needed. Another co-op moved into a laundromat and worked on it for seven months to get it ready--the Briarpatch group took only ten days for cleaning and remodeling, even though there were fewer than 100 members at that point. Many of the members have special skills they contribute to the store. For instance, if a cabinet is needed it can be built to specifications--with found lumber--by a carpentry-wise member.

The Cooperative Market, which opened March 4, 1975, is a relatively new Briarpatch business. But already the members have learned some useful things they'd like to share with others who might be interested in starting a food co-op:

What to look for in a building:

1. Find a space that's large enough. Don't underestimate the space needed and do allow for growth.

2. Find a place that doesn't need too much work.

3. Check zoning regulations and also check with the Health Department and the Building Inspector. Don't rent a place, move in, and then have the authorities come down on your head because you haven't met all the requirements.

People and money needs:

1. Have a good, dedicated group together before you start.

2. Be sure your capital base is large enough. In our case, by law we couldn't spend our share money until we had a fund of $10,000.

3. Be prepared to lose money in the first few months. Food inventory alone is a high expense.

Patti of Rabat (Briarpatch import store on 24th Street, San Francisco) organized a group of 15 stores into a "pyramid" for alerting each other to shoplifters. If one store has been ripped off, and the proprietor has a description of the shoplifter, he or she phones the top store on the pyramid (Rabat); Patti then phones two other stores, each of which phones two others and so on. Within 3 to 5 minutes, all the stores in the pyramid have been warned of the shoplifter's presence on 24th Street.

-the planters

We figure Johnny Appleseed was a charter Briar. His spirit continues in a modern-day organization called International Association for Education, Development and Distribution of the Lesser Known Food Plants and Trees. It has two major aims: to combat world hunger and to make life more interesting and/or economical for everybody. Dues for members are $7.50 a year; address is P.O. Box 599, Lynwood, Calif. 90262. Here are some excerpts from their newsletter:

"Help us get more trees planted that will provide food crops. Trees will grow where it is impossible to grow other crops, on hills, in rocky soil, yes, some will even grow with their roots in water. Trees prevent erosion, help to prevent floods and provide cover for wild life. Trees make shade and provide timber and a replenishable fuel.

Fruit trees could be planted in the parks, as street trees, around the houses in the poorer sections of the towns. They would need to be checked and a little care taken of them for the first couple of years after planting, then they would provide needed food and vitamins for the children in the area. Sadly, in many areas, instead of more trees being planted, they are being cleared away to make room for more houses and plowed fields.

One very interesting fruit is the cashew which can be grown under a great variety of conditions. We know it for the delicious nut but this nut grows at the end of a large receptacle called the cashew apple from which juice, wine and jelly can be made and which, when dried, tastes like something between a date and a fig.

People in rural and suburban areas are often short on their food supply and money and still throw away their beet tops and such items while ignoring the nearby vacant lots and fields where dandelion, sourdock, pigweed, lambsquarters, plantain, poke, purslane and numerous other good, edible food plants grow rampant."

56

Couples and Money

By Michael Phillips

For people concerned with having healthier and more honest relationships with friends and sexual partners, money is a difficult subject to handle. In writing The Seven Laws of Money, Salli Rasberry and I worked out some rules for dealing with money on a very personal and open basis, but devoted only one page to couples and their money. Since then I have worked with Annie Helmuth in developing some useful guidelines in this area. Annie is a strongly independent woman with extraordinary sensitivity to the relations between people.

Annie always pays for herself and so do I. Any exception to this personal rule requires a great deal of thought and extensive discussion of the unspoken and hidden assumptions involved in letting someone else pay for us. Why? Because letting someone else pay for you produces a subtle (often hidden) change in the relationship. Something is being bought and what it is is not out in the open.

Fifteen years ago, young people used to joke, "I paid for her dinner and a movie but all I got was a kiss," or "He thought the price of my dinner included more than just my company." Although people don't talk in those terms so much any more, those or other assumptions are still there. Annie feels that a man's paying for her is simply not fair to her or to him. On my part, the hardest thing in not paying for a woman is the fear of being considered a cheapskate; yet when I treat someone else I feel like her parent, and I expect her to behave in some appropriate way.

If you're responsible for yourself, you pay for yourself! I used to alternate "treats" with friends, paying one time and having the friend pay the next. Then I realized that it is nonsense to carry around those mental balance sheets detailing who owes whom what. I now share equally with dates, or where that is inconvenient settle within a day or two.

57

How do you pay for yourself in an ongoing relationship where there is a difference in income or wealth? The tendency is to let the argument "I can afford it more than you" prevail and forget about the openness and equality being sacrificed. The rule I find works best is, "The one with less money chooses." If we're going to a restaurant, we go to one that is chosen by the person with less money to spend on dinner. We try to pick a restaurant that has a wide range of prices.

This rule can be applied to nearly everything: shows, vacation places, etc. Suppose, however,.that both people want to go to the theater but the one with more money wants much more expensive seats--what then? The solution is that both pay the minimum seat charge and the one with the desire for the more expensive seat pays the difference between that cost and the higher one of sitting together in the more expensive seats.

In long-term relations where the money differential is significant, a second rule, I have found, is useful: "The one with more money provides the capital." By this I mean that if one has

a car and the other doesn't, they split the gasoline expenses and bridge tolls evenly but the one with more money (presumably the one who owns the car) pays the other costs of car-owning--insurance, repairs, and depreciation. If both own cars, but one is smaller and gets better mileage, the gasoline cost of running the one with the better mileage is the cost that is split by the couple. Where one has a house and the other an apartment, parties are held at the house and the person with more money bears the costs of broken glasses and cigarette burns on the rugs; food and drink expenses are shared equally.

58

In the beginning, keeping track of money and keeping the issues out in the open is a constant emotional struggle. It's always easier to say, "I'll treat-- let's forget the petty splitting of expenses." However, both Annie and I find that the system I've outlined above has strengthened our personal integrity and that our relations have grown more open and honest. <u>Now</u> we enjoy figuring out ways to solve problems of sharing expenses, and the calculations are so commonplace they are second nature. Most of our friends expect everyone to pay for himself or herself so we seldom talk about it, but new people we meet find it hard and question whether it's worth doing.

Our solutions, "The one with less money chooses" and "The one with more money provides capital," work well for us. We'd like to hear more about this from others.

Pricing

Pricing of new products in the Briarpatch is an ongoing question. Annie Helmuth and Michael Phillips brought back a large number of kimonos they had bought in Japan. The cost was low and the demand high. The discussions on pricing ranged from one view that the prices should be based purely on costs, with low calculations for hourly wages, to the suggestion that the kimonos be auctioned off to the highest bidder to find out what the market would bear. The solution was that two of their friends joined them in pricing each kimono; the pricing was on the basis that "the kimono is to be sold to a friend." The next evening friends were invited to a private sale, and the following day the remaining kimonos at the same prices were sold to the public. Price as though all your customers are your close friends!

Briarpatch Cooperative Auto Shop

By Kristin Anundsen

Autos in for repair (above)
Keith scheduling jobs (below)

The Briarpatch Cooperative Auto Shop in Palo Alto never was designed to make a big profit. On the other hand, it wasn't intended to lose money either. Nevertheless, for some time after its incorporation in April 1973, it was operating in the red, and although its membership was increasing rapidly, its fiscal future looked a little wobbly.

Then, about a year ago, Keith Williams took over as manager and the Auto Shop's prospects took an upturn. "We had to clean up our act," Keith explains. "We needed to become more businesslike in our dealings with our membership and our suppliers. Our original goal was to operate 'without profit,' but when we got a CPA in here he enlightened us to the fact that you have to have contingency funds. You have to start putting money away ahead of time for things like moves, sick pay, vacations, and so forth. We were operating so close to the wire--our checkbook balance was always minus, and the bookkeeper was just counting on certain funds to come in on time."

Another problem was record-keeping, or awareness of cash flow. "Our member/customers were writing up their own bills, and even though the board of directors had decided that there would be no accounts receivable, credit was being extended. The previous manager sometimes gave things away. Also, expenditures were not always accounted for and too much money was tied up in inventory," says Keith.

Today, the Auto Shop operates in the black, transactions are systematically recorded, and parts and supplies that weren't necessary have been sold. The working account usually has a balance of at least $1,000, according to Keith. (There is, in addition, a capital account, a tax account, and an immediate-parts account.) The shop is also operating more smoothly as a service to its customers.

One of the oldest Briarpatch businesses, the Cooperative Auto Shop was started by Bill Duncan (who is now in Appalachia setting up a land-based community). At that time Keith Williams was running his own business: "on-the-street auto repair." Bill "took my partner away from me," recalls Keith, "and I came down to find out what was going on." The three of them, plus another mechanic and an office assistant, set up the business with the aid of an Agape Foundation Grant. "We determined our own salaries," says Keith. "We'd get together at Bill's house to decide who should make what. We never did really clear it up. The primary criterion was need. I'm the highest paid because I have the largest family." As in most other Briarpatch businesses, everyone's jobs are considered equally valuable.

In order to use the shop's facilities, each customer must become a member by buying a $15 share for each vehicle to be serviced; this share money is used for capital investments. The co-op owns everything but the building, which is leased. There are now close to 1,400 shares outstanding, of which about 50 have been refunded. Staff includes general manager Williams, three full-time mechanics, a full-time parts person, a part-time apprentice, and a CPA.

Major policy decisions are made by the board of directors, who are elected by the membership. Every Monday morning one board member, the manager, and one other staff member meet to review operational problems. Other decisions are made on the spot by the staff members themselves. "Our overriding objective is high-quality, honest auto repair and maintenance," says Keith. "When I have to decide something, I just think of that concept and the decision is usually made."

He adds, "I couldn't see myself going to work in anything other than a collective business or my own business. If you have the traditional employee-employer orientation, you're not going to get what people are really capable of doing."

Finding people of Briarpatch values to join the staff is difficult, Keith admits. "We recently lost two mechanics, and so far we've only been able to replace one. We interviewed one person who was so into money that he couldn't have been happy working here. He couldn't see it as anything but just a job." Mechanics who are hired are put on a trial basis for two weeks or more on half commission on their labor. To work permanently, a staff member must feel, and show, that he or

she truly likes dealing with people on a personal basis.

The shop's labor charge is $16.50 an hour, which covers basic expenses, pays the mechanics $700 a month, and leaves a small surplus for emergencies and expansion. Charges for most jobs are determined at a "flat rate"-- based on the time a competent mechanic should take to do the job well--even if the job takes a little longer or not quite so long. Mechanics try to give the maximum realistic estimate of the price of a job. Parts cost between 10 and 20 percent less than list price.

In addition to having their cars repaired by staff mechanics, members have the option of renting space at $2 an hour, which includes using

Steam cleaning and electronic tune-ups

the shop's equipment and periodic advice from staff mechanics, or $5 a day for use of the bench only. Mechanics will also service the car and rap with the owner about it during the process; the cost is the regular repair rate of $16.50 an hour. The shop stocks a healthy collection of manuals to aid the do-it-yourselfers. All members of the co-op are asked to give two hours of work to the shop a year.

The idea of providing auto repair that isn't a rip-off—and, in fact, educating customers to the point where they can actually take over many repairs themselves—is a major catalyst in maintaining the enthusiasm of both staff and member/customers. Member Dick Daniels finds the shop constructive in the sense that "Even if I end up with a big bill, I can learn something. I don't feel manipulated." Keith Williams, who once quit a job with a large organization when it got into defense work, says, "To every one of us, this is more than just a job. Most auto shops don't relate so closely to the car owners. The work load is extremely demanding, but everyone likes taking responsibility for what they're doing. We feel we _are_ the Briarpatch and we're willing

to do a lot. One time we all came in on a Saturday and painted the building."

Lee Swenson, who has been a member from the beginning, says that the Briarpatch Cooperative Auto Shop's evolution "has really been a struggle. First of all, running this kind of business with cars is difficult in itself; if there's anything people are neurotic about, it's cars and money. Also, at first there were problems with quality control, since the staff had to service so many different kinds of cars. Most people's patience is short, mine included—we expect everything to run smoothly from the first and are judgmental when it doesn't. The Briarpatch Shop needed a growing period. Now, with more practice, better machinery, and better pacing, it's going very well. To me, the most important thing it's done is to stay honest."

An eight-page Briarpatch Cooperative Auto Shop report, giving the latest financial statement, the share agreement, articles of incorporation, bylaws, and prices, is available from the shop at 2901 Park Blvd., Palo Alto, CA 94306 or from the Briarpatch Review office, for $1 a copy to cover postage and handling.

Gary Warne has two major occupational involvements: a used-book store, called Circus of the Soul, and Communiversity, which offers free classes and interest groups. Communiversity, formerly affiliated with San Francisco State University under Gary's direction, is now run collectively and operates out of the bookstore's storefront office. Shared with the San Francisco Roommate Referral Service, the storefront, at 451 Judah Street, San Francisco, is open daily from noon to 7 p.m.

Demystifying Business

by Gary Warne

At my first and last Renaissance Faire I asked a stained-glass window maker how he worked his craft. He wouldn't tell me, and I guessed that was because he didn't want me making windows myself. Another time I went into a bookstore to ask some questions about how to price old books. The people there implied that I must be crazy-- why should they take their time to help me set up my own business? Neither of these people were Briars, to my way of thinking. One of the important values to a Briar or a Briarpatch business is that of shared information. Whatever a Briar learns in his or her work and in setting up a business should be available as a resource for others to learn and grow from as they begin their own ventures. A Briarpatch exists to bring people together to share what they've discovered and to discover what they have to share.

Lately I've been thinking about other qualities that identify a Briar, and about how Briarpatch values show up in my own behavior. Besides shared information, here are some other basic Briarpatch motives:

Self-sufficiency. It's important for us to take our lives into our own hands, to seek personal growth through personal responsibility and independence from hierarchies, employers, and corporate empires--which are actually overextended communities. We seek self-dependence (on our own creative powers) and interdependence (with friends).

Concern with the people we do business with. A reciprocal exchange agreed upon between two people--that is, a buyer and a seller agreeing that a price is fair--is certainly a major goal. In my own activities I like to go beyond this to look at the needs underlying the exchange. Why is that person really in my store? Consumption is habitual and impulsive; what people are feeling is not always directly related to what they are buying. I like to try to find out whether the person needs the product or service I'm selling or something else entirely. If the business person treats people in such

a way that the money in their hands is the relevant thing about them, these people feel processed. If the medium is the message, the way people are dealt with is as important--maybe more important--than the product or service they are dealt.

Pricing is a central point in relating with people who come into a store. To me, it's essential not to be locked into a pricing scheme. I deal in used books so that I don't have to pay a fixed list price for them and sell them for a fixed price. Whenever possible I accept non-money exchange (barter). If a person says he or she really wants a particular art book but can't pay the money for it, I say, "Okay, maybe you could bake me some bread instead."

The Communiversity offerings are free. The person or persons who advertise interest groups in our catalogue state what their own personal needs are; if those who sign up can meet any of these needs, fine-- but they don't have to. The catalogue itself is paid for by such things as selling food at the New Games Tournament or holding a garage sale.

Simple living. The more simply you live, the less you have to charge for your products or services. Lifestyle determines business style. My needs are really very simple. At the store I don't even have a phone--I don't really need one.

I feel that when a business is just starting up, prices should be high enough to allow for contingencies such as taxes, recessions, and unexpected foul-ups. Later, as the entrepreneur learns to use resources more effectively in personal and business life, prices could be lowered. I've just started the bookstore; if it makes more money than I need, I'll lower my prices. I think that some-times business people raise their prices as the business progresses just because they're bored with what the business itself is doing. They want to make more money to titillate themselves.

Community involvement. A Briar, as I see it, should have an understanding that the business and the customers share the same environment. The money that is spent on the goods and services is part of the community's--the neigh-borhood's--resources. So the business person has a respon-

sibility to be an integral part of that community, to understand it and to contri-bute to it.

When I got the storefront my main idea was to create a "living room." People stop by all the time to talk or sing or play the piano. The Roommate Referral Service that shares our storefront brings in six to twelve people a day, and we hold many of the Com-muniversity sessions there. In the course of having a good time together, people buy things and tell us about their own needs. We try to help the neighborhood groups in ways they can't help themselves. For example, we helped the Inner Sunset Food Store, an emerging new nonprofit co-op,

by suggesting that we run an ad for them in the Communiversity catalogue. The ad was for a "class" on starting a co-op food store. Like most of the Communiversity offerings, it's not really a class, but an interest group with no "teach-ers" or "students"--just people who want to exchange

ideas and skills. Twenty
people signed up for the food
co-op group.

Continuity of values. If and
when I should decide to sell
my bookstore, I would sell it
only to someone who shared my
own standards and values.

Most of these standards and
values are related to one
overriding idea: demystifying
business. In today's society,
in order to save time we
often pay for something we
could make or do ourselves.
In doing this, we are usually
also paying to remain separated from our creative
forces--paying to remain mystified.

To me, the Briarpatch idea of
posting financial statements--
to make everyone aware of
where the money comes from and
where it goes--is very important. What I want to do beyond
that is to state what I want
to do in the future if the
business should bring in more
money.

As a Briarpatch business grows,
more people should be brought
in to learn the service or
skill. Then more people would
be creating the goods and
living a meaningful work style,
and the business and creative
process involved would be de-
mystified to increasing
numbers of people.

Advertising

We don't accept advertising
in the Briarpatch Review.
We publish material that we
think would be of interest
to our readers, and we assume that people buy the
Briarpatch Review because
of its contents. If we
sold ads it would be asking
you to pay for the Review
and shoving some else's material (the ads) into your
magazine. If the content
of the ad is as important
to our readers as the rest
of our contents then we
should run the ad as regular text.

So what we have tried to do
is to pick a business we
would like to advertise and
pay them to design an ad for
us to run. We offer $25.
Our first invitation went
to Communion Restaurant.
They didn't want an ad--
they are already swamped
with business without do-
ing any advertising or
promotion. We gave them
the $25.

With this issue, Briarpatch Review inaugurates a new department, "Simple Living." To help Briars avoid being caught up in the kind of desire for "things" that gets in the way of concern for other values, this department will offer suggestions for living fully but simply, with a minimum of expense.

Our first contribution to this new department comes from Kathleen Person Buchanan, who identifies herself as a "maker of good things to eat."

Simple Living

A Week of Soups:

Start with a large oven-proof container. Add a pile of soup bones, odds and ends of vegetable scraps, a sliced onion, and three or four buds of garlic. Take a piece of rag and a few teaspoons of herbs such as parsley, sage, rosemary, and thyme (hopefully fresh from your garden). Tie the spices and herbs into the rag and toss it into the container. Turn on your oven to 250 degrees and roast the goodies for a couple of hours. They will turn a lovely golden brown. Throw in a couple of cups of wine and let it all simmer for another hour.

Remove from the oven and put everything into a very large kettle. Add enough liquid to cover. The liquid could be broth, boullion cubes dissolved in liquid, wine, vegetable juices, or whatever meets your fancy. I prefer a mixture of 1/2 wine and 1/2 vegetable juices. Simmer slowly for about four hours. Turn off heat and let the pot sit on top of the stove overnight. In the morning remove the fat from the top and strain the liquid. Taste and add sea salt and pepper if you wish.

Measure the liquid and add three cups of additional liquid (such as above) for each cup of starting liquid. To this base add ingredients in the order of cooking time. If beans take two hours, add them first, then in the last 15 minutes of cooking time add things that take only 15 minutes to cook.

The soup is now ready. Refrigerate it after you have had
some, and bring out the soup from the refrigerator each
day and bring to a boil before adding new ingredients.
As to the basic liquid decreases, simply add a cup of
additional liquid each day.

My choice for soups of the day for one week:

Day 1--Add rice noodles to the
liquid, remove them, and serve
them in small bowls along with
side dishes of condiments such
as bowls of fresh sliced
vegetables, chopped nuts,
relishes, or curries (a la
Thailand).

Day 2--Throw in leftover rice
noodles; add sliced scallions,
bamboo shoots, mushrooms, and
bean sprouts (a la Japan).

Day 3--Add a variety of grains
(a la Zen).

Day 4--Add fresh vegetables
(American vegetable soup).

Day 5--Add more fresh vegetables and some odds and ends
of pasta (Italian minestrone).

Day 6--Add Indian curry sea-
soning and some exotic vegetables such as squash, cauliflower, eggplant, etc. (Indian
vegetable curry).

Day 7--Just reheat the pot and
serve soup in small bowls along
with several bowls of condiments such as raisins, sliced
bananas, coconut, sliced fresh
oranges (African).

69

Production and Distribution

The second Briarpatch Review ("Springtime 1975") was printed in an edition of 5,000 by a dedicated group of Briars who worked tirelessly doing production and assembling the Review for mailing and distribution.

We're pleased with the response to the format and the color mimeograph process and the only change we're making in this issue is to do the non-color pages on offset. A mimeograph machine is funky and warm, but it starts spitting ink at you and the paper when somebody new walks into the room or your consciousness wanders for an instant. Good practice.

We contacted bookstores and Briarpatch stores in the Bay Area to ask them to carry the Review. City Lights took ten copies and so did The Tides and The Mill Valley Book Depot. Like many other small press publications, we had to build our own distribution network, so we sent out letters to all the people we thought would be interested in the Briarpatch Review and were delighted to get orders from far-off places like Chicago and Fresno. These are the Briars who ordered ten or more Reviews:

Cody's Books
Berkeley, California

Whole Earth Truck Store
Menlo Park, California

The Catbird Seat
Portland, Oregon

Whole Earth Access Company
Berkeley, California

The Distributors
South Bend, Indiana

Pacific Distributors
San Diego, California

Kepler's
Menlo Park, California

Rational Distributors
Seattle, Washington

Light and Sound Distributions
Tampa, Florida

Sparrow Natural Foods
Fresno, California

Sailing Equipment Warehouse
Olympia, Washington

Briarpatch Food Coop
Menlo Park, California

Plowshare Natural Food
Chicago, Illinois

Banyen Books
Vancouver, Canada

The Aquarian Age
Lompoc, California

Tree Frog Trucking Co.
Portland, Oregon

Shakti Distributes
Decatur, Georgia

Serendipity Couriers, a service oriented distributor of large and small press publications in Sausalito will carry the _Review_ to Bay Area bookstores for us. We hope more Briars will sell the _Review_ to local bookstores and newsstands. Five or more copies of the Review are available to individuals and retailers for 70¢. Send orders with full payment (postage paid) to the _Briarpatch Review_, 330 Ellis Street, San Francisco 94102. We'll give full credit for unsold copies returned in good condition.

Annie Helmuth

Costs

3,000 copies printed
Printing costs:

Mimeograph	– free
Offset	– $145
Paper costs	– $441
Mailing costs	– $ 85
Office expenses	– $ 65
Total	$686

Income since Spring
issue – $619

All labor donated.

Gift Giving

NOTES FROM THE BAY AREA BRIARPATCH NETWORK

Let's see, it's been six busy months since the last Briarpatch Review. The Bay Area Network expanded its scope, membership, activities and the amount of fun we've had.

We've established a "Briarpatch Pledge" which is the amount of money each Briar can afford to give the Network for a six-month period (six months seems to be our number). It's very important to us that our network be self-supporting and the pledge is a move in that direction. Seventy-one Briars have given between $30 and $120 each as pledges. About twenty of these people have given additional time and energy, offering skills and materials that help keep the network flowing. For example, Allen printed our envelopes, Mike and his computer handle our mailings, and Dan provided us with 100 wooden boxes.

Our Wednesday Pier 40 consulting sessions have expanded to five Briars regularly offering their specific knowledge of the business world; Mike for finance, Rich for management, Steve for legal questions, Bonnie and Bart for taxes and bookkeeping, me for marketing, and all of us for overlap. We're developing a good group and the feedback from people coming to Pier 40 (about six businesses a week) is very positive. As a reminder, our Wednesday Pier 40 meetings are open to people who have specific questions about their present or future business. Appointments are made in advance through the Briarpatch coordinator (me) and are available to anyone who feels in tune with the Briarpatch.

Over the past few weeks Mike Phillips and I have visited individual Briarpatch businesses a few mornings a week to find out more about them and how the network can be a greater help. Seeing someone's business "on location" offers us a more fundamental picture of what's going on--also Briars without "problems" don't come to Pier 40 sessions, so we're going out to them.

We held two workshops over the summer. Together with the Number's Game (Bonnie Moore), we organized a day-long workshop on taxes and bookkeeping; and with the New Dimensions Foundation (Mike Toms, et al.) an evening seminar on advertising. Both were successful in terms of turnout and useful information received by participants. Later this fall we'll be presenting a series of four Tuesday evening seminars on public relations, media, direct mail and graphics followed by a day-long work session. Flash, of the Imaginators, will also be offering a workshop on silk screening for Briars in late October. We've got a lot of talent in the network and it's nice discovering ways to share it.

Another exciting project we are developing is a group health insurance plan for Briarpatch members, with wholistic approaches to medicine included in the coverage. Interest in the plan has been high and we are now compiling the individual data on members before finding a specific insurance company to give our good business to. (New Briars are always welcome.)

And then there are the parties. The Briarpatch hot tub party had fifty of us soaking (not all at once) in Liz's Japanese bath after the New Games Tournament in June. We celebrated Father's Day with a pot-luck dinner and dance at the Imaginators' warehouse. Three bands, 250 people and a Cherokee Sun Priestess blew the adage that business people can't have fun (you know, thinking all the time about cash flow, inventory and accounts payable). One beautiful woman in her fifties, who had been invited by a Briar, came to me with an incredible look of bewilderment; she was expecting men and women in BUSINESS. And we just finished celebrating our first Birthday Party with pot-luck desserts...more than 350 Briars feasting, drinking, dancing, and connecting. Outrageous!

by Andy Alpine

BRIARPATCH REVIEW

CONTENTS

The Briarpatch Review is a product of the Briarpatch network: a group of people interested in simple living, openness, sharing, and learning how the world works through business.

This issue was put together by:

Kristin Anundsen	Annie Styron
Kathy Mayer	Michael Phillips

Cover by Kris Handwerk

Photos by Alan Gould - pp. 20, 22, 23, 27, 36
(omitted credit Winter issue - pp. 3, 10, 34)
Photographs by Robert Foothorap - pp. 14, 15
Photograph by Laird Sutton - p. 18

being in the briarpatch

The Briarpatch starts with a state of mind and grows to become a community. How can you become a part of it?

You may already have the state of mind. You may already be a Briar. You <u>are</u> a Briar if you're trying to live more simply using fewer resources, if you're sharing your resources and experience with others, and if you're seeking your right livelihood.

People have asked us, how do you become part of a Briarpatch community? You may have to create it. The community begins with small groups of people who are Briars and grows until it can be as large as it is in San Francisco with an intricate sub-economy having over 100 businesses and several hundred active Briars.

A Briarpatch community grows organically. It needs careful tending and the right environment; it can't be made to happen. You can't put out a printed flyer inviting small businesses to join; that's a Chamber of Commerce or Rotary Club approach. You create the environment by talking with friends, having parties, working on projects and waiting patiently like a good gardener until there are enough Briars to spontaneously call yourself a Briarpatch. When that happens, you'll have your financial records open to everyone, you'll probably need a part-time coordinator supported by voluntary tithes and bartering, and you'll begin helping each other on a large scale.

- Michael Phillips

Messages
from the Briarpatch

We had a wonderful collection of letters this quarter... even though we didn't have room to print them all, we <u>appreciate</u> them all. Many of these Messages from the Briarpatch invite comment from other Briars--maybe even continuing dialogue. Please keep the lines of communication open by responding to these letters as well as to articles in this issue. We print the addresses of our Message writers in case you want to respond to them directly.

PRIVILEGED DROPOUTS?

Even though we're far away, I want to be a part of your network because so much of what you do fits my conception of what we're working/groping toward. Right now we're moving into the black for office overhead and trying to work out how we support ourselves and others who want to work here.

One big conflict I feel is between wanting to provide services regardless of ability to pay and hearing sympathetically the wishes of upwardly mobile women who are tired of being poor and would like to look forward to a decent income. I recognize that I grew up rich and had the chance to do lots of things many women haven't. So my choice to live on less has a different context that I feel hesitant to apply to others. I feel the contradiction of suggesting to women that they settle for less $ when they've been doing that all their lives and now have a chance to rake it in. I've made my choice that humane and invigorating work conditions are more important than high salaries-- but how do you know that if you haven't been there? I'd rather hitchhike than fly--but I was raised on private planes.

What I'm asking is, how do you keep the Briarpatch from becoming the bastion of privileged dropouts? In the long run I want everyone to quit overcon-

suming our limited re-
sources--but in the short
haul it just seems like
I am stepping aside to
give someone else a crack
at overconsumption.

This doesn't just apply
to money. The same holds
true of power and status.
I downgrade the value
(worth) of degrees yet
realize I do so from the
position of having one.
What can I say to women
who are working for a de-
gree now about climbing
to power on the backs of
even less privileged wo-
men (the still undegreed)?

I would like to hear
others in the Briarpatch

address these issues and
grapple with the contra-
dictions involved. I
know the answers aren't
easy and maybe just keep-
ing the question before
us is a major step for
the present.

            Rae
            Seattle Institute
            for Sex Therapy,
            Education & Research
            100 NE 56th
            Seattle, WA 98105

THE FLOW OF WORK

        Been curled up reading
the latest Review. I read
them all cover to cover with
great pleasure.
        We've been doing fine
and learning lots. The
article called "Japanese
Business Lesson" turned me
on as it went well with views
I've been developing toward
work. We recently hosted
Bill and Akiko, who wrote
The Book of Tofu. He de-
scribed how an apprentice
to a Japanese tofu master
spent the first 6-7 years
just helping and never
being told directly how
to make tofu. During this
time the master spends a
good deal of energy telling
his apprentice to leave his
ego and flow with his work.
The idea that the attitude
toward the work is more
important than the work
skills holds water. Barbara

        cont'd. on page 111

a garden for learning and right livelihood

By Kristin Anundsen

"Everybody talks about 'getting back to nature,' but who's really doing it--who really knows how?" asks Raymond Chavez.

The question, coming from him, is rhetorical. Raymond is part of an educational experiment that is dedicated, in his words, to "marrying all the elements of man's relationship to nature." Under the direction of a noted British horticulturist, Alan Chadwick, Raymond and his fellow staff members and apprentices are "doing it."

They are part of the Round Valley Garden Project in a remote area of northern California. Alan Chadwick has developed a method of gardening so economical in terms of land and natural-resource use that at least one journalist has described it as "the answer to man's age-old problem of hunger." The project participants, however, are not in it just for this reason. They are there to find their own personal form of right livelihood.

Stewardship

The project was started in 1972 on a donated 15-acre plot near the town of Covelo. Using the master/apprentice system, it is training people in stewardship of the earth. Its chief element is something called "biodynamic horticulture," a complicated amalgam of not-so-complicated techniques. The school includes studies of orcharding, vegetable and flower culture, growing of soft fruits, landscaping, herb culture, nursery work, plant propagation, bees, and poultry—and interrelates them all.

In planting, everything is considered: appearance of the plants, height, time of blossoming, nutrients they add to the soil upon decomposition, insects they attract, degree of sunlight they need, benefits of being near certain other plants, etc. Productivity is considered a byproduct of beauty and harmony, and at this unusual school, apprentices can study classical poetry, dance, singing, and even mime and deportment in order to get their own beings in tune with nature and to sharpen their awareness.

The biodynamic techniques the apprentices learn are very

practical. For instance, seeds or seedlings are planted close together, so that when the plants mature their leaves will just touch; the resulting leafy environ-

ment retains moisture, protects the microbiotic life of the soil, and thus helps provide higher yields. Virtually everything is done by hand, from digging beds to cultivating to harvesting. Each plant is given attention and an opportunity to reach its fullest potential in relation to the other plants. The biodynamic method has been studied in a test plot in the Stanford Industrial Park, and the tests indicate that it uses a tiny fraction of the water, space, and energy ordinarily needed to grow a given amount of food.

Nature Knows Best

Emphasis is placed firmly on getting back to the natural state, or the way things grow in their original wild form. Over the years, restrictions imposed by machine technology and the demands of commercial marketing have brought about an overspecialization in farm plants. In order to breed for certain characteristics, farmers bred other characteristics out, and plants lost the vitality

of their original form. They
declined in nutritional
quality, flavor, and productivity. The soil became
unbalanced, chemicals were
added to correct it, and
things got worse. Nature
knows best, say the Round
Valley gardeners, and they
seek to get as close to the
origin as possible.

Raymond points to a line of
conifers at the edge of the
garden and explains that the
raspberries were planted a
certain distance from the
conifers because that's the
way they grow in their original
state. He adds that the
clump of borage planted next
to the raspberries will
attract a certain kind of
bees that will pollinate the
berries. The garden may look
somewhat haphazard, with
fruit trees interspersed
among other plants and herbs
scattered about, but there's
a reason for everything.

Chemicals, of course, are
anathema in the garden. The
gardeners are learning which
chemicals are, or can be
induced, in the soil naturally.

Attitudes

The Round Valley educational
process is based, says Raymond,
on "observation, sensitivity,
reverence, and finally obe-
dience to the laws of nature."

Many of the apprentices and
staff members seem to have an
almost religious feeling about
nature and the man-in-nature
relationship. Yet they are
not all spiritualists, nor
do they all share any particular belief system. They're
not even all vegetarians.

Raymond came to Round Valley
when the project started. He
was fresh from the University
of California at Santa Cruz,
where Chadwick had had an
experimental garden. Having
grown up in the sixties,
Raymond retains a spirit of
revolution, and he considers
the garden to be his own
"revolutionary statement."
(However, he is not really
political and has no interest
in discussing the politics of
man-on-a-tractor versus man-
with-a-hoe.)

Another viewpoint is exemplified
by Richard Joos, an architect
who once had, as he puts it,
"high-technology answers to
everything." Eventually, he
says, "the trees told me I
was doing something wrong."
He had heard of Alan Chadwick
and finally managed to track

82

him down at Covelo. Now he is on the staff. "In the process of working this way, something happens to you," Richard says gently. "You get connected through the digging, through really seeing what's going on."

His conversation often sounds anthropomorphic. "The birds will tell you," he says seriously. Later he notes, "We don't weed just for the sake of weeding. We don't do it until the weeds actually start to interfere with the plant. Weeds have one outstanding characteristic: they grow fast. Have you ever noticed what happens when someone next to you is working fast? You start working faster too." One is left with an image of a competitive young plant putting up shoots furiously, with sidelong glances toward the industrious weed next door.

Applications

Some outsiders get the impression that the Round Valley gardeners are "mystics" who want to close themselves off from the rest of society. On the contrary, they are very much concerned with how

their work will affect the rest of the world, and they hope the Peace Corps and similar organizations will be seeking people with their kind of training. Most of them are learning for the purpose of teaching others.

One way the method could be used, some suggest, is in city backyards; families could grow all their own food in very little space. "A lot of unemployed people are just sitting around," says Richard, "when they could be gardening. Even employed people could spend an hour in the garden after they come home from the office instead of having a cocktail--it's just as relaxing."

Apprenticeships

At present there are 25 apprentices at the Round Valley Garden Project--the capacity for that particular site. Later, they hope, there will be more sites. There are six horticultural staff people, besides Alan, and two carpentry instructors who teach the apprentices how to build sheds, cold flats, and glass houses. Tuition is free, but apprentices must put in full days of strenuous labor in the garden. They

cont'd. on page 100

How to Find a Storefront

By Gary Warne

Gary Warne, proprietor of Circus of the Soul, a used-book store, shares a storefront in San Francisco.

If you want to start a business and need a place to start it in, start walking. That's the first step in finding a storefront, and it's a pleasant one. You really get to know the city and you develop a feel for where you would like to be. You may be surprised, too--as I got re-acquainted with San Francisco my feelings changed a lot.

As you walk, keep your eyes open for a good location. This doesn't mean looking for a nice store that says "For Rent." The chances of your finding something that way are nil--forget it. There are only two ways to search out a storefront: ask other shopkeepers in the area you like (realty companies also if you come across any); and locate dimly lit, painted-over, or unused-looking stores.

The name of the owner or landlord will never be posted on such stores. So how do you find out whom to contact? First, call the Public Library and ask to speak to the office that has the "City Directory." This book is the opposite of the phone book--it has street addresses (from 1 Broadway to 3001 Broadway, for example) listed first, followed by people and phone numbers. So if you know the address, you can call the number at that address. If there is no listing for that address in the City Directory, don't give up--there's another approach: call the Assessor's Office at City Hall and ask for the owner's name and number listed in the "Realty Index." This book is organized the same way as the City Directory except that it has names of owners, not renters. (This book is printed privately in San Francisco, however, and I'm not sure other cities have it.)

Once you've found your storefront, the owner will want to know how you're going to finance it. There are two simple credit checks you'd better be prepared for. One is the length of time you've had your account at the same bank --the longer the better, so don't switch banks if you know you're going to be looking for a storefront. The other is something called a "credit rating," which the realtor or landlord will find out by calling the bank. The bank won't tell exactly how much money you have in your account, because that's against the law. But it will divulge a number that gives an indication of the amount. For example, if you have from $100 to $399 at Wells Fargo, your credit rating is given as "Low 3." If you have $400-$700, you're a "Medium 3," if $1,000-$1,400 a "Low 4," and so on. The rating is different for different banks.

This credit rating is based on that day's balance; it's not an average. So you can change your credit rating by depositing--temporarily--enough to change the computation. Maybe you can borrow the money from a friend for a month.

The best (often the only) way to cut your rent down is to share your storefront with another business. If your business takes up a lot of room, find one that doesn't.

A storefront sharer will bring you more customers as well as helping with the rent. Even if you can manage the rent yourself, you might consider taking in a free social service of some kind just to center people in your store--or better yet, you might create a free service of your own.

Wilbur Hot Springs: a healing refuge

By Annie Styron

I got addicted to hot springs in 1968 when six of us were driving back from Albuquerque after doing travelling production for the Whole Earth Catalog. We found a bone-warming, renewing hot springs one cold evening and along with everybody else I've been looking for hot springs ever since.

My favorite hot springs is Wilbur, located in a valley 120 miles northeast of San Francisco and 22 miles from the nearest town. It is so quiet and peaceful that we find ourselves talking in whispers or very low voices most of the time. Wilbur is a stressless space to be-- alone or with others. The hotel has 11 bedrooms, a large, well-equipped community kitchen, a main diningroom, a small diningroom, a library-livingroom with a Franklin stove, and a new, redwood-panelled community meditation room. Built around 1918, the hotel is entirely lit with kerosene lamps. A bathhouse is across the dirt road from the hotel with five baths heated with mineral waters from 95°F to 125°F. A naturally heated outdoor swimming pool (cold in summer) is right next to the bathhouse.

Kathleen de Wilbur, a director who specializes in cheerful survival, told us how it all began:

"As long ago as 1897 this was a health sanctuary. My great-great grandfather was Francis Wilbur who founded Wilbur Hot Springs in 1865. Up the road was Blank Hot Springs run by Mrs. Blank as a gambling hall and saloon where all the miners hung out. At that time there were 1,000 people living between Wilbur and Blank Hot Springs and the hills. My grandfather loved to gamble and he lost Wilbur to the Blanks from going down the road too often and gambling. I grew up with this story being told to me and always remembered it. I came up here with Richard Miller in 1971 and have been here ever since. We have a young daughter, Sarana Richka de Wilbur

Lawson y Miller, who was de-
livered on January 29, 1975."

*Richard Louis Miller, who con-
ducts Liberal Arts Awareness
Training at Wilbur, has a
Ph.D. in Clinical Psychology,
is a gestalt therapist and has
taught at universities and
growth centers. Although
Richard would like to share
the responsibility for Wilbur
equally with the staff, he is
definitely the main organizer
and provides most of the
strength for the development
of Wilbur as a health sanctuary. Here's his account of
his own involvement:*

Gestalt Kibbutz Dream

"In the late 1960s and early
70s my partner Larry Bloom-
berg and I had a clinic in
San Francisco called the
Gestalt Institute for Multiple Psychotherapy. We were
developing an interest in
moving our entire practice to
some place in the country to
develop a consciousness-
raising community (a Gestalt
Kibbutz, as Fritz Perls called
it). A group of 10-15 friends
including Bob and Alice Hall
and Richard and Katherine
Heckler were also interested
in the idea, so we had meet-

ings on a weekly basis and started looking for land. We also told friends and real estate people about our plans. We took so long to find land that the meetings fell apart and people drifted away to Hawaii and New Mexico.

"Then, Larry found Wilbur Hot Springs. He was driving along the road going from one hot springs to the other and there it was! The hotel was condemned by the Health Department and it was in terrible condition, badly vandalized, with huge piles of junk everywhere. Where the swimming pool is now was a falling-down 20-room bathhouse. Other rotting buildings were scattered around the land. There were old, rusting vehicles, a few hundred pounds of broken glass, several tons of old wood, old burned mattresses and couches, toilets, rags and miscellaneous debris.

"We rented the house next door to the hotel in September 1971 and started coming up on weekends. I later rented the hotel itself from the woman who owned it for weekend seminars of 20 to 30 people and we held Gestalt community workshops once a month. We used the dining-room and kitchen as they were pretty habitable. Since the rent was cheap were were able to cut the price on the work-

shops as a political statement.

"I met Kathleen and we started coming up here together. Then she moved up full time and we began living and working in the middle of the squalor. We hauled everything we needed, including drinking water, and started cleaning up. The health inspector showed up and fortunately we got along quite well, since we were both concerned with health. I made a deal with him to have the seminars here, though we couldn't be open to the public until more work was completed.

Foreclosure

"After we'd been there a while, the County Sheriff nailed up a foreclosure no-

Afternoon in the baths

88

tice on the front door. The
landlady had floated three
mortgages and hadn't paid a
dime for five years, not even
taxes. So Kathleen and I went
down to Colusa County Title
Company to bid on the place.
This took place in the street
in front of the title company
where they traditionally have
foreclosure auctions. We
finally bought the place although the title wasn't clear
and I was taking a chance of
buying a gigantic lawsuit and
losing any improvements made.
We did get title insurance
after two years of worry and
work.

"We had bought ourselves a
hot springs. We started seriously cleaning up and I decided to close my practice in
the city and live at Wilbur
and write for a year. It was
during that time that the idea
of opening as a health sanctuary occurred to Kathleen.
Kathleen is a major force here,
I don't know if I would have
wanted to hang around without
her. I watch her as the guru
here. I feel that her opti-
mism is important, taking life
lightly. I did a 25-page
prospectus of the renovation:
planning and organization is
my trip. Kathleen walks
around smiling and getting
things done.

Kathleen and Richard

Free Labor

"We led three free workshops
with help from our friends at
Esalen, and at one of them
125 people showed up. We
asked people to give us two
hours a day of work. One
group of 50 people walked
around picking up debris and
formed a pile that took a
bulldozer to move.

"One of our biggest concerns
was that when people would
come to stay we had to make
sure no one would get near
the rotting buildings. But
there were such good vibes
from people that a man broke
his leg, didn't sue, didn't
tell anybody and still comes
back regularly.

Small is Just Right

"I can see Wilbur developing into a small 'consciousness town'. My only concern about the town is how to support these people who would live here. Wilbur was a town once and everybody who lives in the town could be involved like they once were. But instead of miners and gambling saloons or Woolworth's, there would be centers for Tai Chi, Aikido, Yoga, and herbal shops to fill out and complement the ongoing program at the Hot Springs.

"We feel that every detail of the environment is important: the colors, temperature, cleanliness of the rooms (not too clean, but not too dirty), so that you feel like being in it and leaving it clean. So there's a political and philosophical message. While we're all here to serve, no one is a servant. People take responsibility.

"At this point the average number of people on a weekend is 25. We charge $15 for the first night and $10 for the second. We want to encourage people to stay longer than one night because it takes at least two days for them to unwind and benefit from being here.

"I'm committed to Wilbur Hot Springs being kept small to do what we're trying to do. We'd like to see another health sanctuary started elsewhere rather than expanding our facilities. I hope we serve as inspiration for others as the work is hard, the air is clean and our lives are high. For me, a health sanctuary means a place where people like us, who have spent many years working with people and their habitats, can put energy into creating an environment that offers people enough space and nourishment to grow and learn as well as heal themselves."

You can go to Wilbur to restore yourself or to participate in the Liberal Arts Awareness Training.

Call Kathleen de Wilbur (916) 473-2306 or write Wilbur Hot Springs, CA 95987.

We Started Our Own Spinning and Weaving Supplies Business

By Marcha Fox

My partner, Brenda Kroon, and I are recent transplants to Utah from California. We knew each other before we came here and planned to live near each other so we could homestead and enjoy each other's fellowship. We are concerned with becoming as self-sufficient as possible and that is one of the reasons we started our own spinning and weaving supplies business. We are totally enjoying our business since we love the craft we are promoting.

Starting on $30

We launched the business the first part of November, 1975. In about two weeks it had paid us back our initial outlay and since then we have built our inventory solely on the money coming in. We started with a retailer's license, a supply of letterhead stationery on which to write to wholesalers, some drop spindles, and an ad in the paper. The total cost was about $30.

The boost we got in operating capital came from teaching classes. We really got in on the ground level here, since there was no one else teaching spinning. There used to be plenty of spinners and a spinners' guild, but the guild had fallen by the wayside and none of the local spinners taught. Quite a few of our initial students already had spinning wheels and were just looking for someone to teach them! Others took our classes because they were getting into self-sufficiency skills and homesteading and still others simply because it sounded like fun. Our students are of both sexes, and occupations range

from firemen, anthropologists,
and hydrochemical technicians
to housewives, secretaries, and
students. We teach the classes
in our homes, so we have no rent
overhead.

At first we didn't take home
any of the profits. Now we are
paying ourselves a few dollars
a week for expenses (gas and
babysitters, when we have to
track down supplies or run
errands) and using all other
income to buy inventory.

Since anyone serious about
getting into spinning will need
to purchase tools and supplies,
we can just about count on each
student's buying these things
from us. These purchases are
spaced out over the length of
the course, and as we bring in
money for one item, we use that
money to order what we need
next.

Growing and
Spreading the Word

We are considering building up
our inventory so that we can
open up a shop for the public,
but this may not really be
necessary or even desirable
since most of our customers
will be our students and people
here are not that impressed by
a commercial establishment.
Most businesses of this sort
that have a downtown location
don't make it for long because
of their overhead, and we figure

we wouldn't get enough walk-in
business to make it worth it.

Salli Rasberry Spinning

We have advertised in the town
newspaper and the local throw-
away and have narrowed it down
to the throw-away since the
majority of our students found
us in there. Word of mouth is
now taking over too. The
population here is about 90
percent Mormon and the LDS
(Latter-Day Saints) church
preaches self-sufficiency, so
the interest in our classes is
quite high. Add to that the
fact that there is a university
in our valley and you can see
that we are in a fantastic
location. And as I've mentioned,
we have very limited competition.

We are looking forward to the County Fair, where we will have a booth, the State Fair, and various other fairs where we will be able to promote our craft, classes, and supplies.

When our inventory is large enough that we can fill orders directly, we hope to expand into the mail-order business. We are working on a mail-order price list and a lesson manual, and we are building an inventory of spinning wheels so that eventually we can supply people with them without the long wait they can expect from ordering through companies. Our husbands are making as much of the equipment as possible, which further enhances the profit margin.

A Productive Partnership

Our partnership is ideal-- Brenda studied spinning in California for a couple of years and is a very capable teacher; I am self-taught and cannot teach with as much proficiency, but I have had substantial bookkeeping and business experience. Brenda is the instructor and I am the business manager. Neither of us could run the business without the other, and the feeling of dependence is a good one.

We feel that it's absolutely essential for anyone trying this kind of business to be an experienced spinner. You have to be aware of the sources available for supplies. Of course, you could be the best spinner in the world and a crummy teacher. Our talents seemed to fall in the right areas and the rest took care of itself--with a little help from elbow grease, naturally.

As time goes on we hope to expand into other areas of self-sufficiency and hold mini-courses in such things as soap making, tanning hides, and field trips. Ideally, some day we will be a self-sufficiency center for Cache Valley. So far we are growing beyond our original comprehension and we feel we have been blessed in obtaining our goals. We've had no problems getting the business rolling--we've had more problems keeping it in hand so it doesn't engulf us in tons of work!

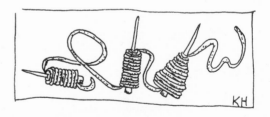

Pioneer Handspinning Supply Co.
565 East First South
Hyrum, Utah 84319

Zen Center's Grocery

By Michael Phillips

*left to rt. Bruce Halberson,
Terry Gragg, David Chadwick,
Jim Bockhorst, Melody Kean.*

The Green Gulch Greengrocer
in San Francisco, a new member
of the Bay Area Briarpatch
Network, was opened last
summer by the San Francisco
Zen Center. This is an
extraordinary business,
although to outward appear-
ances it is similar to other
groceries and small busi-
nesses.

Understanding how this grocery is unique is the key to
the lesson it offers the
rest of the Briarpatch.

Visually the Green Gulch grocery doesn't look too different. It is cleaner than
most groceries--much neater
and less cluttered even
though it has less than
1,000 feet of floor space.
The real difference is the
<u>feeling</u>. It feels warm,
comfortable, truthful, and
inexpensive. Actually,
when I shop there I spend
more money than usual be-
cause I buy more.

There are two reasons for the
unique quality of this store:
(1) the original motive for
opening it and (2) its ongoing decision making process.

The motive for opening the
store was to serve the neighborhood. The Zen Center is
in a low-income neighborhood;
more than 50% of the people
are black. Previously the
only store in the neighbor-

94

hood was a small, high-priced grocery. It closed early last year and for months there were no interested renters. As time passed, the Zen Center felt the need for the kind of community focus that a store can offer--specifically, a low-cost grocery.

As the need for a store was growing, so was the produce crop at the Zen Center's monastery/farm located in Green Gulch in Marin County. The farm was nearly three years old and its organically grown crops were becoming greater than necessary for the needs of the Zen Center itself. The surplus was ideal for supplying fresh, organic, and low-cost food to the city of San Francisco. So the Green Gulch grocery was opened by the San Francisco Zen Center across the street from the San Francisco Zendo (medita-

tion hall), and operated by the practicing Zen students.

Conscious Decisions

From the time the store was opened until today, the second reason for its unique quality has been apparent: Each and every detailed decision is made very, very carefully. Each decision is weighed in terms of service to the neighborhood--service in the form of a community focus and low prices--and one prime motive is the opportunity for the Zen students to serve others, which is consistent with their practice.

One of the first decisions was to build a check-out counter in the middle of the store. This was done because Baker-Roshi, the teacher-leader of the Zen Center, wanted the employees to be physically close to the customers and to be part of the movement within

95

the store, rather than to
act as processors standing
at a check stand on the end
of a dull production line.
A counter in the middle does
make the store less efficient
than those with ordinary
check-out stands, but it
enables the employees to
chat with the customers,
give advice, and answer questions. When you are in the
store you feel a continual
interaction with the people
who work there, and of
course they feel much closer
to their customers. The
customers, in turn, seem to
enjoy bagging their own
groceries, which partially

compensates for the ineffi-
ciency of the check-out
counter.

Each "Little"
Decision Counts

The store has many unusual
little things about it, which
taken together have a great
impact. Example: Produce is
marked with tags that are
green, yellow, or orange.
Green means it's definitely
organic because they've
grown it themselves or seen
it grown with their own eyes;
orange means it isn't organic
at all; and yellow means in
between or maybe. Annie
Styron asked David Chadwick
about some yellow-tagged
potatoes while shopping and
David picked up the phone,
called the wholesale supplier
and asked him if he personally
"believed" that they were
organic. The answer was yes
and David relayed to Annie
his feeling that the supplier
himself is a very honest
person. That is really willingness to help a customer!
Another example: The store
buys from many more than the
usual number of suppliers.
This takes more time, but
they want to deal with "small"
suppliers as much as possible
and they want to shop around
enough to find the occasional
low-price deals on good products (like the papayas with
poor skins that are excellent

inside and sold to customers for as little as 12¢ apiece).

Still another example is the way the "spoilage" problem in produce is handled. Consistent with Buddhist tradition of using everything fully, produce that has become discolored and too old to sell is (1) put into a half-price box, (2) served in delicious casseroles to the students at the Zen Center, (3) when fruit is involved, juiced and sold, and (4) what little is left, returned to the farm for compost.

To the Green Gulch people, "serving" doesn't mean making decisions for the customers. This store is neither a health food store nor a typical politically organized community store. In both health food and politically managed stores the people making business decisions have "ideas" of what is good for the customer. Health food stores generally don't carry so-called breakfast "junk" cereals. Politically oriented community stores don't buy from giant agribusiness distributors.

Green Gulch Greengrocer carries some "junk" food because the people in the neighborhood want it and would have to walk many extra blocks to buy it anyway; they also carry some food from large whole-

salers because it is sometimes very cheap.

Novel Pricing

The store is right now trying an unusual pricing pattern. Most of their prices are multiples of 5¢, with no emphasis on the 9¢ that all other groceries have (39¢, 3 for 99¢, etc.). The reason they're doing this is that there is no desire to mislead or confuse customers and 5¢ and 10¢ are much easier for the customer to add than 39¢ and 99¢. Of course that makes it easier to add the totals at the checkout stand too.

There are many more things I could say about the store but it would be more of the same--about how small details and careful attention to every decision have shaped the appearance and nature of the store and helped it grow successfully. It is now eight months old with $21,000 gross revenue and hires neighborhood people to work there. With this continuing healthy growth it will probably reach its peak revenue of $35,000 in six months and be able to return a small surplus to help make the San Francisco Zen Center more self-sufficient.

AD AWARD

Each issue we provide advertising space to an outstanding business we select from the Briarpatch and give them $25. (we reward our advertisers). This issue it's GREEN GULCH GREENGROCER. They chose not to advertise, but we're giving them $25. anyway.

ETHICS OF ADVERTISING

The following excerpt from United Focus Journal sums up, we think, a "right livelihood" attitude toward advertising.

It is our opinion that any group, any publication, any medium taking advertising from another organization or individual does so in exchange for something else. The question then arises as to discrimination, and where the line is drawn as to what is acceptable and what is not....No matter what claims are made, the medium accepting the advertising "ties into the energy of the advertiser" and thereby implicitly endorses his product, organization, etc.

TRAVELERS' DIRECTORY

Tourist homes are back and better. A handy little book called the "Travelers' Directory" lists places to stay with kindred souls from Klein Ochsenfurt, Germany to Davis, California. The Directory includes names, addresses, telephone numbers, ages, interests and offers of hospitality to travelers. The obvious advantage is a huge savings in the cost of lodging, but best of all you participate in native life, sharing information and experiences about traveling. The Directory is a reciprocal hospitality exchange which is not for sale. You must list yourself in it in order to get one. The cost is $8.00 per year.

The Travelers' Directory
Tom Linn - Editor
6224 Baynton Street
Philadelphia, Pa 19144

Helpful Exchanges in the Bay Area Briarpatch Network

-Ralph Heins at the Biofeedback Center needed some extra secre-
tarial help and decided to trade two hours work at the typewriter
for one hour on the biofeedback equipment. It's been working fine.

-Flash of the Imaginators needed some mathematical expertise to
simply explain formulas to figure volume in non-square terrariums
and aquariums in a book he was working on. Ken Nonomura, an engineer in the Network, went over to Flash's warehouse and filled the
need. Before Ken left, Flash, with his flair for design and low
cost production, had completely organized Ken's concept of a low
cost sensory deprivation tank ("Lilly tank").

-A woman wanted to buy a hardcover book on photography from Gary
Warne at his Circus of the Soul used book store. She couldn't
afford this coffee table type book; discussed it with Gary, left
for a few hours and came back with her own freshly baked pound
cake. The deal was closed.

-Andy Alpine needed leads on manufacturers of display racks for
the Common Ground Directory. As a teacher of the Communiversity
he was able to put out the word through its bulletin of course
listings. Allen Schaaf, from Black Sheep Press, immediately
called Andy and presented 76 racks that he had lying around his
print shop, and offered them as his next Briarship pledge.

-Helen Crosswhite of Making Ways really was impressed with the way
Ron Johnson put together our health insurance plan; mentioned it
to the folks in another organization she works with and within a
week they had a new dental plan.

-Richard Weiss and David Riordan met at a Network pot luck dinner
and during our sharing of what we were into and our needs found
out that they could and should work on an educational filmstrip
together. They are and today recorded an accompanying soundtrack.

-Since Flash knows about plastics, David Riordan was getting some
leads from him for the fan housing on the inflatable environment
David's producing. Why go to others? They decided to make it
themselves.

--Andy Alpine

Cont'd. from page 83

get to eat the fruits--and vegetables--of their labors but are otherwise responsible for their own expenses, including housing.

Apprenticeships begin in September and last for a minimum of one year, sometimes as long as three years. And before you even get to be an apprentice you must work with the project for a trial period of at least two weeks.

Instructors currently receive $100 per month, which comes from grants and from the modest sales of fruits and vegetables to the local farmers' market. Coordinating support for the project's activities is the Institute for Man and Nature. The Institute is inviting individuals to become Friends of the Garden; for $10, a Friend can participate in special events such as Garden luncheons or poetry readings, receive a newsletter, and obtain Garden seeds.

Although exciting in their potential, the Round Valley Garden methods will probably

not spread fast. First, they take a long time to learn. Second, widespread application will require a gradual but significant shift in values. This labor-intensive way of gardening doesn't make a lot of money, so it won't appeal to everyone. "Our society has come to believe that all systems that make money are good systems," says Richard. "But what about the other values--quality of life, sensitivity, permanence?"

The Round Valley gardeners, for whom these values are paramount, are planting seeds in more ways than one. If there is enough nurturant soil, the ultimate result may be the flowering of a new awareness of humankind's relationship to the natural world.

For a detailed description of Alan Chadwick's method, see How to Grow More Vegetables, a review of which appears on page 30 of this issue of Briarpatch Review.

For more information on the Round Valley Garden Project, contact the Institute for Man and Nature, P.O. Box 67, Covelo, CA 95428. Inquiries about apprenticeships should be addressed to Alan Chadwick, Round Valley Garden Project, Covelo, CA 95428.

A garden grows
on the roof

By Judith Skinner

In the spring of 1975, I was hired to put a garden on the roof of the Glide Office Building in downtown San Francisco. On hand were six containers: one large redwood box, 15" x 10', and five slatted boxes capable of holding four 7" pots.

I wanted four more containers--round barrels at least 4' in diameter to match the scale of the redwood rectangle--but getting anything custom-made proved prohibitively expensive. I compromised with four sets of three wine barrels, each 24" in diameter, $7.50 apiece, from S. DeBella Barrel Co. on Harrison Street.

After arranging the large containers in a simple pattern, with the rectangle in the center and the barrels in a broad circle around it, I scattered the slatted boxes of pots at uneven intervals from the entrance to the roof to the door of the Briarpatch Review/Point office at the far end.

As I worked, a house finch sat on the TV antenna and warbled his long, loose song, and so I

Judith and the snow peas

bought one more container for him: a birdbath.

Joe Cohen of the Zen Center drilled drainage holes in the bottoms of the barrels, and together we stapled screens over them to allow water, but not soil, to escape. He filled all the containers with a mixture of equal parts of redwood compost, Tillo (rice hulls, sewage sludge, coffee grounds), manure, redwood fines (coarsely chipped redwood bark), plus a small amount of soil. We did not add much soil as it was so heavy to carry. The redwood fines provided the necessary coarseness to make the whole mix light and loose.

I topdressed each barrel with 2 tbsp. fish meal (nitrogen), 2 tsp. bone meal (phosphorus), and 4 tbsp. kelp (potassium). For the 7" pots, I cut that ratio in half; for the redwood rectangle, I doubled it. This is a rich topdressing, designed for a crowded planting. I wanted the plants to flower and fruit abundantly, to tumble over one another and over the edges of the containers.

Planting

I thought of planting fruit trees, but it is windy on the roof, and lower, bushier plants seemed more suitable. I planted the central rectangle with white daisies, and each set of barrels with a combination of three fra-

grant roses: orange "Tropicana," pink "Fragrant Cloud," and yellow "Golden Masterpiece." The daisies will have to be replaced every second or third year, but the roses are a permanent planting.

Around the daisies and roses I put a variety of medium and low annuals (bachelor buttons, nemesia, lobelia, asters, phlox, marigolds, portulaca), herbs (prostrate rosemary, spearmint), and vegetables (cucumbers, San Francisco Fog variety cherry tomatoes).

In the 7" pots I mixed violas and ageratum, and surrounded the birdbath with a ring of peppermint. It was hard to forego petunias, but their fuzzy leaves pick up all the grit in the air and they usually look terrible in the city.

Summertime

Spring turned into summer, the roses bloomed, and the daisies billowed over the rectangle in the center. The spearmint climbed down the sides of its barrels and the annuals flowered in many colors.

The cucumbers rotted almost immediately, soon to be discreetly covered by a layer of blue lobelia, but the cherry tomatoes thrived, beyond all reasonable expectation, producing edible fruit well into the next winter.

In August I fertilized everything again, and deadheaded old blooms.

Wintertime

By early December it was time to prune the roses and the daisies and to replace the spent annuals with new ones: stock, forget-me-nots, and johnny-jump-ups. I filled the pots with cineraria, parsley, and a variety of bulbs: Darwin tulips, daffodils, and rose freesia. In among the daisies, I nestled a few Dutch iris "Wedgewood."

In the barrels near the Briarpatch Review/Point office I set out snow peas, which are full of fruit as this article goes to press. Last week I planted another set of barrels with anemones and California wildflowers.

As I replant each container, I fertilize. So far I have had no burning as I use fish meal for nitrogen; others have told me blood meal does burn if planted immediately.

Later this spring, when the snow peas finish, I plan to set out lettuce, chives and thyme. This summer might be a good time to try strawberries and camomile. And some day, I would like to cover the back wall with a veil of flowering vines: honeysuckle, jasmine, bougainvillea, blue plumbago, orange trumpet creeper.

cont'd. on page 110

books

HOW TO GROW MORE VEGETABLES*
* than you ever thought
possible on less land than
you can imagine

By John Jeavons

Published by: Ecology Action of
the Midpeninsula, Palo Alto,
California, 1974
82 pages, $4.00

*Using this book I grew the most
incredible vegetables last year.
In a 15 x 20 foot space I had so
much food--tender, beautiful
carrots; dark, crisp spinach--
that I had trouble giving it
away. My friends grew used to
having shopping bags full of
chard, broccoli, lettuce, beans,
left clandestinely on their
doorstep.*

*The book basically is a clear,
concise step-by-step explanation
of the biodynamic and French
intensive methods of gardening
brought to this country by Alan
Chadwick, once mentor of the
gardens at U.C. Santa Cruz.
Overall, it is a how-to-do-it
book, but still it presents the
philosophy and general approach
to life espoused by Chadwick and
others who work with him.*

*If you want to know how to grow
a lot of luscious food in a small
space, how to prepare good, organic compost simply, how to
utilize natural plant controls
to fight pests, and how to have
a harmonious, balanced garden
where plants and pests get on
together--you might spend some
time with this book.*

- Clifford Janoff

Excerpts from the book:

"The method is exciting to me
because man becomes important
again as he finds his place
in relation to nature. In the
method man helps provide for the
needs of the plants instead of
trying to dominate them. When
he provides for these real needs,
the plants bounteously provide
more food."

"When planting seeds or seedlings, remember that the most
important area for the plant
is the 2 inches above and
the 2 inches below the surface
of the planting bed. This is
because of the mini-climate
created under the plants's
leaves and because of the important protection of the
upper roots in the bed by the
soil. Without proper protection, the plants will develop
tough necks at the point
where the stem emerges from
the soil. A toughened neck
slows the flow of plant juices
and interrupts and weakens
plant growth of the plant.
These areas are also important
because in a very real sense
the roots are leaves in the
soil and the leaves are roots
in the air."

"Normally (about 90% of the
time), insects only attack
an unhealthy plant. Just as
a healthy person who eats
good food is less susceptible
to disease, so are healthy
plants that are on a good
diet less susceptible to
plant diseases and insect
attack. It is not the insect
which is the source of the
problem, but rather an unhealthy soil. The soil needs
your energy, not the insect.
The uninterrupted growth
stressed by the biodynamic/
French intensive method is
also important to the main-

tenance of plant health. In short, we are shepherds providing the conditions our plants need for healthy, vigorous growth."

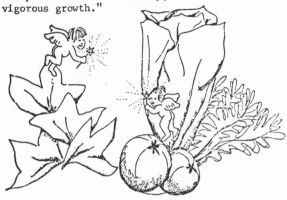

THE FINDHORN GARDEN
Pioneering a New Vision of
Man and Nature in Cooperation

by Findhorn Community
Forward by William Irwin Thompson
Harper & Row, Publishers,
New York, 1975 $10.00

The Findhorn Garden is a book about a remarkable garden and community in Scotland, renowned for giant vegetables growing in the sand, roses blooming in the snow and the spirit of community in shared consciousness that makes it all possible. It is a story told by five people. Beginning with Peter's history, the tale grows in richness and beauty as Eileen, Dorothy, Roc and David add the petals of their perspectives. Together they offer an expanded vision of environment which includes levels of consciousness not ordinarily taken into account.

"Findhorn and the garden straddle the past and the future. By drawing us back into myth and legend and into cooperation with the Spirits of Earth, the elves and fairies and gnomes, Findhorn invites us to a more ancient time when man was young and shared his world knowingly with these beings. This priceless gift of wonderment invites us to become as little children, dancing in an elven ring of quicksilver delight and walking near the· majesty of the great god Pan....Yet at the same time, Findhorn proclaims the image for humanity of a new image, the birth of the consciousness of participatory divinity."

The photos fit into words and pages like windows into the Findhorn world. Looked at lingeringly these glimpses take you from peering in to inside the realm.

This book goes far beyond gardening. "Whether you tend a garden or not, you are a gardner of your own being, the seed of your own destiny."

- Barbara Janoff

A poem, Old New England saying, and Briarpatch principle, all in one:

Use it up,
Wear it out;
Make it do,
Or do without.

The Joy of Business

By Michael Phillips

The Briarpatch is really about fun. It's also about business. For us the two can be the same.

Andy Alpine and I visit Briarpatch businesses every Wednesday to offer help and learn how each Briar can help other Briars. We always come home on Wednesday night very exhilarated. Business in the Briarpatch is fun.

One of the things about Briar business is the pace. It's very human, most of the time. When we visit a business it's common for us all to go out for a sauna to talk. Some Briar businesses even have hot tubs on the premises and we do our visiting in the tub. Our conversations are usually relaxed. We often do unusual things during our visits--one afternoon we went flying and another afternoon we tried out biofeedback devices. If you take "making a lot of money"

off the list of reasons for being in business you can pretty easily replace it with "fun" as a reason for being in business.

Business Instead of School

I personally like business because it is a wonderful and exciting way to learn. It is quite unlike school, which emphasizes ideas and logical processes and rewards conformity and smart talk. I couldn't stand school. I disliked almost every grade and every class after kindergarten. I love business! I find that the people who are happy in their work and do well in business don't place an undue value on ideas, routine, or "talking" about things.

In Briarpatch businesses we "do" things. We keep trying new things, always in small increments, so we can see the effect. We're always changing things a little so we can LEARN how to serve our customers. Even after we've found something that works well we still try again, to see if there is something else that will work better. These are not the result of preconceived ideas that we have; they are continual experiments

with reality so we can learn. We judge the results of these experiments and changes by increases in revenue, decreases in cost, or more free time.

An experiment: In a bookstore we recently visited I noticed in their financial records that their revenue from magazine sales was quite high for the small amount of floor space it occupied and I suggested trying more magazine space. The idea was tested and magazine sales picked up, as did all other sales because more customers came to the store. It was a service the neighborhood wanted. The result could have been the opposite and we would have learned just as much about what the neighborhood wanted. The point is that we experimented and learned. We couldn't have looked up that result in a book.

You Learn by Doing

Business is such an extraordinary place to learn that there is no textbook. At least there are no good books on how to start and run a small business that will really give you an idea of how to do it. The reason for that is that business is pure experience. People who are already in business always tell people who are starting out, "There's not much I can tell you; you just have to jump in and learn for yourself."

One of the most enjoyable things for me is to look at the books (financial records) of a small business and be able to ask questions. The books always reveal some trend or pattern that the person in the business is too close to to see, and it's fun to view the learning experience right before your eyes.

One of my favorite stories is about a small bakery whose books I was examining. I noticed that sales were higher each day of the week than the previous day—except Tuesday, which was always lower than Monday. I asked the owner why this happened. He thought for a long time and could find no explanation. I asked what he did on Tuesday that he didn't do any other day. The answer was that he cleaned the floor and the bathroom with a disinfectant. His eyes lit up when he realized that the smell of bread in the bakery was one of his most important products and that probably customers were avoiding the store on Tuesday mornings because of the smell of disinfectant. The answer all came from looking at the books.

urban predators

Country folk know that they have to be careful to protect things from predators. Urban folk aren't usually so careful. In the country a garden without good fencing will be eaten by deer, rabbits, and snails; chickens will be eaten by coyotes; and garbage will be scattered by raccoons. Living in a city or suburb, you are likely to lose your bicycles, motorcycles, and cars if they are left outside. Urban predators will take them unless you plan ahead. Chains, locks, and alarms are usually useless.

The way to discourage urban predators is to make your tools unappealing to them. The finest operating tool will be unappealing if it is dull and used looking, has no shiny chrome, and is very personalized.

Three examples are shown here. Margo St. James has a bicycle

that is four speed, light as any racing bike, and as finely tuned a machine as one could want, but it is intentionally ugly and it hasn't been stolen. I have a 1970 Suzuki motorcycle with rusty chrome and identifiable personal touches like a leather-covered gas tank and a securely fastened flag on the back. It's very well tuned with new parts throughout the engine...but has no appeal. A number of my friends drive finely tuned cars with deliberate dirt and dents; they don't worry about theft.

There's no need to be angry about thieves. They are now part of urban life and we can deal with them the same way country folk deal with deer, raccoons, and other predators.

--Michael Phillips

Briarpatch Health Insurance Plan

For the past year or so we've been discussing various ways of insuring the health of members of the Briarpatch Network. Ideally, we would like to create a plan where we ourselves underwrite each other's health (see article on Dr. Sam in Spring 1975 Briarpatch Review). In the meantime we have put together a group health insurance plan for Network members. It's a combined life, medical and dental plan which covers hospital costs, doctor's visits and fees, complete dental care and more. Through the diligent efforts of our brokers Werner and Ron, the Briarpatch plan also includes coverage of wholistic approaches to health such as acupuncture, iridology, homeopathy, biofeedback, osteopathy and others when prescribed by a licensed M.D. Chiropractic treatment is directly covered. Early in March representatives of the Briarpatch businesses interested in the plan voted on the specific options available and we expect coverage to begin May 1st.

- Andy Alpine

If you are a Briarpatch business and would like more information on this plan, write to Andy Alpine, 461 Douglass Street, San Francisco 94114.

Cont'd. from page 103

Borrowed Scenery

The garden is growing, all
atangle, as the Hilton Hotel
rises a stark 40 stories above
it. There is a Japanese landscaping term which means "borrowed scenery." It refers to
a method of landscaping which
consciously harmonizes a distant
view of mountains, for example,
with the design of a garden in
front of it. When I first saw
the roof, I felt hampered by an
ugly bit of "borrowed scenery"
in the Hilton. But if the Hilton
is not much as "borrowed scenery,"
it is excellent as "borrowed
climate," for it creates a small
banana belt as light and heat
reflect off its surface. San
Francisco in the summer is often
a discouragingly foggy place
to grow things, but every time
the sun dared to shine, it was
intensified by the Hilton next
door and the plants thrived.

Should the Briarpatch Network
ever need a truck garden, the
roof of the Glide Office
Building might be just the place
to garden, as well as "live
in the cracks."

The greening of the Hilton

Dutch iris and daisies

Cont'd. from page 79

had a similar experience at a natural foods bakery. She apprenticed two years--got the flour, washed the pots and pans, learned to do everything at the right time to make it flow. She was never given the recipes during that time. When she finally got to bake herself, she found she could do it well and had lots of confidence in taking on any baking task. Why? She knew the pace, the timing, and the right attitude. Interesting.

So often we are in a hurry to "do it" and after a while we want to do something else "more interesting." I think the idea behind the apprentice system changes all that. By stretching out the period before we get to "do it" our egos finally give up waiting and learn to be content with what is happening now in our work. When attitudes are foremost, then our challenge becomes getting our inner selves to flow more beautifully with our work--that could keep one going for a lifetime. When we get to "do it" right away we can get hooked on the rush of

fresh conquests. As soon as we get a skill down we get bored with it and begin wanting to do something new.

David Copperfield
Well-Being Magazine
Box 7455
San Diego, CA 92107

We ran an article about Well-Being, the healing magazine, in the last issue of the Briarpatch Review. We forgot to include their address (see above) and the fact that subscription rates are $3 for 5 issues (add $1 outside U.S.); $10, one-year supporter; $100, lifetime. Well-Being is published every six weeks.

COMING CLEAN

After years of reading ads, hearing and seeing commercials (and disobeying Gen. 12:1), I demanded to finally get clean. I gave up all the soaps which made me "glamorous" and "sexy" and "nice." And took up kosher kitchen soap. My skin is at last clean and I feel right at last.

Carol Ohmart
P.O. Box 242
Beverly Hills,
CA 90213

DELIGHT AND DISMAY

My first issue of Briarpatch Review (winter '76) was both

a delight and a dismay. A
delight because we (as a
family) identify with you
people and believe in your
simplified versions of living
--a dismay because my sixth
sense tells me many of you
are not building on firm
enough psychological grounds
to develop staying power.

To wit--Charles Parsons is
doing a fabulous job of
raising his son, Justin,
alone; even Charles's grandmother says so. Charles and
Justin Parsons have found the
father-son relationship not just
bearable by blood ties, but
absolutely beautiful. This is
great! But Charles comes on
like any other possessive parent. Justin is his and his
alone. Even if he should re-
marry, he threatens to keep
Justin solely for himself.
How can Briarpatch communities
grow if their members refuse
to grow in the art of loving
selflessly--the prime ingredient for any productive,
communal society?

Then there is Salli Rasberry,
conceiving, then creating a
child in her own image and
likeness. Their story reads
like a Judy Garland movie.
But my concern is not for
Salli, who "...was used to
doing things my way and I
couldn't give it up." My
thoughts keep going back to
Sasha, who "...was often angry
at having to share me."

What happens to children who
have been a lone reservoir for
a parent's emotional needs?
Do these children automatically
mature into emotionally stable

adults, capable of making
lasting commitments of love?
Or do they repeat the only
human growth pattern they've
ever known?

Even my husband's reactions to
Michael Phillips' article on
the ethics of using unemployment insurance won't offer you
a change of pace. He (my
husband) views the whole dis-
sertation as ethical hair
splitting. If unemployment
insurance isn't needed to make
a transition from the old
lifestyle into the Briarpatch
way of living, then why would
one take it? If it is needed
to effect the change, why
should it be viewed as some
albatross? Surely Briarpatch
people aren't renouncing
society completely, are they?

We see, too, something of a
contradiction in Michael
Phillips' use of situation
ethics to advance the legal
use of marijuana, psychedelics,
and sex (consenting adults)
but he suddenly becomes an
ethical purist on the use of
unemployment insurance.

In the meantime, back at the
ranch, we have almost survived

another Michigan winter. It's not the erratic weather that threatens us directly, it's what it does to mason work. Despite this, we survive, raise a big garden, can, freeze, make our own bread, and generally count our blessings amid some happy grumblings.

I teach part time for money and tutor for free in the summer. (Charging for tutoring stigmatizes the child, insults the efforts of good teachers, and asks parents to pay their school tax twice! I feel much freer without money involved, anyway.)

My sincerest good wishes to all of you. Be good to one another.

Elaine Roberts
125 Saginaw
Byron, MI 48418

costs

2,200 copies printed

Printing:	$624.49
Office expenses:	205.86
Advertising award:	25.00
Mailing costs:	111.22
	$966.57
Income since Winter issue:	$1,092.58

All labor donated.

distributors

Serendipity Couriers
Sausalito, CA

The Group, Inc.
Daytona Beach, Fla.

Distributors
South Bend, IN

Christopher Constantine
Philadelphia, PA

Turtle Island
Indianapolis, IN

Sparrow Natural Foods
Fresno, CA

Ten or more copies of the Review are available to individuals and retailers for 50¢ each. Please send payment with orders and we will ship them Book Rate postage paid. From Briarpatch Review, 330 Ellis Street, San Francisco 94102.

BRIARPATCH REVIEW

farm in the city
simple living conference
new pioneers in iowa city
cross—country caravan

"trust" your land
selling a briarpatch business
who's minding your health?
briarpatch business gardens

Contents

This issue was put together by: Kristin Anundsen, Barbara Janoff,
Kathy Mayer, Annie Styron, Michael Phillips and Tamra.

Art & Photo Credits:

Cover photo: Walker Evans, Roadside Stand Near Birmingham, 1936.
New Games Foundation - 3
Tamra - 6, 7, 13, 17, 26, 28, 32, 37, 38, 39
Alan Gould - 8, 9, 14, 15, 24, 25
Michael Phillips - 10, 25
Kris Handwerk - 27, 34, 35, 36
Marilyn Jones - 33

*The Briarpatch Review is a journal of the Briarpatch Network:
a group of people interested in simple living, openness,
sharing, and learning how the world works through business.
It is published every three months at 330 Ellis Street, San
Francisco, CA 94102 Tel. (415) 928-3960. Subscription rates
are $5 per year (add $2 outside U.S.); supporting membership
$25. Single issues and back copies are $1.25 postpaid. We
welcome feedback and stories about your own Briarpatch.*

Being in the Briarpatch

Earth Ball at New Games Tournament

The Briarpatch starts with a state of mind and grows to become a community. How can you become a part of it?

You may already have the state of mind. You're a Briar if you're trying to live simply and share your resources with others, if you're seeking right livelihood rather than wealth for its own sake.

A Briarpatch community begins with small groups of Briars and grows until it can be as large as it is in the San Francisco area, with over 100 businesses. You can't make it happen in a hurry; it needs to grow organically with careful tending and the right environment. You create the environment by talking with friends, working and playing together, and waiting patiently until there are enough Briars to call yourself a Briarpatch. By then you'll probably need a part-time coordinator supported by voluntary tithes and bartering. Your financial records will be open to everyone and you'll be helping each other on a large scale.

Messages

from the Briarpatch

HAYSTACK AT ARCOSANTI

Representing the Haystack at Arcosanti program, I am happy to enclose a $5.00 year's contribution.

No doubt you are familiar with Arcosanti, visionary architect Paolo Soleri's environmental reformation project, located in central Arizona. Haystack School of Crafts, located in Deer Isle, Maine (a nonprofit summer school offering courses in ceramics, weaving, jewelry, printmaking, woodwork, etc.), initiated a craft program at Arcosanti last spring, consisting of a four-week session.

This fledgling endeavor was quite successful, and for the last six months we have been hard at work preparing a program for this coming fall. There will be two four-week sessions in weaving, blacksmithing, ceramics, and stonemasonry. The theme is crafts people addressing the future and the quality of life.

Honoring frugality as an attitude fundamental to getting off the merry-go-round of destructiveness, the work will be in locating, preparing, and using raw materials indigenous to Arcosanti's locale, in conjunction with recyclable and commercially available ones as needed.

We're hopeful that there might be some folks in the Briarpatch network who'd be interested in participating in our program, and whom we might like to associate with. The cost of participation is $125/week, covering room, board, and tuition.

David Zatz
Haystack at
    Arcosanti
225 Eastern
    Parkway #4A
Brooklyn, NY 11238

NEW COMMUNITY

The intentions and business practices of Briarpatch seem to be very much what we here at Pulga are evolving into.

We are a small community, 12 adults and 8 children, living on 66 acres in the Feather River Canyon in Northern California. In addition to our gardening, building, and the care of the land we are on, we have members doing business in stained glass work, ceramics, general carpentry, the weaving, dyeing, and sewing of fabrics , and fine furniture and cabinetmaking. So far the most income has been from Pulga Designs, the furniture and cabinet shop.

This is a business that
three of us operate. It is
our intention to design and
build honest, high-quality
furniture, cabinetry, and
architectural specialties at
a price people can afford,
and that in turn supports us
and our trip. We have been
in business three years now
and as the saying goes, things
are getting better all the
time. We feel that this has
been largely possible by the
sharing of our resources and
skills and by our communal
life style, which allows us
to live so much more cheaply
than if we were each trying
to do it all individually.
This in turn allows us to
be able to charge less for
the work that we do, so
everyone seems to win.

We would like to become
even better players in this
game as well as being able
to share our experiences with
anyone else interested in
playing, so enclosed is our
check for a <u>Briarpatch Review</u>.
Please feel free to contact
or visit us at any time.

Jon F. Violette
Pulga Designs
Box 1
Pulga, CA 95965

RECYCLING

Right now my friend and
I are entering the "do it"
stage. We hope to start a
recycling, bartering, junking
business in Los Angeles.
Having spent parts of the
last year in borrowed trucks
making runs to swap meets,
junkyards, and recycling
centers, we see a need that
we can fill--a rechanneling
of some of this scattered
energy flow. No significant
monetary gains were made;
however, we learned many
beautiful lessons in transforming one man's junk into
another man's tool. We
would like to go into the
business full time now and
would appreciate any sug-
gestions.

We are new to the
business world, a little in
awe but determined. Saving
for our own truck and a lot
for storage of slower-moving
"tools." Any and all help
will be gratefully utilized.
Wonder if you folks know of
any organizations that offer
grants in the recycling business. Also interested in
business counseling, loan
information, and contact
with other "junkers."

Karin Kempa
4521 Kingswell
Los Angeles, CA
90027

Cottonfield is a fabric store that handles only 100% cotton fabric and thread--things hard to find in these synthetic times. Modelled on the idea of an "old-fashioned store", it was started by Jane Reardon, a young woman who grew up only a few blocks from College Avenue in Berkeley where Cottonfield is located.

COTTONFIELD

by Annie Styron

To me, Jane typifies all the qualities of a "Briarpatch" entrepeneur. Cottonfield is designed to fill a real need in the community: the kind of place people can come to ask for help or advice on the things they are making. While I was there, a woman came in with a pair of readymade pants and Susan, one of the two young women who work with Jane, got down on the floor and pinned them up for her. The women feel that this willingness to help people creates exactly the kind of atmosphere they want in the store.

Jane told me, "We have a good time here. We all like to do things for people and I don't care if I don't get paid for everything we do. We do,

however, charge for things like making buttonholes."

An important activity the store offers is sewing classes for children and adults. There are three classes for children, two high school age classes and two patchwork and quilting classes for adults. There's a nine-year-old in the adult class because she's a whiz.

In addition to adding revenue, the classes give life to Cottonfield because the kids come by after school and on

120

Saturdays to help in the store by doing things like writing sales checks for the customers. The women take turns teaching the classes which are held during business hours. Katy, a ten-year old student, did a window for Cottonfield of things kids had made.

New Business Values

Jane, Debbie and Susan had all worked in a fabric store, and their experience convinced them they wanted to have a place unlike the one they had worked in. They also felt good about collaborating and working with women their own age with similar ideas about business values and lifestyles. They wanted Cottonfield to be a place where people would come not only to buy goods, but learn a self-help occupation. They've found that people are grateful they're learning a skill, and the fee for classes is kept as low as possible. As Jane says, "It feels good to be able to help, and they've become our friends."

Sewing Ecology

There's a box in the store that says: "Used Sewing Patterns. Don't throw them away. Donate them. Our collection is growing." Cottonfield has worked out a way to reuse discontinued

patterns even though the pattern companies insist they return the envelopes. They cut out pictures from old pattern catalogs and paste them on envelopes to identify the old patterns and loan them to their customers.

As part of the effort to be unwasteful and ecological and to counteract the tendency of most businesses to ignore the waste of boxes and packing materials they:

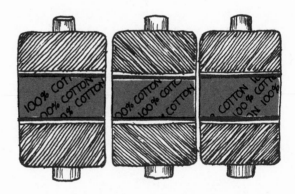

-Give thread boxes away to customers.
-Try not to stock things in packages, for example, loose buttons, instead of attached to cards.
-Order tape on rolls.

Salesmen said they couldn't survive having only 100% cotton items and tried to discourage them from getting unpackaged things.

The women feel that packaged zippers are wasteful and are trying to find a source for unpackaged ones.

There is a wood case stocked with spools of thread in glowing colors that are impossible to buy retail elsewhere. It's 100% cotton thread used by the manufacturing industry. The store sells a wooden adapter with the thread so the spools can be used on home sewing machines.

Jane told me, "We try to tell our customers what we're doing and why we're stocking unpackaged items. We try to explain that what they think they want isn't necessarily the best. For example, use pins to make markings on things instead of tracing paper."

Debbie instructing.

Briarpatch Advice

Jane spent two weeks researching everything she thought she would need to open the store, including estimating how much capital was needed. She called places to find out about such things as the cost of getting a license, cost of fixtures, wood prices, and figuring how much rent she could afford.

After estimating that she would need $8,000 to capitalize the store, she talked to Michael Phillips and Andy Alpine at a Briarpatch consulting session. Michael felt that all of her preliminary estimates and research done before coming to the Briarpatch for advice clearly showed that she had a good idea of all the necessary elements that go into making a business work.

Michelle looking at thread

Cottonfield has been open for eight months. They had been paying all the overhead expenses including salaries, rent, utilities, excluding patterns and fabric. Now Jane reports sales have doubled to about $4,000 per month which is above break-even.

Location Matters

The location is important for several reasons. They spend less on advertising because the street is well-known for its shops that appeal to people who just like to browse. Also, the neighborhood association is active in trying to keep small businesses and maintain the residential quality of the neighborhood.

According to Jane, "People are really supporting small stores. I knew it was that way before opening Cottonfield, but I didn't realize how strong that feeling was until experiencing it. We try to meet the needs of people in the neighborhood who shop here."

Jane Riordan, Debbie Wendel and Susan Dague at Cottonfield.

Is Briarpatch a New Culture?

By Michael Phillips

New cultures are often the result of major technological changes. The Briarpatch is a cultural reflection of the most recent change, and as such it is part of a new economic system that is quite different from any other I know of.

Three Eras

I identify three major technological changes that have created new cultures. The first was the use of <u>agricultural</u> technology. Beginning about 8,000 years ago, it edged out a nomadic hunting/gathering culture. It was a function of large city populations where written records were created; it used complex trade and led to the development of money and central social management (government).

The second technological change came 150 years ago with the widespread use of <u>mechanical power</u> (originally steam engines). This created a culture of enormous material consumption, intense resource competition, broad-scale literacy, great population growth, and great physical mobility.

Now we are in the midst of the third change, brought about by <u>information-communication</u> technology. The United States is well into this info-communication change; more than 55% of all employed people are processing information rather than physical products. We spend our days in meetings; on the phone; making or using TV, radio, or movies; writing to each other; filing paper; talking face to face with all kinds of people.

Information, this commodity we are spending our time on, has a distinct quality that makes it different from nearly everything else in the economic system: Its value is <u>not</u> based on its scarcity--in fact its value increases with its abundance. If I give or sell you some physical product, such as tea, then I have less of it. And if that product is in short supply generally, the price will be high. The opposite is true with information. The more phones connected to the network the more valuable each telephone is. Also, if I give you information I have not lost anything--in fact it helps me as well as you.

The Value of Openness

The new culture born of the info-communication revolution is reflected in the Briarpatch in a special way. You could even say that the Briarpatch is a new culture itself. The way the Briarpatch works is based on our knowledge that

you can give information away
and be better off. Unlike the
older society that we still
live in, which tries to make
information scarce by using
patents, copyrights, and
secrets, Briarpatch people want
to share everything we know
and feel.

We have found that keeping our
financial records open helps
other people to start low-cost
businesses where we can buy,
and openness lets other people
help with advice and suggestions
that make our work much easier
and more fun. All of our openness, our writing, talking,
smiling, and hugging, helps
each of us get more emotional
support from others. Our lack
of secrecy automatically
creates a noncompetitive
climate where people want to
help each other.

The consequences of this community of helping and sharing
make it possible for us to live
on fewer material goods. We
don't need lots of fancy things
for social status to get
emotional support; we've got
that kind of support. When we
physically share re-usable
resources like trucks, houses,
records, and tools, we don't
have to buy our own. Above
all, with the enormous sharing
of information within the
Briarpatch the entire world
works better for us, so we
feel freer and happier and
less dependent on goods.

We know information is a commodity that is more valuable
the more it is spread around.
So we gladly share what we can
and appreciate the openness of
other people.

A Farm in the City

By Kristin Anundsen

Cars and trucks whiz by on the Bayshore Freeway leading to/from San Francisco, but although The Farm is right under the freeway, its denizens can't hear much noise. The freeway is hollow, see, and the air inside apparently cushions the sound.

A farm under the freeway, you ask? Yes, a farm, and more than a farm. It's a community center, but more than that too. It's a center for the arts, a place for potluck dinners and other events, and a wide, warm, funky space for just being.

Crossroads

"I've always had a thing about freeways," muses Bonnie Sherk, an artist who, with musician Jack Wickert, is a prime mover of The Farm. (Both of them live there.) "I guess it's my karma." To her, freeways are both sculpture and symbol. She appreciates their surreal form but also sees them as technological, monolithic structures that separate people and communities from each other. A main purpose of The Farm is to bring people and communities back in touch, to "integrate a lot of the elements of life, <u>including</u> the freeways, and to make visual connections." In fact, the full name of the place is "Crossroads Community (The Farm)."

It really is a farm. Right next to the concrete roadway is a garden overflowing with herbs, flowers, and vegetables, flourishing because of the tender loving care it gets as well as the sunny weather. There are fruit trees in the front yard, and a nearby barren, rocky piece of land is destined to be a meadow someday. At one side there is a small greenhouse.

In the basement of one of the two spacious, connected buildings is the "Raw Egg Animal Theatre," an indoor-outdoor environment that houses

126

three rabbits, a rooster, lots of hens, and sculpture designed for these animals. The animals also helped to create the place by moving things around and building nests. The "theatre" has been used for a life drawing class and for instructing children about farm animals; also, the chickens produce eggs for eating. A dog and assorted cats have the run of the whole Farm. When asked if she owns the animals herself, Bonnie says vaguely, "Oh, I don't think in terms of ownership."

Cooperation

Everything at The Farm is a cooperative, integrative venture, and it has been from the beginning. The idea began in May of 1974; in August the main building, a former pillow factory, was rented. Besides Bonnie and Jack, a dance group called Tumbleweed and a theater collective called The Jones Company moved in. Tumbleweed and The Jones Company each got a grant from the Zellerbach Foundation, Bonnie worked as a waitress, and Jack drove a cab in order to make the rent payments of $1,000 a month. Eventually, The Farm as a whole—a nonprofit corporation—was able to get a grant from the National Endowment for the Arts.

Everyone who uses the space now contributes something—money, work, or materials. Furnishings—doors, tables,

pianos, curtains, whatever--
have been scrounged, built,
or solicited. "Also, sometimes people just lay things
on us," says Jack. "The other
day we found that round table
on our doorstep." Maintaining
The Farm was and still is a
tremendous amount of work,
and no one is ever idle.

Right now The Farm's greatest
needs include a typewriter and
some help in installing a
sprinkler system, fire exits,
and insulation.

Bonnie hopes The Farm will
become more and more self-
sufficient. "We could have
a cafe here," she says. "We
could serve things that are
grown on The Farm and have
performances by the groups
that are involved with us.
The foods could be cooked and
served by a changing crew of
artists, children, and other
community members so we could

garden under the freeway

have a good ethnic mix in our
cuisine."

Ecology

Among the many groups that
have used The Farm for rehear-
sals or meetings are the New
American People's Opera; a
theater workshop directed by
Judy Berg; the San Francisco
Artists' Caucus; the Pickle
Family Circus; a children's
performing arts workshop; tap
and jazz dance classes; the
annual New Music Festival; and
the San Francisco Mussel Group.
Which of these does not seem
to fit with the others? Mussels? Well, they may not be
art, but they're ecology, and
integration of art and life
is part of what The Farm is
about.

Recently, a new organization
has moved to The Farm to share
its space on an ongoing basis:
Earthwork, "An Urban Center
for the Study of Land and Food,"
which was started by some
former San Francisco Ecology
Center people. Earthwork's
mission is to share and dis-
seminate information on food
production and distribution,
and among its resources are a
library, a converted school
bus for field trips to agri-
cultural areas, booklets and
filmstrips on food buying
clubs, and people who can
arrange classes, workshops,
and urban/rural work exchanges.
Earthwork's staff has fixed
up a comfortable space on the

kitchen at the Farm

"garden floor" of The Farm, and it's open to community residents.

"We wanted Earthwork in here with us because we felt it was important to balance the performing arts with other life elements," says Bonnie.

Learning and sharing are part of The Farm's integrative process; the idea is for various participating groups to communicate with and help each other. They share any talents they have. On one recent evening, following a Chinese potluck dinner, Robert Burkhardt of the Pickle Family Circus showed slides from his trip to China. Robert, in addition to being a photographer, is also a plumber, and it was he who had put in The Farm's gas lines and sink.

The Future

Future plans for The Farm include:

· More programs involving children and the elderly.

· An amphitheater with hillsides for spectators, built from piles of broken-up concrete, fill, and topsoil. "The National Guard will dig up the concrete," says Bonnie, "and if the city will permit it, we'll use it to build the hillsides."

· Conducting of tests to determine what the modern automobile environment does to growing things. This will be done in conjunction with the Department of Agriculture, university science departments, artists, children, and others.

· An international film series. This is contingent on getting the vast performance space insulated.

The Farmers are engaged in a continuing dialogue with city, state, and federal governments in order to acquire additional open space. Meanwhile, the space they have is developing into a true community center-- not a cold, institutional one, either, but a homey place that Bonnie hopes will appeal to everyone, on some level. "The Farm gives me a lot of hope," says Robert Burkhardt. "We need more places like it to encourage small community groups."

NEW PIONEERS IN IOWA CITY

By Craig Mosher

Like a lot of other folks, I had my consciousness raised (directed is perhaps a more accurate word) during the political struggles of 1968-1971. I became impatient for change, worried that we had little time left to "save" ourselves, our communities, and our planet. I wanted "revolution now!" I thought in terms of large-scale projects; government, private, or university funding; even nationwide organizations and impacts.

Five years later I find myself persuaded that most "revolutionaries" will only succeed in replacing one centralized, intolerant, authoritarian regime with another. So I am seeking a change theory which recognizes the necessity of ·evolutionary change based on human values. The i Ching offers such a concept:

Kua (hexagram) #53
DEVELOPMENT (Gradual Progress)
...development proceeds gradually, step by step.
...within (below) is tranquillity, which guards against precipitate actions, and without (above) is penetration, which makes development and progress possible.
This principle of gradual development...is always applicable where it is a matter of correct relationships of cooperation.
Gentleness that is adaptable, but at the same time penetrating, is the outer form that should proceed from inner calm.
The very gradualness of the development makes it necessary to have perseverance, for perseverance alone prevents slow progress from dwindling to nothing.

SUN - UPPER TRIGRAM (WITHOUT) - The gentle, wind, wood, penetration, adaptability.

KEN LOWER TRIGRAM (WITHIN) - keeping still, mountain, calm tranquility, stillness.

130

Like a growing tree...the work of influencing people can be only gradual. Progress must be quite gradual.
...the inexhaustible source of progress is inner calm combined with adaptability to circumstances.

These words of ancient Chinese wisdom are echoed by many other people on both the personal and community levels. Gurdjieff says that fundamental personal change comes only through lifelong work. Barry Stevens reminds us, "Don't push the river; it flows by itself." The Beatles sing, "There will be an answer, let it be." And the steady tortoise crosses the line ahead of the dashing hare.

But How?

Pondering the notion of gradual progress and knowing that the social, political, and economic changes that seem so crucial may take decades, I wonder how to manage perseverance. Part of an answer comes from Mike Phillips' "First Law of Money," which ever so simply states, "Go ahead and do what you want to do...do not worry about the money." When we are working on the right things in the right place at the right time they will grow; people and energy will gravitate to these projects. The experience of so many alternative and cooperative projects seems to bear this out.

How do we know what is right? Mike Phillips suggests that one way to recognize right livelihood is when you feel you could go on doing the activity for a long time, even a lifetime. Another way to recognize it is when "the good intrinsic in your livelihood is also good in terms of the greater community." Also, when there is a focused relationship between your work and yourself, money will become secondary.

Organizational and community growth also will occur naturally under these circumstances. Right activity for an organization, like right livelihood for an individual, can be recognized by the extent to which (1) the or-

On THE MOUNTAIN, A TREE,
The image of development

131

ganization's collective identity
(defined by purpose, structure
and procedures, values, and
membership) is integrated with
the group's activities; (2) the
group sees itself as being around
a long time; (3) the greater
community benefits from the
group's activities.

A Midwest Example

Here in Iowa City, a midwestern
university town of 50,000 on the
banks of the Iowa River, the New
Pioneer Cooperative Society
provides an example of a cooperative group's development.
New Pioneer has grown in five
years from a small natural foods
buying club to where it now
includes a large natural foods
store and warehouse, a restaurant
and bakery, an auto repair
garage, a memorial society, and,
most recently, a credit union.
The group's purpose is to provide
natural foods and other community services at low cost,
utilizing members' volunteer
labor. Decisions are made at
monthly membership meetings by
consensus, reflecting a value
placed on activities that are
cooperative, small scale, non-
institutionalized, natural,
diverse, and that meet present
needs in the community.

New Pioneer is working toward
buying a building to house its
activities--evidence of the
long life we expect for the
co-op.

A prime criterion for cooperative
ventures, going back to early
co-ops, has been that they
provide services which are
needed in the community. An
example of this in New Pioneer
is our credit union. When we
began planning for a credit union
we sent out a questionnaire to
members asking how much they
would deposit, where they worked,
and how long they planned to
stay in Iowa City. We were
surprised by the responses,
which showed us to be more numerous, wealthy, employed, and
stable than we had imagined.
The strength of this response
not only convinced us that there
was a real need for a co-op
credit union in town but also
convinced the State Department
of Banking to grant us a charter
and incorporation papers.

Gradual Growth

The credit union will give us a
mechanism for concentrating and
utilizing our own limited capital
for our collective and individual
purposes. It will allow us to

132

meet members' and groups' needs for small amounts of start-up money for new projects and activities. Thus, our development will remain gradual; our activities will be able to expand as our membership grows.

New projects are begun out of members' personal resources, inner convictions, and felt needs. We do not seek outside funding or large contributions which might accelerate our development beyond our own members' pace and abilities. The bakery is now debating whether to try to fill some large orders from profit-making food stores with a staff that is still inexperienced and somewhat transient. A sense of right activity will likely lead them to choose to supply only our own members, at least until the business grows strong enough to meet the demands of commercial competition.

"Trust" Your Land   Cont'd. from page 141

WHO WE ARE. The Northern California Land Trust is a trust, leasing it for life to low-income farming families or groups. Lessees are selected on the basis of need, ability, and the desire to farm using environmentally sound methods. We welcome various means of acquiring land: purchase, gift, or some beneficial combination of these. A donor of land may continue to live on this land for life.

tax-exempt, non-profit corporation which seeks tax-deductible gifts of land or money to buy land. We then hold this land in perpetual

More information can be obtained from the Northern California Land Trust, 330 Ellis St. #504, San Francisco, CA 94102; the Trust for Public Land, 82 2nd St., San Francisco, CA 94105; or The American Land Trust, P.O. Box 2076, Arlington, VA 22202.

A NEW AGE JOURNEY

By Richard Goering

The Briarpatch is spreading its roots east this year with Project America 1976, a cross-country walking and bicycling tour devoted to sharing ideas for simpler, more joyful, ecological lifestyles. Project America 1976 is the 103rd member of Briarpatch, and its business is described on the mailing list as "spreading knowledge." Actually, the project is a two-way learning experience, and those of us who are participants are learning as well as teaching.

The project consists of about a dozen people, including two Japanese members, who are bicycling and occasionally hiking from Santa Barbara to Philadelphia. We are accompanied by a propane-powered resource bus, "Hope," which has files of information and books to sell on alternative energy, nutrition, simple living, personal growth, and other such topics. We started bicycling February 6, and plan to arrive in Philadelphia in late October.

Project members are providing information and offering workshops on yoga, folk dance, aging, French intensive/biodynamic gardening, origami, new games, and nonviolent social change, among others. We also learn what we can from people we meet, and do a lot of networking. We go out and talk to people in communities we visit, and learn about their lifestyles, attitudes, and concerns for the future.

Bicycling through New Mexico --

I suppose you could say we're a kind of travelling alternative lifestyle medicine show, a counterculture caravan going into the heart of Middle America. Whatever we're doing, as far as we know, is unique. There have been counterculture caravans before, but not many tried to relate to the man or woman on the street in Clayton, New Mexico or Henderson, Kentucky.

Because of what we're doing, we've adopted a slightly more conservative image than one might expect of an alternative-oriented cross-country trip. Our bus looks like it could belong to a church group, and we plug into the "Bicentennial" label. We emphasize meeting and listening to people rather than converting or confronting them. We often find that our ideas aren't so far apart—especially when we talk about self-reliance, cooperation in communities, and the need to conserve energy, money, and resources.

Reaction

We've been in cities like Phoenix and Albuquerque, where there already is an "alternative" community, and towns like Indio, California, and Truth or Consequences, New Mexico, where "New Age" could just as well be an advertising slogan. We're meeting a broad cross-section of people, although most people we actually work with are already interested in new kinds of life-styles.

At first, we'd come into town, announce our workshops, and find there was not much response. Now we're working more with specific groups in the community that already have an interest. Our book-selling and information tables do best on campuses or in front of food co-ops. We meet many "Middle Americans" in our travels, and we have had generally cordial and interesting discussions; but by and large, these people don't buy a lot of books or come to workshops.

Nice things happen—at times, when we need them most. In Indio, after a frustrating day trying to sell books outside of Gemco, we sold books on energy, nuclear power, and gardening to the city planner—who thanked us

135

for "expanding my mind." In Tucson, a metallurgical engineer read about us in the newspaper (we've had good local publicity, usually) and came out to talk to us about developing a "more satisfying" lifestyle. In Truth or Consequences, we were greeted at the city limits by a sign that said, "Our High School Supports Free Enterprise--the American Way." Next day we were at the high school, showing films on nuclear power and giving workshops on creative dramatics and nonviolence training.

We've met people with fascinating ideas for the future. In Arizona we toured Arcosanti and met Paolo Soleri, architect and visionary of ecological cities. In Tucson we stayed with people from the L-5 society, which advocates space colonization as a way of solving energy and population problems. We met Steve Baer in Albuquerque, toured his solar energy research facility, and found him as resistant as ever to the idea of government grants.

Finances

It's hard financing a business whose product is "spreading knowledge." Mostly it's been from our savings, about $100 a month, and we're starting to get some income from books and small donations. We're getting less bashful about asking for money for workshops, and we're open to the idea of outside work. Of Course, this is cheap living--what with not owning cars, staying in churches or private homes, and buying food in bulk.

Norie Huddle, the woman who originated the project, received an advance on a book to be written about if from a Japanese publisher. (She lived in Japan for four years studying pollution, and wrote a book about it called Island of Dreams.) The advance, and a small grant, helped start the project; but we have not yet realized visions of making it self-supporting.

Ourselves

We're learning how to live and cooperate with a group of people in a very tight space. Our bus is crowded, and we've had to adjust. We've also become aware of the need for personal space, and we're trying to balance that desire with the need for more group planning and coordination. It isn't always easy. Someone told Norie recently, "You're putting yourself in a hotbox when you do a project like this. And you'll get all your buttons pushed."

Buttons get pushed, and sometimes it becomes an energy drain. Disorganization and unclarity are problems. We schedule meetings and time together as needed, and try not to let grievances pile up. On those quiet evenings out on the desert, we've been telling each other our life stories and devising games we can all enjoy.

We're moving on...through California, Arizona, New Mexico, Kansas, Missouri, Illinois, Kentucky, West Virginia, and Pennsylvania. We're planning a ten-day retreat/event in the Ozarks June 25-July 5, open to friends. Anyone who wants to get in touch with us may do so through the Ecology Center, 13 Columbus, San Francisco, California 94111.

Leaving Santa Barbara February 6, 1976.

Selling (and Buying) a Briarpatch Business

By Michael Phillips

One Briar sold his business to another Briar a year and a half ago; we now have enough experience to say that everyone benefited from the terms of the sale.

The business is Raskinflakkers, an ice creamery in San Francisco that carries Bud's ice cream (a local favorite). Raskinflakkers was launched by Phil Groves, one of the earliest people to join the local Briarpatch Network. Phil started the business in December 1973, and by the end of 1974 it was averaging about $4,500 a month in gross revenue. Phil felt burned out by the work involved in starting and running the business and decided to sell it. The buyer he found was the Divine Light Mission, which purchased Raskinflakkers in January 1975 and soon thereafter joined the Briarpatch. The store is very successful now, reports manager Mike Sredl; it provides regular jobs and fun for 10 members of the Divine Light Mission.

Mike Sredl scooping ice cream

Terms

The business was sold for $15,000, a modest price for a going concern with more than $5,000 worth of equipment. However, the neighborhood is not wealthy, the ability to continue getting Bud's ice cream was not assured, and the store is on a month-to-month tenancy with no lease. On the other hand, the conditions of the sale reflected Phil's trust and willingness to share in the risk.

138

The terms were: nothing down; 8% of gross revenues for the first six months, which was applied to the purchase price; two years to pay off the balance; 10% interest on the declining balance.

The interest rate was very fair to both sides. A bank loan to the Mission would have been at least 12%, and a secure return for Phil from a bond would have been 8%, so the 10% loan starting after six months was halfway in between.

Satisfaction

Both Mike and Phil are extremely happy with the way things worked out. Phil had thought the 8% of gross revenue for the first six months would be modest--based on his average of $4,500 a month the Mission would have been paying him $360 each month. But the new management, with longer hours,

some decorating, and hard work, increased revenues to more than $8,000 per month during those first six months and were paying over $600. When the six months ended and payments began on the regular 24-month loan at 10% interest, payments dropped to $500 a month.

The store's average sales now range from $8,000 per month in the winter to $10,000 in the summer. Very good revenue for a 600-foot store in a low-income neighborhood. Openness (including open books) and trust on the part of both buyer and seller contributed to the feelings of mutual satisfaction.

Buying a cone

139

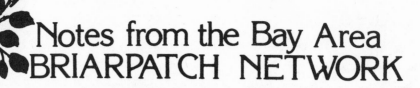

Notes from the Bay Area
BRIARPATCH NETWORK

By Andy Alpine

There's been a lot going on in the Briarpatch Network over the past few months. We had a party for members and seventy-five of us took turns sharing who we are, what we're into and what some immediate needs are. Our Health Insurance Plan got under way on May 1st and is working well. We published our first Skills Exchange Directory and Newsletter. And we're planning to help start a group for women in the Briarpatch to share thoughts, problems, needs, etc.

Rather than go into the details of what's been happening in the Bay Area network I thought I'd put out a feeling that many of us have experienced and are experiencing. It concerns Work and our relation to it.

In The Prophet, Kahlil Gibran speaks not only of Love, Marriage, and Friendship, but also about Work:

"You work that you may keep pace with the earth and the soul of the earth. For to be idle is to become a stranger unto the seasons, and to step out of life's procession, that marches in majesty and proud submission towards the infinite."

"When you work you are a flute through whose heart the whispering of the hours turns to music. Which of you would be a reed, dumb and silent, when all else sings together in unison?"

"To love life through labour is to be intimate with life's inmost secret."

"And what is it to work with love?...It is to charge all things you fashion with a breath of your own spirit."

"Work is love made visible. And if you cannot work with love but only with distaste, it is better that you should leave your work and sit at the gate of the temple and take alms of those who work with joy. For if you bake bread with indifference, you bake a bitter bread that feeds but half man's hunger."

"Trust" Your Land

Some of our readers have asked us for information on land trusts. The Northern California Land Trust, in a recent newsletter, explains the concept by quoting another publication (from the Sam Ely Land Trust in Maine) and then goes on to define its own operation.

WHAT IS A LAND TRUST? A land trust is defined as a "legal entity chartered to hold land in stewardship for all human-kind, present and future, while protecting the legitimate use-rights of its residents." More than a mechanism for common ownership, it is, rather, ownership for the common good.

The land trust as an organization, and as a social movement, has three concerns: environmental, economic, and social. Environmentally, the trust encourages intelligent land use and discourages environmental damage. It effects these goals through land-use planning and prevention of profit on land sales. Economically, the trust seeks to reduce speculation and to ease access to the land, which it effects through prohibiting the sale of its land and through creative financing of its leases. Socially, the trust seeks to create a new system of land tenure by providing lower-cost land, putting farm land back into production, and encouraging people to work cooperatively.

The trust holds only the land. Improvements such as buildings are owned by those who lease the land--individually, collectively, or cooperatively. The goals of the trust are protected by its charter (and perhaps by deed restrictions of land donors).

The trustees do not control the land or the lives of the leaseholders. The trust is a relatively passive agency, as far as its land-using members are concerned. Use-rights are secured by long-term leases which are renewable and inheritable. This lease protects one's position on the land as well as the land itself. The main thing lessees give up is the "right" to profit by selling the land.

cont'd. on page 133

Gardens in Businesses

By Rosemary Menninger

San Francisco has one of the most varied community gardening programs in the country, involving gardens by neighborhoods, schools, and institutions. But there are virtually no gardens as yet that are associated with businesses. Briarpatch members with access to a yard, or even pavement, could become community gardening leaders with very little effort.

The City will deliver free compost upon request. It's not necessary to dig; just pour the compost into any containers that will hold soil

and drain water. Plant, then
water nearly every day, weeding twice a week.

If several Briarpatch businesses had gardens on the
side, bounty from one garden
could be traded for surplus
at another--especially practical in this city with two
climate zones. In general,
cooking greens, salad greens,
and all members of the cab-
bage family, which includes
broccoli and cauliflower,
grow well in the fog. In
the Mission district, tomatoes, peppers, sometimes
eggplants, and even melons
flourish. Potatoes and
root crops grow great all
over here.

The food grown in business
gardens is like a fringe
benefit for employees. A
garden I helped General Motors
start, at their assembly plant
in Freemont, yields an acre
of food; but GM also says it's
the first time their management and labor have worked
side by side and without rank.
In a small business garden,
this can be equally true.

A great potential lies in
small businesses throwing a
garden, like a party, for
the surrounding neighbor-
hood. Inviting nearby residents and workers to join
your garden can bring you
business and publicity.

San Francisco Community Garden

Nine or ten business-
initiated gardens would be
in effect a gardening
program--the first of its
kind in San Francisco, another first for Briarpatch,
and an inspiration to small
businesses that they can
become community leaders.

*If any Briarpatch Businesses
are interested in starting a
community garden program,
please write Kathy Mayer,
413 Litho Street, Sausalito,
California 94965.*

143

Who's Minding Your Health?

By Chuck Clanton

I am...a person, a man (trying to be more of the former and less of the latter), a scientist (an observer and analyzer of patterns--only sometimes for fame and profit), and a nascent physician. The last has proven to be the least of me because there is much in organized medicine that I cannot accept or tolerate. That is my perspective. Now for my premises:

--I am my body. You are your body. Each of us should know as much about our bodies as we know about any of the other things we live with.

--Doctors are not gods, nor are they demons. They are people with a system of beliefs about the world (sometimes called knowledge) that sometimes proves useful to some people with some diseases. Their world view is limited, but so are mine and yours.

--Most sickness is not abnormal. Throughout our evolutionary history, the body has been exposed to disease and has developed mechanisms for coping. Therefore, I am skeptical of anything that purports to improve on our natural defenses, whether that be radiation therapy or vegetarianism.

--Every course of action, including inaction, has its advantages and disadvantages. Oftimes the outcome is uncertain, and judgement must be based on the application of individual values to the probable benefits and risks. These decisions can be very difficult, but each of us must make them. That is what it means to take control of your medical destiny.

--When something is wrong, organized medicine should not and does not preclude other health resources, including religion, alternative health professionals, and the like. They should not preclude medicine either.

Instead of discoursing at length on what I think medicine should be and do, it may be more useful for me to apply these premises to how a person can use the medical establishment to obtain the best care possible.

How to Find a Doctor

A personal or family physician provides a valuable service by telling you when the problem is serious. Look for a general

144

practitioner (family practice "specialist," pediatrician, or internist) who meets these criteria:

1. You like him (her) and can talk to him (her) easily.
2. The price is okay (discuss it!).
3. (S)he shares decisions with you (you may have to request/demand this since some patients do not want to know that there are risks and benefits to everything, including inaction).
4. (S)he is willing to help you seek consultation with a specialist for serious diseases.
5. (S)he lets you recover from non-serious diseases without treating symptoms that you do not feel the need for suppressing.
6. (S)he explains the nature of your disease and the reason for treatment so that you understand and can make your own decisions.

The best way to find such a physician is by personal recommendation. However, you will not necessarily get along well with your friend's doctor, even though (s)he is just right for your friend.

If you have something serious, see a specialist. Cheap, in-humane, time-consuming, but generally high-quality medical services are available in clinics at medical schools. Expensive, sometimes more humane, much less time-consuming, and generally high-quality medical services can be obtained by seeing a staff or attending physician at a medical school as a private patient. The clinic or department will provide names.

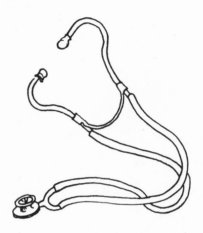

How to See a Doctor

A major problem with medicine is lack of communication between doctors and patients. On your first visit, discuss the fee schedule, let the doctor know that you do not want to be treated for symptoms that are not bothering you excessively, and show your concern and active participation in the process by asking questions about how the diagnosis was arrived at and how certain it is. Refuse treatment until you understand

its ramifications. Ask
about alternatives and the
risks and benefits of each.
It's your body. Do not
pretend that you can give up
your responsibility.

If a drug is advised, find
out why. Is it to alleviate
a symptom? (Does that symptom
really bother you?) Is it to
eliminate a causative organism?
(Has the presence of the organism been established? If
not, why treat it?)

Doctors expect you to trust
them with your life even if
you have never seen them before.
That is ridiculous. If you
have something serious, get
another opinion--from an
appropriate specialist. The
doctor is <u>your consultant</u>
on the vital issue of your
health, but ultimately it's
your body, your decision, your
life.

As a general rule, see a doctor
when you become concerned or
when you have a symptom which
does not fit--as insurance.

It's worth the price to find
out it's (usually) nothing--
and you can ask all those
questions to find out more
about your body.

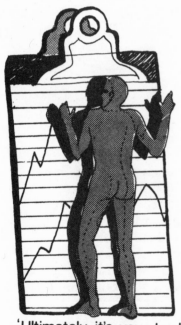

'Ultimately it's your body,
  your decision, your LIFE...'

MEDICAL SELF-CARE MAGAZINE:
ACCESS TO MEDICAL TOOLS is a new
quarterly medical journal for
laypeople. It carries reviews
of the best popular medical books
and articles teaching paramedical
and preventive medical skills.
Editor Tom Ferguson, a Yale
medical student, is eager to
correspond with potential
contributors and subscribers.

Subscriptions are $7, sample
issue $1 from P.O. Box 31549B,
San Francisco, CA 94131.

book

Garbage Housing

by Martin Pawley
120 pages, black and white ill.
Architectural Press, London
Halsted Press, New York

This book does not tell you
how to make homes or domes
from your garbage can or its
contents. It is a plea for
the application of mass production methods to solve the
worldwide housing shortage.
Sounds obvious but, as author
Martin Pawley points out, the
housing crisis is culturally
determined and not a technical
problem. Using a machine gun
barrage of statistics, he
nails our governments "for
making pious appeals for restraint after preaching spectacular consumption for decades."

Of necessity in the Third
World and Asia, people do use
garbage for building materials.
Pawley cites examples from
Easter Island to Vietnam. But
in the West we fail to see the
building brick lurking in
every beer bottle. Alfred
Heineken, head of the giant
Amsterdam brewery, was an exception with his WOBO bottle/
brick, but he was defeated by
the combined forces of cultural prejudice and his own marketing department. Pawley
goes on to describe garbage
housing experiments conducted
in Chile and with his students
at various English and American schools of architecture
"filled with empty studios
and crowded bars." Always the
same sad story.

Author Pawley at home.

Founder of the legendary London weekly, Ghost Dance Times,
Martin Pawley has spent years
shouting down the ear trumpet
of the English architectural
establishment. Still on the
rebound from rationing, English
nouveau consumers scoff at
ecological concerns. A profit without honor in his own
country, Pawley is now living
in a '63 Cadillac at
Rensselaer Poly.

-Lucinda Hawkins
London

Briarpatch Members

*If you would like a list of
Briarpatch Network members and
what they do, send 50¢ to the
Briarpatch Review, 330 Ellis
Street, San Francisco 94102.*

147

Simple Living Conference

By Eleanor McCallie

On Feb. 28 and 29, 1976, the Second Annual Simple Living Conference was held in Ukiah, California. More than 100 people helped organize and run the conference, which was sponsored by the Ukiah Community and the Rural Institute.

Even before the conference started, the local newspaper congratulated the organizers: "They have harnessed and channeled the energy that is everywhere in our community, but which too often remains scattered and apart."

"Come Learn, Come Teach" was the theme on the poster for the conference, which was a community effort toward reeducation. In this regard, the style of the Simple Living Conference was as important as the content. People shared what they'd learned--some things new, some things old and tried, and some things just revived.

More than 2,000 people in the county came to the conference. Upon entering the large hall at the Fairgrounds, you

were met by a four-ring circus of practical skills and folk learning. In each corner of the room people gathered for particular workshops. The form of the workshops was informal, a somewhat organized style of over-the-fence neighborly conversations about "how I tried this" and "well, last year we got good results this way."

Changes

I'd like to share not only a sense of the conference but also how the conference reflected changes that have taken place in this community. Ukiah is the county seat for Mendocino County, an area known for redwoods, grapes, and pears. Its hills hold pockets of homesteads carved out of the

148

wilderness, late and old, embodying the theme of the "agrarian self-sufficient lifestyle." People have tried to do it on their own. The movement in the last few years, however, has been from the hills back into town. As one homesteader put it: "We tried to be self-sufficient on our own and then we came to know that our security depended on the well-being of the whole community. We're trying to find ways to do it together now."

The conference reflected these changes. There were lots of workshops on self-reliance skills such as beekeeping and poultry, rural first aid, fire prevention, building peasant dwellings (yurts and umbra cones), and alternate energy sources. People showed ways to use sun, wind, and manure to make electricity to run your car, your car to run your TV, your wood-burning stove to run a hot shower, water to run your drill, and even how to get steam out of your privy by composting waste for your garden.

Workshop Topics

More prominent than "do your own" was the theme of cooperative effort. Many workshops centered around what people were doing together and generated energy to start community projects. Such workshops included:

Community Gardens: Moving in the direction of county self-reliance through grow-

a yurt

ing the food we consume.

Rural Transportation: Alternatives such as "backwoods transit" (public transportation into the woods), car pools, and transportation co-ops.

Local Cooperative Health Insurance: Alternative participant-owned health insurance.

Community Canning: The concepts and organization of community canning...a community canning plant will be starting in Anderson Valley.

Legal Clinic on Cooperative Land Ownership: Methods of land ownership that reflect

cooperative values--partnership, limited partnership, trusteeship, corporate non-profit, cooperative.

Cooperative/Collective Food Distribution: How Ukiah can participate in the alternative food distribution from several warehouses in Eureka, Arcata, Santa Rosa, and Sacramento.

Cottage Industries and Job Sharing: Processes to employ more people.

Workshops on local politics and current issues included ways to make the local government more responsive to the community needs, building codes, land use and the environment in Mendocino County, National Land for People and the 160-acre irrigation laws in Fresno, nuclear power, and appropriate technology which is budding in Sacramento. In due respect for the interdependence of all life, there was even a course on "integrated systems for urban folks."

There will most probably be a Third Annual Simple Living Conference in Ukiah and no telling what changes will transpire by then. For reports from the conference or more information pertaining to any of the presentations, contact
Simple Living Conference
Ukiah Community Center
225 E. Perkins St.
Ukiah, CA 95482
(707) 462-4357

Preventing Dental Disease

By Philip Hordiner

Cavities and gum disease are almost entirely preventable today. Prevention is so simple that it is a wonder that so many people still are in the habit of allowing their teeth and gums to go bad.

The traditional approach is to allow cavities or gum disease to occur and then to have a dentist repair them. As a dentist, I can tell you that it is far better to avoid the repairs altogether.

For those of you who are bothered by gums that tend to bleed, or recurrent cavities, this is the simplest way I know of getting on the road to good dental health.

Assume that bacteria grow on your teeth much the same way as mold grows on food. They utilize sugar to form a sticky mass which sticks them to your teeth. They grow in this mass and within 24 to 36 hours, they form a plaque which is what actually harms the teeth and gums. The bacteria are protected by the plaque so that mouthwashes cannot penetrate and harm them. Sugar, however, is rapidly absorbed into the plaque and within 20 seconds is converted to acid by a process of fermentation. The acid then dissolves a little of the tooth where the plaque is stuck to it.

After about 5,000 contacts with sugar or foods containing sugar, enough tooth structure is dissolved to form a visible hole in the tooth. Plaque also forms other byproducts which destroy the skin where the tooth contacts the gums.

If your gums bleed easily when you explore with a toothpick or dental floss, you know that the skin has been destroyed in that area. The gums are stress-bearing tissues and will not bleed if they are healthy.

Since the gums heal fast if given the chance, you will find that if you scrape the plaque off your teeth once a day for five days, you will not be able to make them bleed.

Toothpick Technology

The simplest way I know for removing bacterial plaque is with an ordinary round toothpick. Start by looking carefully at your teeth and gums in a mirror. Pull your lips and cheeks back so you can see all parts of your teeth. Notice where the gums and teeth meet. Do you see some white sticky material stuck to the teeth? Take an ordinary round toothpick and holding it like a pencil, insert it in the groove where the gums meet the teeth. Run it along in the groove the same way you would clean your fingernails. The gums may feel sore if the skin in the groove has been destroyed. As you scrape the plaque off, you may get quite a bit of bleeding in some areas. Note that

the areas that don't bleed won't feel as sore. Clean all areas around all teeth in this manner. The gums may be quite sore for the first few days. You can ease this by rinsing your mouth afterwards with a teaspoon of salt in a glass of warm water. The important thing is to clean all the way into the deepest part of these grooves.

After about five days of doing this you will experience a marked change in how your gums look and feel. Enjoy this new feeling and keep it up. Experiment with different ways of using toothpicks. Try breaking them in various ways to get into difficult spots.

Break them off so you can reach inside the lower teeth!

152

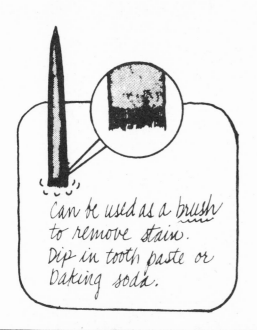

Can be used as a brush to remove stain. Dip in tooth paste or baking soda.

If you try these simple methods, let me know what results you get. I will do my best to answer your questions. I learned much of what I know from other toothpick users as this was not taught in dental school.

Philip Hordiner is a dentist in the Briarpatch network. He can be reached at:
3412 Geary Boulevard
San Francisco 94112

Distribution

Our distributors in the Bay Area are Serendipity Couriers and the Whole Earth Access Company. Andy Alpine drops off copies of the Review when he visits Briarpatch stores in the Bay Area, and other Briars distribute copies in likely places.

Stores in other parts of the country order ten or more copies at our standard discount of 50%. If you know stores you think would be interested, we'd be glad to send you postage paid, ten or more copies for 50¢ each. Send payment with orders to: Briarpatch Review, 330 Ellis Street, San Francisco 94102, or call (415) 928-3960.

Costs

2,200 copies printed

Printing and production:	$641.55
Mailing:	259.67
Office expenses:	33.23
Misc.:	48.30
Ad Award:	25.00
	$1007.75

Income since Spring issue:	$881.99

All labor donated.

153

BRIARPATCH REVIEW

Ron Jones' Network   Rightlivelihood
A Novel Record Emerges   A Service not a Store
Classic Corporate Dropout   Womenergy
Health is Freedom   Small Time Operator

Contents

This issue was put together by: Kristin Anundsen, Annie Styron, Michael Phillips, Tom Hargadon, Deon Kaner, Beverly Muir, Sheldon.

Art & Photo Credits:

Cover drawing by Kris Handwerk;
Walker Evans, Roadside Stand Near Birmingham, 1936.
New Games Foundation, Tamra, Alan Gould, Michael
Phillips, Deon Kaner, Jim Winterstein, Kris
Handwerk, Pauline D. Baynes (Permission Ballantine
Books).

The Briarpatch Review is a journal of the Briarpatch Network: a group of people interested in simple living, openness, sharing, and learning how the world works through business. It is published every three months at 330 Ellis Street, San Francisco, CA 94102 Tel. (415) 928-3960. Subscription rates are $5 per year (add $2 outside U.S.); supporting membership $25. Single issues and back copies are $1.25 postpaid. We welcome feedback and stories about your own Briarpatch.

Being in the Briarpatch

Earth Ball at New Games Tournament

The Briarpatch starts with a state of mind and grows to become a community. How can you become a part of it?

You may already have the state of mind. You're a Briar if you're trying to live simply and share your resources with others, if you're seeking right livelihood rather than wealth for its own sake.

A Briarpatch community begins with small groups of Briars and grows until it can be as large as it is in the San Francisco area, with over 100 businesses. You can't make it happen in a hurry; it needs to grow organically with careful tending and the right environment. You create the environment by talking with friends, working and playing together, and waiting patiently until there are enough Briars to call yourself a Briarpatch. By then you'll probably need a part-time coordinator supported by voluntary tithes and bartering. Your financial records will be open to everyone and you'll be helping each other on a large scale.

Messages

from the Briarpatch

I recently read the account of the history, philosophy and operation of the Briarpatch network. The support and sharing of resources, skills, energy between/among people into the evolution of organic, humanistic ways of living and healing our society, culture and land is critical, if not the key, to me, you, us being "successful."

I am presently working with social and environmental educational and alternative development people in Toronto, Canada. I am researching the concept, philosophy and basis for developing learner-oriented resource-sharing networks as a tool to adult education in the neighborhoods and communities. I would appreciate any information or resources that you may have on the above. I would also be open to sharing information/feelings on what I am doing and some of the Toronto projects (that I am in touch with) with anyone who would find this equally profitable.

How about this...I want a Briarpatch pen pal.

Enclosed is a money order for the Review.

> Bruce Craig
> 231 Palmerston Ave.
> Toronto, Ontario
> Canada M6J 2Z3

Sure is nice to get the mailings telling about the happenings around the Briarpatch. I never seem to get up that way but here is a token amount of $ to help with the mailing, etc.

Thought you might like to hear about our reorganized construction company. Used to be that five of us worked for DiLorenzo Construction Co. Now, at the inception of every new project we six entities sign a legal "joint venture contract" which designates responsibilities, profits, etc.

Before, the Co. would do supervisory work, hassle payroll, etc. as well as what they do now--have the licences and liability insurance, get financing, handle billing, and sell the houses. They would add 75% on to all our labor bids to cover their costs. Now they take a straight 10% of what we bid. Much more equitable.

Before, if we bid $1,000 they would call it $1,750 (1,000 plus 75% of 1,000). If we did it for $800 they would have kept the difference. Now, we bid it at $1,750 and they take 10%-- $175. It's up to us how much we will make. We split it: supervisor $8.50 an hour, assistant $7.50, others $5.50-6.50 plus a bonus at the end (a % depending on

number of hours worked) if
there is $ left (which there
always is).

Result: the company is
happy. They do their financial fiddling and make $ on
the houses, not on us. We
are overjoyed. Released from
the "puttin' in time for
money" blues. We get paid
for building the house, not
for putting in hours. The
faster we work the more we
earn, but interestingly
enough, since we are responsible for the finished house
and are earning more money
than before, and are more in
charge of our own fate, we
have tended to do better as
well as faster work.

Bob Intersimone
Los Agrinemsors
Carmel Valley, CA
93924

Will be contacting the
BPers in L.A. who are into
"junk" as in cars, trucks,
etc.; I've been long into
"junk" that is trash-nothing
made into elegant objects
of art--useful to body/soul/
mind/spirit. I've been
collecting a long time, as
when the NOW comes for "my"
school, a shop shall be
attached for junk-exchange
and to make money for the
non-profit school. (Five-
Point-Five Lodge, a school
for metaphysics of the
spirit, arts, sciences, etc.
and a sacred ONE retreat.)

Pass-alongs: I do not
have any bugs on or near my
tomato plants! Besides TLC,
I also use whole peppercorns
near...also in all cupboards,
under couches, etc. Bugs
HATE peppercorns, or even
ground pepper. What few can
resist pepper hate garlic and
dry mustard.

Rice (NOT "minute rice"!)
can be popped like popcorn,
then cooked and seasoned--
unique flavor.

One candle before a triple
mirror gives plenty of light.

Egg-shells burnt on stove
good for most plants.

Clothing wrapped in news-
papers discourages moths, etc.

Old cotton handkerchiefs
make excellent coffee filters.

Detergent "soaps" need
softeners--real soaps do not!

If anybody wants to send
me some pass-alongs, I will
pass-along too.

Carol Ohmart
P.O. Box 242
Beverly Hills, CA
90213

Building an Educational Network

RON JONES

This thing called Zephyros--educational materials--started three years ago. It came about out of my frustration with textbook publishers, schools of education, and professional organizations. Like the toothpaste vendors that came before them, the big three of education were selling things I didn't want or need. The teacher organizations were selling credit, tires, and trips to Las Vegas. Schools of Education were hawking the latest learning theory. Corporate publishers were selling old books with new covers. All of this activity didn't help life in the classroom. And like the disappointment over toothpaste promotion, they didn't help my personal or social well-being.

If fact, they made things worse. As a classroom teacher I didn't want new tires, didn't need another theory, and hated the idea of passing out books no one would use. What I wanted was a way to

160

trade ideas with other teachers. I wanted somehow to feel important without becoming a school administrator or Ph.D. candidate. And perhaps most intriguing of all, I felt the need to be a part of a community. I'm sure my grandparents wouls shake with approval at this desire to take responsibility for my own destiny and at the same time help some neighbors raise a barn. Lacking a barn and a frontier, I decided to find some like-minded friends and build textbooks.

In the fall of 1972 I completed work on a textbook that was

Yickees, we did it! We had written and printed our own textbook. We had taken direct responsibility for what our children would read and act upon in the classroom. It felt good. I was proud of our book and amazed at what happens once you get into print. Almost immediately after our book started circulating the superintendent of schools called to say hello. The local union wanted to know who financed us. And most interesting of all was the reaction within the school itself. Teaching strategies that were once chastised as being foolish were applauded

... we had taken direct responsibility...

to be called <u>Your City Has Been Kidnapped</u>. Teachers, children, and friends all helped in this venture. It was a delightful workbook depicting ways to see and investigate a city. It wasn't a big book, and it was of little concern to schools of education, professional groups, or commercial publishers. But it was an important book because it became the responsibility and creation of people who used it. We financed it ourselves--printed on newsprint. It cost about $900 for 5,000 copies.

once they appeared in print.
Teachers who were once scorned
became published and instant-
aneouly respected as inservice
consultants.

Now What?

After all this hoopla calmed
I faced the real consequence
of such adventure. My garage
was full of books. Inasmuch
as my car doesn't like sitting
out in the fog, I decided to
mail copies of the city book
to teachers in other parts of
the country. With each copy
of the book I enclosed a letter
detailing an "educational exchange." I figured that if
teachers could write their own
books they could also actively
share and trade lesson plans.
The letter I wrote on this
topic went something like this:
"If you are tired of textbooks
that don't work, why not join
with us (that's me, a garage
already full of books, and
several friends) and we'll
print and circulate ideas that
teachers develop in their own
classrooms." I proposed that
these ideas would be placed in
primers and mailed out twice a
year in a big box. "It will
be a unique way to see and use
what other teachers are developing. We can call it the
Zephyros Education Exchange."

To finance this exchange I requested $10 yearly membership.
If corporate publishers could

infiltrate the schools using
an army of salespeople and con-
vention booths, I could do equally well with one V.W., postage stamps, and the grapevine
of communication that exists
between teachers. It worked.
Teachers from all over the
country began sending their
favorite teaching activity,
games, and lesson plans. With
each letter came an idea,
money to create the next
primer, and words of friendship and encouragement. As
the mail piled up close friends
jumped in to help.

Work Party

To assemble the first Zephyros
box in 1973 we called our
friends and invited them to a
work party. About 60 people
arrived with various express-
ions of anticipation. After

all, no one had ever done a
"Zephyros box." They were
teachers, artists, children,
parents and even a few grandparents.

We scrounged and bartered for
books, games, records, anything
we thought teachers could use.
Placing all these items in
piles along the street we made
a human assembly line, each
person filling up a box as
they moved down the line.
Others worked on labeling. At
the end of the line the boxes
were sorted and placed in mail
bags. Someone brought a radio.
People began moving. Neighbors
viewing this strange site
came by to see what was happening. The local street gang
came by to get in on the fun.
There was this rhythm of
people stuffing bags and
talking. No one had to give
directions; it was as if we had
all done this thing together
in some other place or time.
Everyone worked. No, it wasn't
work. It was barn raising.
I wondered out loud if this is
what it felt like living and
working in China. Within three
hours it was over. The boxes
were piled on trucks and into
car trunks.

During the past three years we
have printed 15 primers and
sent out six different "Z"
boxes. Over 46,000 teachers
around the country are using
Zephyros in their classroom

and submitting practical ideas
to future issues. Other than
that things are still the same.
Our home remains our place of
work. All work is still voluntary. And yes, the garage
is still full of books. A
friendship alliance of 60
or so Bay Area teachers, artists, and parents gather twice
a year to ceremoniously pack
the "Z" boxes. This community of friends has remained
the heart of Zephyros. All
the money that comes in goes
right into the next project;
we don't use Zephyros funds to
support ourselves.

Staying Small

In the past year the chorus of
activity by Zephyros has been
acclaimed by a host of journals
as the nation's number one in-
novative publisher. Being

number one is quite a problem. Long ago we decided against becoming a big business...Lord known this country doesn't need another big business. The future of Zephyros is therefore destined to stay small and committed. We will continue to produce primers full of activities and twice a year send out a box of goodies.

Sometime soon I would like to initiate something called spontaneous publishing. I think this follows the tradition of small but intensive publishers. Whereas serial publishing implies a standardized journal of some kind coming out in regular intervals, spontaneous publishing means just the opposite: the power of a person who gets an idea to simply publish it as a one-time statement--and then send it to all his or her friends. This means that if you were teaching and developed a play, you might print it and make it available to anyone interested in your work. If large numbers of the general public became their own medium, the exchange of ideas would be very exciting. We have been trained to be consumers, but what if we became producers?

There it is again, that creeping populism, that faith in people charting their own destiny, that stubborn independence. Yes, I think you and I can write our own textbooks, maintain exchanges, press our own records, open our own stores and in general reclaim life from the franchise kings. Yes, we can learn to cooperate rather than compete and we can trust and support each other. Yes, it sure beats watching television.

How to Figure 'Included Sales Tax'

By Simple Simon (Richard French)

For simplicity's sake, many small businesses sell their goods at a "tax-included" price, then figure out later how much of what they collected was sales tax.

Here's how to make that computation:

1. Divide your total "Sales and Tax" by 1.065 to get Sales.

$ 5000.00
  1.065
$ 4694.84

2. Multiply sales by 6-1/2% to get Sales Tax Collected.

X .065
$ 305.16

3. Add sales back in to check for accuracy.

+ 4694.84
$ 5000.00

A Novel Record Emerges
From The Briarpatch

*Gurney Norman was one of the world's first Briars: founding
midwife editor to the first Briarpatch Review in 1973; author
of "Divine Right's Trip," a folktale/novel that was part of
the Last Whole Earth Catalog; contributor to CoEvolution
Quarterly. Gurney has a kind of dual residency in the Bay
Area and Eastern Kentucky. Son of a coal miner in Hazard,
KY, he lived there 30 years before moving to Menlo Park,
CA, nine years ago. A major element in his writing is a
fascination with folk culture; now, he says, "I look for
the suburban equivalent of the old folk life I used to live
as a means of staying sane. Life is possible for me in the
suburbs because, after nine years, I see that folk equivalent
everywhere. The interest among suburban people in ritual,
ceremony, and certain exotic cottage industries encourages
me enormously."*

*Gurney has now produced his second "novel," which he describes
here:*

I'm a novelist running loose in the cosmic briarpatch--have
written a novella-length folk tale called Ancient Creek. A
story about conflict between old traditional folk culture
and modern consumer culture, it's an 80-page piece of writing
read aloud to an audience of Kentuckians in the studios of
JuneAppal Records last October (1975).

It's taken a year to get the record out. It will be distributed exclusively through Briarpatch-type channels:
personally by hand, through local stores, via small regional
distributors. (The Bay Area distributor is Robin Cohen,
phone (415) 431-4312.) JuneAppal Records is very much a
Briarpatch-type company too--it exists to help talented
musicians and storytellers in the Appalachian region get
their work recorded and find an audience. It's an alternative to the Nashville approach of merchandising folk
materials for mass consumption.

cont'd. on page 192

Classic Corporate Dropout

By Kristin Anundsen

Robert Paul's Moment of Truth came one day in 1970 when the news of Kent State blared over the airwaves. At the time--after successive careers as a diamond merchant, a teacher and a master's degree candidate in linguistics--Robert was a successful investment banker in New York. "I was riding high," he recalls. "I had lots of money and power--I'd reached the pinnacle people dream about."

Working near him were two stockbrokers, father and son, one age 60, the other 20. Robert felt close to them and identified with both of them alternately; he could perceive in their struggle his own struggles with his father and his son. He saw Kent State vividly through the son's eyes, and what he saw shook him up. "I realized that my whole way of life, and what I did for a living, put me on the side of the National Guardsmen."

He stayed away from work for a couple of days. "I was disoriented. For years I had slaved, worked day and night, doing the things that promise you success...and now I realized that success was an empty thing." He

..success was an empty thing ...

166

also realized that he had internalized the values embodied in balance-sheet analysis: what increases profits is good and what decreases profits is poor. Finally, he called the office and said he wasn't coming in anymore.

After a while, he decided not to stay in New York, but to head for San Francisco, where his ex-wife lived with their two children. He had made the trip back and forth from New York several times, and now it seemed more or less logical to go and live there. He was planning to make the trip in a van, "but on the eve of my depature, my van was ripped off. I had to take the plane." It seemed an inauspicious beginning.

Actually, however, it was pretty much uphill from there. After a stint as a car salesman, he decided

he wanted to be a "hippie carpenter." He didn't know a thing about building, but he didn't consider lack of knowledge an obstacle. He plunged into community development projects. "I was willing to work for nothing in order to be doing what I wanted and to train myself in building," he recalls. "I lived on about $90 a month then." He built a tutorial center, an art gallery, and a play yard and taught carpentry to kids. He then worked (building) for an open-classroom-type school, and finally he got a chance to remodel a house in Berkeley. "I learned all the building trades there," he says.

Robert is apparently one of those enviable people who take to new occupations naturally. "I can just look at things, see how they're made, and go ahead and build,"

he says. He now does carpentry, design, engineering, and construction, on all types of projects from furniture to buildings to fixtures for stores and restaurants. He is happy to be a builder, delighted to be operating independently, and glad to teach the people who work for him on various projects.

He pays his employees from $4 an hour (for someone who has no tools, vehicle, or experience--only willingness) to $15. If his work crews do the job well and fast they get even more. Everyone knows what everyone else is being paid. Robert takes 75% of the profits on a given job, where he works right along with the others as well as supervising. "I unload trucks, do framing--everything; but I'm still definitely the boss," he asserts. "I'm didactic and high-handed. I see to it that our clients get what they need and not what they don't need. But all the workers have a vote in matters like whether to work in inclement weather or whether to take a job that requires risky work or a long commute."

Without advertising his services, he has acquired plenty of work. "I've always ended up with ongoing work because

I developed tight relationships with my clients," he says, "so I started a side business: building maintenance."

He is interested only in making "what I need to live on" --which, for himself and his two children, he figures is $20-25,000 a year.

Robert is a Briarpatch Network member, and what he likes most about being in the Briarpatch is sharing resources. "Other people have always come to me for advice or encouragement or a kick in the ass," he explains. "I'm one of those 'resource people' who can teach, juggle, tell you where to buy a dozen refrigerators...whatever." (He admits that he is usually on the side of giving advice or resources rather than receiving.) Another thing he likes about Briarpatching is "being in contact with other people who fly by the seat of their pants." He doesn't miss investment banking.

Health is Freedom

by Salli Rasberry

My experiences with doctors have been shallow relationships with me in the role of dependent child and the doctor playing paternalistic authority figure who knows everything about dispensing medicine and nothing about me...offering pills instead of insight. With our meetings squeezed into ten-minute time frames, we have briefly discussed my symptoms, avoiding the significant questions.

Bill Gray is a doctor of unique breed; sensitive, bright, a good listener. He practices homeopathy in Mill Valley and is representative of the wholistic health movement. Homeopathy is difficult to explain. I think Donna, who works with Bill, has a good definition: Homeopathy is a non-toxic method for stimulating the body's own healing forces, resulting in cure." The following is an interview I did recently with Bill.

B.G.: I learned from my studies in Greece with Homeopath George Vithoulkas a very powerful definition of health: Health is freedom. Freedom from bodily anger, from having to put undue attention on your body; freedom to experience emotions without being trapped by them; freedom from confusion. Most people are conditioned to think of health as the absence of disease. Where the "allopath" tries to rid people of their symptoms, we deal with the life force itself. The absence of disease is not the same as a positive sense of well-being, which is a very positive state to be in.

S.R.: *Many of my friends feel that if they get a cold or flu, they are somehow to blame, and they feel guilty for being ill.*

B.G.: Having the flu doesn't mean that there is a poor state of health. Actually, getting a virus can be a good thing; it can mean the body is trying to heal itself, which is already a sign of strength. People who are unable to react to colds and flu can be the ones in real trouble.

Really sick people, those with chronic disease, often don't get colds and flu. The best thing to do when you get a cold or flu is the traditional stuff: bed rest, fluids, <u>plus</u> learning whatever your lesson might be--more relaxation, exercise, a better diet.

Flu that would ordinarily take two weeks to get over can clear up within 12 hours when treated with homeopathic remedies. These are natural substances that speed up the body's healing processes in a way we don't understand but know works. The remedies are carefully chosen through a matching of

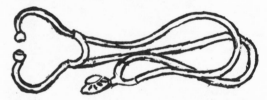

the patient's reaction to illness with substances that can aid their body in healing itself.

I differentiate in my practice between the person who is basically healthy and develops an acute illness (such as a cold or the flu) and the person with a chronic disease. I limit my practice primarily to chronic disease. When I do see a person with an acute illness I act mainly as an adviser, for if I give them a remedy a dependency develops with the responsibility for their health on my shoulders.

I help people take responsibility for their own well-being by developing their own basic habits of health. Naturally, people come to me at all different levels of understanding so I try to come in at their level and take them as high up as they can go. Once they become sensitive to the rewards of good nutrition it's easier for them to get in tune with the amount of rest, relaxation, and exercise they need.

S.R.: What about swine flu?

B.G.: It may or may not happen. Flu runs in cycles of approximately 10 years and our last major epidemic was over eight years ago. If there is a major epidemic, thousands and thousands may die, because it is a very virulent strain which traditional medicine is powerless to control. If the flu becomes life-threatening, homeopathy would be very helpful because we don't have to go through the elaborate detective work to discover what caused the illness but rather can concentrate on who the person is and how they are reacting to the situation. Based on that information, and how the person deals with obstruction, we can help the

person stimulate the life force.

During the 1918 epidemic a pathologist in San Francisco compared allopathic and homeopathic methods of dealing with flu patients. Of those patients treated in traditional methods and admitted to the hospital, 50% died, which is an extremely high mortality rate. Of the 5,000 patients treated homeopathically, only one died.

S.R: What is your financial position?

B.G.: If you employ the wholistic approach, as I do, you're dealing with the whole person

and must spend a lot more time than with traditional approaches. To evaluate all the factors in someone's life can take a great deal of time. I am limited as to how many patients I can see in one day, and in order to spend the time the patient needs and still meet overhead expenses I must charge accordingly. (The more traditional approach would be to say, "I know what my overhead is so I'll see more people and spend less time with them.") Instead of charging by the patient I must charge by time. My fee is now $60 an hour.

Because that is such a high
rate for some and not for
others, I've opted not to
make payment decisions for
my patients. I _ask_ $60 an
hour but the patient decides
how much to pay. People must
examine their own priorities.
In wholistic medicine the
patients take responsibility
for their own health, and
they are responsible in my
practice for their own bills.
I share with them my cost; if
their health has high priority
they will find the money.

For tax records I must keep
track of charges I make but I
keep no record of patients'
names. I have no idea who pays
me and who doesn't. My philosophy is that if I'm important to people they will keep
me open and if I'm not then
they won't pay and I won't be
open. Institutions shouldn't
stay open just because they

exist. I provide a service
and I'm confident it will all
work out.

_S.R.: How _is_ it working out?_

B.G.: It's close. Last month
I lost $500. I have yet to re-
solve the Medi-Cal situation.
The way it works is the doctor
submits a bill with a diagnosis
on it which is then passed
through standard channels.
This works out for most doctors,
since because of their large
volume of patients they can
charge within certain guidelines set up by someone as
"the" fee. In my case, my
charges are often outside the
minimum standard and must go
before a committee of doctors
who decide whether fees are
appropriate. I usually end
up with 20 to 30% of what I
asked for. For instance, if
a person has allergies and
is not in touch with themselves, I might have to work
really hard to decide what
remedy would help them; if it
takes me an hour and a half
I have to charge $90. If
that doesn't match with the
committee's idea of how long
doctors should spend with a
patient and how much they
should charge, then I'm
screwed. Part of why I must
charge so much is to make up
for these losses.

Also, and I've resisted this
fact, in my experience Medi-

Cal patients frequently don't show up for appointments or are late. If I schedule an hour for a person and they don't show up, I have lost that hour. A regular doctor schedules his patients 10 or 15 minutes apart, so if they don't show up it doesn't hurt as much as in my case. Since Medi-Cal is probably the model on which national health insurance will be based, soon everyone will be receiving Medi-Cal and for wholistic practitioners that could be disastrous.

S.R.: It's hard to find an insurance company that will reimburse patients for wholistic services.

B.G.: It's strange, because it's cheaper for them in the long run. Chronic disease patients treated traditionally must return again and again to their doctors for treatment, medicine can be expensive, and often they must be hospitalized--all of which may cost thousands of dollars.

The same patients treated homeopathically are often cured in a year with no medicine needed.

There is a vast difference in the cost to society between wholistic medicine and traditional medicine. There are several issues at stake here besides the doctor-patient relationship: the pharmacist-convalescent hospital, big business syndrome, and political issues too. For instance, it should not be necessary to be a medical doctor to practice wholistic healing; as a matter of fact, by training the doctor is the person least likely to comprehend our methodology because an M.D.'s training is so much in the opposite direction. Doctors deal with pathology--the abnormal condition of the body--whereas the wholistic practitioner is specifically not approaching it from that point of view. Wholistic health practice is evolving into a creative movement, so the traditional definitions no longer apply.

RIGHT LIVELIHOOD

Michael Phillips

Right livelihood is one of the hottest issues I've seen lately. Talks and workshops on the subject are on a "standing room only" basis. I think there has been a significant shift in work values. In the past it was considered reasonable for people to develop a marketable skill and pursue a career that would earn them enough money to do the things they really wanted to do. People worked at their jobs so they could do the things they wanted on weekends, go where they wanted on vacations and in some cases earn enough to retire "early" and then do what they wanted. Now our peers are saying, "That's nonsense; why should I do something I don't like 70% of my life so I can do what I want 30%?" They want to combine what they enjoy doing with their livelihood.

The Tough Question

Now that more people are thinking about doing, working at, and being what they want, the really tough question becomes, "What do I want?" The person who goes camping every weekend doesn't necessarily want to be a forest ranger, nor does the weekend sailor want to be in the merchant marines. Hobbies, interests, and avocations don't always translate directly into full-time activity. Finding right livelihood is difficult and takes plenty of time, often many years. Right livelihood is a concept found in Buddhism (one of the eight-fold paths), Sufism, and early Christianity. It is part of a whole view, part of being a whole person. It is a fundamental element in the Briarpatch. We want people to enjoy what they are doing fully, and to do it for the intrinsic rewards.

My personal list of the qualities that describe right livelihood are as follows (and are necessarily sketchy): First, it should be an area of great passion. Second, right livelihood is something you can spend your life doing. Third, it should be something that serves the community. At last, it should be totally appropriate to you.

Passion in your work? I list it first as a criterion for right livelihood because it conveys the sense of excitement, joy and fun that being alive is all about. The whole person will feel the passion of life and the excitement of living if it is part of his or her continual day-to-day livelihood. Most of the time right livelihood means you get up and look forward to the day with the same excitement that we feel on vacations. That means hours that fit us, people with whom we feel happy, light, air and humor.

Spend your life doing something? This means the livelihood should have within it the room for your constant curiosity; it must give you room to keep learning, to grow in compassion; and it should offer you challenges that will try you and yet appeal to you time and again. Most livelihoods actually have this potential, whether it is garbage collecting or systems programming, because the range of subtle and delicate refinements is always present; but often it is the co-workers, the prevailing social attitudes of the company's day-to-day environment that keep this from happening.

Service is a vital quality of right livelihood. You should feel that you are completely serving the community in what you do or you will have a longing as you get older to do something else and may have regrets. You should not be doing one thing and feeling that others, nurses or psychiatrists, do more for people than you. But nearly every livelihood has enormous potential to serve people, and you will be serving people best when you are using your unique skills most fully.

A Challenge

Using your unique skills totally is both a criterion and a challenge because the answer to it will lead to your right livelihood. Many people aren't sure what their unique skills are or how they can be used in the most fulfilling way. Personal skill inventories and reviews of experience and interests can be helpful, but if you aren't already certain of what your right livelihood is, you must give yourself the time and space to try many things. Many livelihoods have to be created, and many require long years of apprenticeship and practice. Each of us needs the diligence and sensitivity of an artist in practicing and striving to find the qualities within us that we can uniquely use.

OF BRIARS

Excerpted from *New Age Journal*, July/August 1976.

By Paul Hawken with assistance from Kay Rawlings and Brer Rabbit

A small, alternative business has many strikes against it: it does not have the financial leverage that larger companies employ; owners lack practical know-how and experience; banks demand success before they offer loans; and most start with insufficient capital to accomplish their goal properly. Altogether, this spells trouble, and the fact that most small enterprises turn belly up within the first year underlines the point. Compounding these challenges is the fact that a small business cannot afford the kind of professional advice that would help it through those difficulties. But now there are hundreds of businesses organized together to help and support the process. They call themselves the Briarpatch.

The Briarpatch is comprised of people who are learning to live in the cracks of society with a joyful consciousness of abundance. They define themselves as "positively oriented' racoons, groundhogs, and rabbits who seek a livelihood that "nourishes and enlivens them." Briars are concerned with the sharing of resources and skills with members of an ongoing community and see themselves as part of a sub-society that is more committed to "learning how the world works" than to acquiring its possessions and status.

It is a crazy-quilt assemblage of the outrageous and conventional, stretched across the San Francisco Bay area like patchwork. From crowded communal flats high above San Francisco's Noe Valley to $300,000 hand-crafted Sausalito houseboats on the bay, from the Montgomery Street offices of the New Dimensions Foundation to the Hayes Street Raskinflakkers Divinely United Ice Cream Organization, from Earthcamp One and Wilbur Hot Springs to Lifestyle Restructurers, Boogie Bands, and Rare Earth Real Estate Brokers of Remote Retreats. The Briarpatch network consists of devoted alternative lifestylers (peppered with a few Republicans) and saxicoline entrepreneurs producing and making exactly what they want to.

And if anyone from downtown thinks the Briarpatch is a trendy hippie puffball that will blow away, they might take note that it is coordinated by Andy Alpine, who has a B.A. in Economics, an M.A. in International Affairs and Chinese Politics, and a doctorate in Law, and has served as an assistant with the United Nations Secretariat, researching Riparian laws and economics; that it was co-founded by Michael Phillips, one-time director of Marketing and Planning for Bank of America and the Bank of California, presently comptroller for the Glide Foundation; and that it received its initial impetus from Dick Raymond, founder of the Portola Institute and a former businessman who holds the mythical M.B.A. from Harvard Business School.

The roots of the Briarpatch network are in the Whole Earth Catalog, the best-selling manual of tools which became a tool in its own right. The catalog was a masterstroke in publishing and it pulled down the National Book Award. Its sales record amazed the industry. With so much energy pouring into the coffers of the Catalog, it answered the question of fiscal integrity by publicly accounting for every dollar spent and received. And when over a million dollars rolled in from the Random House edition, Stewart Brand and publisher Dick Raymond helped establish the Point Foundation to give all the money away. For the first time in a generation's memory, a group put its money where its mouth was and did not compromise its principles for the sake of personal gain.

After the Last Whole Earth Catalog had been published, the Portola Institute went into a long and steady decline. In July 1974, having conceived of the idea and name of the Briarpatch network, Dick Raymond called a weekend meeting for 25 co-earthlings who were then involved with Briarpatch-type activities.

According to Raymond, the meeting was like turning a light on in a dark room and finding a few hundred other people besides yourself, people who were looking for a clarification of the relationship between money,

fine one. It doesn't require a strong institutional leader in order to function effectively."

There are several principles that are the underlying basis of the Briarpatch. The first one is that there should be an alternative to greed, and the best substitute they've found so far is summed up in the word sharing. Greed is condemned not for moral but for practical reasons: it doesn't work. It is part of a closed-end system that inhibits real evolutionary growth--the result of the planetary game that we have

****

an alternative to greed

****

business, and their personal lives.

"If we had tried to do the Briarpatch ten years ago," comments Raymond, "we would have had a foundation, literature, meetings to discuss bylaws, all of which is a silly way to cope with human behavior. The Briarpatch has a quality of non-organization. There is no membership campaign and no formal rules. People hear about the Briarpatch and say 'Oh yeah' and define it for themselves, and their definition is a very

been playing for centuries called "winner takes all." That game leaves a lot of losers with nothing to play.

Briars have decided to abandon that game in favor of a new game, an open-ended game, a game which is evolutionary and noncompetitive. Briars don't see size as a goal, nor sales as a ranking. The success or failure of a Briar business is defined by other criteria. One of the most fundamental is whether the person(s) involved have learned anything about themselves or the world in the process of being in business. If a Briar business fails economically but the people involved have learned a great deal, then that is seen as success enough.

In this open-ended game the Briars play, an important consideration is the distinction between wants and needs, a concept that Briars call "simple living." It is not so much a question of whether one makes four or fourteen thousand dollars a year, but of whether one has an awareness that almost everything we consume is based on some sort

could not find any underwriter to insure them. Each company feared a high potential for smashed thumbs and heads, since Play Experience supervises amateur groups. Werner Hebenstreit, the Briarpatch insurance broker, finally persuaded one company to take the account. The premium, a healthy $1,500, had to be paid before a certain Saturday job, and on the preceding Tuesday, Play Experience had only $500 to its name. Andy contacted the network, and two Briars gave them $700 and $300 as interest-free loans for three months. It is this kind of

****

willing to support each other

****

of preference and usually has nothing to do with needs.

Another criterion Raymond mentions is the idea of networking or alliances. Networking in the Briarpatch means an awareness of the interconnectedness of society and the willingness of each member to be an open and dynamic interflow of ideas, services, and experience.

An example of Briar "networking" occurred when Play Experience, a company which designs and assists in the construction of playgrounds,

willingness to support each other's endeavors fully-- monetarily, with skills, or just faith in the other person's ability to make it-- that has made the Briarpatch into a commercial, yet non- competitive, ecology of synergetic enterprises.

When Dick Raymond arrived in Menlo Park ten years ago, he had successfully initiated and managed several businesses allied with the construction tool industry and had been netting $25,000-30,000 a year. After serving as a consultant to SRI, a western think tank,

he opened his own consulting
firm which eventually evolved
in stages into the nonprofit,
education-oriented Portola
Institute. Fulfilling as it
was, the Portola Institute
depleted his personal resources to the point that he now
lives on $660 a month in a
rented house with his second
wife and their two small children.

One of Raymond's responses to
his reduced income has been
to start "One More Company,"
which manufactures "Shoe
Patch," a tube of gooey plastic adhesive useful for
patching tennis and running
shoes. One More Co. could be
called an arch-Briar company,
embodying every principle and
desirable trait known to its
founders. Shoe Patch comes
in a reusable cannister, which
also contains "Raparound," a
newsletter giving consumer
feedback, listings of some
Briarpatch services, reviews
of recent books, and financial data on the company.
An open file of all company
transactions including board
meetings and present financial
status is available to the
public at the company offices.

I asked Dick how One More Co.
was doing in the less than
merciful world of business.
"Horribly," said Dick, but
perhaps for the best of reasons. One More Company sells
a fine, well-packaged product
which has good consumer response, but the company is
under-capitalized, badly
staffed, and sales are lower
than he had hoped. One More
Company is struggling to make
interest payments on a bank
loan, and Raymond does not
want to rely on the traditional venture capital sources
in order to make it over the
hump. And yet, if he doesn't,
he may not make it at all.
Why?

Dick can only respond meta-
physically. In order to run
a stable company, one needs
competent people, but if the
company has a philosophical
mission at the same time,
one needs people who have a
philosophical understanding
of the company's purpose.

What happens is that in most
cases, these goals conflict.
To stay in business one needs
productive people, and the
two rarely combine.

"I feel this is the fatal deficiency in running an enlightened business. These people
who are trying to run humanistic businesses are going
through the agony of the damned,
trying to find people who can
both work and understand what
they are trying to do. At One
More Company we didn't try to
change dinosaurs into antelopes, but went where the

antelopes were. So what we have is a bunch of antelopes roaming in the Shoe Patch and they don't know much about business. My whole gamble is that they will find out before we go out of business."

An interesting dialectic. Some say greed makes the world go around. The Briars say it is bringing it to a grinding halt. According to Raymond's experience, competence lies with the ambitious achievers, while the idealists are usually inept or disinterested. An over-simplification perhaps, but technology is definitely not antelope country, and the best still lack all conviction. One way the Briarpatch deals with the problem is to have Andy Alpine, Charles Albert Parsons and Michael Phillips available to all members for financial and business consultation.

Andy Alpine first got involved in this kind of open consultation when, soon after the original Briarpatch conference, 10 of the participants met in San Francisco and decided that a coordinator should be hired, someone who could coordinate and relay information to everyone about each other's activities. A few weeks after the second meeting, 12 individuals agreed to put up $25 a month for six months, and on that subsistence wage Andy Alpine took on the job. Today there

are 125 businesses in the Briarpatch, each of which pays a "Briarpatch Pledge" of $30 to $110 every six months. The amount depends on what each member company feels it can afford, and in some cases Briars provide services in lieu of the pledge.

Some of this money covers Andy's small salary and phone expenses (there is no office), and the balance pays for such expenditures as parties which are celebrated on the Briar holidays of Groundhog Day, Father's Day, Brazilian Carnival and Leap Day. These celebrations are an important aspect of Briarpatching, since it is here that most connections between members are made.

When they are not together, Briars can consult the *Skills-Exchange Newsletter*, which lists the resources,

Briarpatch Review crew in tub

knowledge, and skills which
Briars make freely avail-
able to each other. A
carpenter can phone a banker
to get advice about arc-weld-
ing; a writer can phone a
lawyer and get advice about
copyright law. When specific
tasks or materials are called
for, Briars will often barter
rather than use money. That
is not to say that Briars
don't deal with money. They
do, and for that reason Andy's
and Michael Phillips' consultation come in quite handy.

Michael's involvement in
Briarpatch dates from when he
was director of Marketing and
Planning at the Bank of
California. There he met Dick
Raymond, one of the bank's
clients. Raymond had been
shuffled around from one department to another while trying
to get official attention for
his idea that the bank should

provide a space for its customers to meet and get to know
one another. Michael thought
it was a great idea, and during
the three years it required to
convince management, he and
Dick did it on their own, holding informal gatherings at a
downtown Japanese restaurant
on Friday afternoons, meeting
presidents, venture capital-
ists, entrepreneurs, foundation heads, movers, shakers,
thinkers, and priests, until
a small network had been
formed. That was the Briar
prototype. To get the real
Briarpatch off the ground,
Michael left his banking job
and opened up an office at
Pier 40, where he gave free
consultation on Wednesdays to
Briar-oriented people and
businesses.

People who had heard about the
Briarpatch began showing up
from hundreds of miles away.
As news of the Briarpatch

spread, others wanted to join
who knew little or nothing
about it but thought it was a
coming countercultural trend
that they should be a part of.
Some wanted the publicity
(there is none), some thought
they could get funding from
the Briarpatch (wrong again),
and others confused it with a

"hip" Rotary that might help them get more business. Since that time, Michael and Andy have closed the Pier 40 office and now visit individual Briar members on Thursdays.

Despite the fact that Briar-patching has a certain romantic appeal, most people would still rather go around in a Mercedes than a mufti. Americans are too apt to equate with material restraint, conscious limitation, the dollar-sign somehow having become synonymous with freedom in our country. Briars are learning that you cannot serve others if you are only serving yourself. While large corporations battle away at inflation, and each other, the industry of service is wide open. It has no resistance, no enemies, and can never be depleted. Service is a particular kind of currency where impoverishment is self-imposed. If "we" are going to make it on this planet, then we are going to start behaving as "we," which means dropping all the old games of competition and separation. If we are going to stick around for awhile, then perhaps we had best figure out a way to do that, in our businesses as well as our gardens and hearts. The best statement in this regard is a quote from Bucky Fuller which is pasted over the john in a woodworking shop in Sausalito:

> *Take the initiative, go to work, and above all cooperate and don't hold back on one another. Any success in such lopsidedness will be increasingly short-lived. These are the synergetic rules evolution is employing and trying to make clear to us. They are not man-made laws. They are the infinitely accommodative laws of the intellectual integrity governing the universe.*

A Service Not a Store

By Paul Gleye

Books are indispensable tools, so I have started a small business to help people buy them more cheaply and avoid the marketing machinations of the book industry.

The Paul Gleye Book Service is a fully licensed bookstore and member of the American Booksellers' Association. But PGBS is not really a store; there is no inventory, and all books are special-ordered. Since my operating costs are extremely low, I can charge you less than bookstores can for special-ordered books and earn a little for myself.

How it Works

Book discounts to retailers generally vary from 20% to 40%, depending on the type of book and quantity ordered. When a store special-orders for you. it sends a blank check to the publisher; so the store is never sure how much profit it will make from the order. Usually the store will charge the customer at least list price in order to be assured some profit.

It needs a pretty hefty profit on its sales altogether, for a typical bookstore's overhead is extremely high (prestigious location, extensive inventory to purchase and keep track of, and generally small unit sales -- a lot of people make $1.98 purchases rather than $19.98). The result is that the customer is charged every possible penny. Even with the book clubs you end up paying almost list price by the time postage and handling are added.

I believe it is unfair to charge a customer a high markup or even to base the amount of markup on wholesale cost. Since it costs no more to sell a $20 book than a $5 book, the PGBS charge is based on the wholesale cost of the book plus a fixed $2.00 service cost

it costs no more to sell a $20 book

(or list price, whichever is less).

To a certain extent, however, I have come to agree with the conventional wisdom regarding return on an investment. For multiple copies or extremely expensive books, the service charge was too low; it was draining my small capital reserve rather than increasing it. As a result, my service charge for large orders is now based on a formula bringing it to slightly under 10% of the wholesale cost, varying somewhat with my cost to place the order.

Keeping Costs Down

My costs are low because I have no inventory. The business is contained in an old china cabinet in my home, and my only rent is for the Post Office Box. Fixed costs are my annual business license and membership in the American Booksellers' Association ($50 a year), which provides ordering policies and schedules of a few thousand publishers and offers several other useful services.

My major operating cost is

I like the the challenge of ordering

Out-of-print bookstores that offer an out-of-print service usually charge a 100% to 200% markup on any book they find. I charge customers $2.00 to make the search, which is about my cost, and $2.00 over wholesale if I find a copy.

Foreign Books: If you have tried to order books published outside the U.S.A., you have probably found it frustrating; bookstores don't like the hassle. But PCBS will order anything; as a matter of fact, I like the challenge of ordering from obscure foreign publishers.

enough money in the bank to allow me to prepay orders and collect from customers a few weeks later. Bookstores may obtain single copies at a lower cost by prepaying orders. At first I was asking customers for a dollar when the order was placed, since I had so little operating capital. But that proved to be a hassle: too hard to keep track of the dollars, and too hard to insist on receiving them. So now I just bill customers for the whole amount (wholesale plus $2.00, usually) after the book is shipped.

My cost to place an order is fairly fixed. I know what the order forms, envelopes, postage, and other items cost; order costs vary primarily in any follow-up correspondence that is necessary. I have found a bank offering totally

free checking accounts, with no minimum balance, and providing checks that can be written in any currency. That saves me money when ordering from foreign publishers, since I save the $1.50 international bank draft cost.

So far I have advertised by distributing a small brochure among friends, acquaintances, and other personal contacts. As long as the information is spread by word of mouth, I need not be too concerned about being ripped off, I think. Later I may actually advertise.

In the six months I have been operating, I have made gross sales of about $2,800, with a net income of about $330. I have not tried to rely on the business for all my income, and it has by no means

taken my full time. I have started cautiously and am trying to build the business slowly.

Information Freely Given

My philosophy regarding capitalism allows me to be open about my costs and procedures. My ideas were developed before I heard of the Briarpatch, but now I believe the Patch and I are in the vanguard of a new entrepreneurial ethic whose time is rapidly coming. I have no competitive information and no hidden costs. Customers have a right to know how their local entrepreneur works and what they are actually paying for. I am glad to describe the operation in more detail to anybody interested--in fact, one consumers' co-op has already asked me to help them set up a book co-op as part of their operation, and I'll be willing to help out other co-ops as well.

After several attempts, I have found a method of recording all transactions sequentially. Any readers interested in the details of it can contact me directly.

If you wish to order a book through PGBS, first remember that I can't save you any money on most books under

$6.00 (or texts and technical books under $12.00). And cheap mass-market paperbacks are not sold to retailers on a single-copy basis at all. Except for these restrictions, you can pretty much get away from the retail-price level. Just send me author's name, title, publisher, International Standard Book Number if you have it, type of binding desired (hardback or paperback), and your name and address. I'll have the book sent directly to you from the publisher and send you an invoice when I find out the exact cost. PGBS's address is P. O. Box 1201, Santa Fe, NM 87501.

I have found that I am ordering a lot of fairly obscure things...and finding a "hole in the market." Bookstores tend to balk at ordering books from unknown publishers or from overseas, but I find it challenging to order unusual and foreign books which many professional people, for example, need fairly often. In fact, bookstores don't like special-ordering at all because the paperwork is fairly cumbersome and for them the profits are usually not great enough. I am thinking of designing a carbonless form which will simplify the ordering and invoicing procedure to one step instead of the several now required. If I can increase my efficiency, the book service should be financially worthwhile. Most bookstores push mass-market books and bestsellers; my service concentrates on the opposite-- personal orders for individual books, trying to keep prices down, not up.

Notes from the Bay Area Briarpatch Network

By Andy Alpine

Well we're two years old (do networks have birthdays or anniversaries?), membership is at about 165 businesses, and things are running smoothly. The main social event for us over the past few months was a Briarpatch Picnic on Angel Island in the middle of San Francisco Bay. Lots of volley-ball, good food, Sufi dancing, and a cloudless, fogless (it burned off at 11:00), blue-sky day. Our next large event is our celebration of Halloween and Our Making It Through the Solar Eclipse on Friday, October 29th.

In September a group of us "tested out" a friend's work-shop called "Other Ways to Solve Problems." This work-shop on using intuition, subconscious processing and think-ing in non-verbal ways is geared specifically for business decisions. We really had a great time. The Network will be offering this workshop by Arthur Hastings to Briars in November. One of the people attending, a Dutchman living at times in Sri Lanka, told us of a practice that several communities are doing in Sri Lanka and the nine of us present have decided to incorporate it: each day at 10:00 in the morning, each of us takes out a few minutes with eyes closed and wishes health and well being to the other Briars who attended the workshop by visualizing one at a time. We'll let you know our experience. So far it feels real special and it would be great if at some time the entire Briarpatch Network were doing it.

One change coming about on our second anniversary is that the Bay Area Briarpatch Network now has two coordinators. Charles Albert Parsons, a Briar, employment search assistant and nice guy - father extraordinaire (see Review Winter 76) will be handling matters on Mondays, Tuesdays, and Wednes-days and I'll be doing it on Thursdays and Fridays. As of this writing I've moved up to Wilbur Hot Springs (See Review Spring 76) together with Kris Handwerk to join the Wilbur family and to set up and run "The Hermitage." The Hermitage is a place where people can come to be with themselves for an extended period of time to paint, write, meditate, read -- whatever. We're offering three-to-five-day stays from Sun-day evening through Friday morning....Enough advertising!

In closing, just a note that our non-plan for Expansion (letting it happen) is working. Jim Everett, a Network member in Cotati, has put together the beginnings of a Briarpatch Network specifically for Sonoma County. If that's where you live and you'd like to get involved, contact Jim Everett at his business: Living Earth Crafts, 10032 Minnesota Ave., Cotati, CA 94928, (707) 795-4226.

HAPPY ANNIVERSARY

WOMENERGY
Briarpatch Women Get Together

By: Deon Kaner and
Cindy Handwerk

On a Sunday evening in September, the first Get-Together of Bay Area Briarpatch Women was held to discuss matters of mutual interest. The meeting was held at San Francisco Dance Movement Therapy Center in San Francisco.

Twelve women showed up from the network. Each woman shared who she was and what her business experience was like for her. We discussed the assets and liabilities of women being in business for themselves. The people from Cottonfield, an all cotton fabric store in Berkeley, (see Briarpatch Review, Summer 1976) talked about the hassles of trying to communicate with people who always asked for synthetic fabrics and why Cottonfield doesn't carry them. We suggested they print up a little blurb of their policies and philosophy and post it near their cash register, or as a sampler hung in their store.

Levitation

The women from the Granary, an all-women bakery in Pacific Grove, often must lift 100 lb. sacks of flour, which sometimes presents a problem. We levitated one of the women from the bakery to show how to lighten objects. In this demonstration, a woman sat in a chair and four other people stood around her, one at each shoulder and one at each knee. With their hands together and their index fingers pointed, they tried to lift the person (under the shoulders and knees) and couldn't. Next they placed their right hands over the subject's head, one hand above the other, (not touching) and then their

cont'd. on page 192

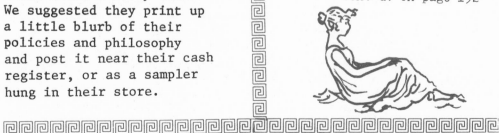

Small time Operator

"Business is pure experience," Michael Phillips wrote in the Springtime 1976 Briarpatch Review. "You learn by doing." As far as management, buying, selling, and other marketing operations go, that statement is 99% true. But when it comes to the business "end" of starting a business--the licenses and permits, the government regulations, the bookkeeping, and a world of other needed information--it would be nice to have some help.

Small Time Operator, subtitled "How to Start Your Own Small Business, Keep Your Books, Pay Your Taxes, and Stay Out of Trouble," offers just such help. It is a technical manual for the neophyte, a step-by-step guide to help a new business-person set up the "machinery" of his or her business and keep it lubricated and well maintained.

The book covers every possible start-up requirement from fictitious name statements and seller's permit to Federal Trade Commission regulations, from financing to a detailed listing of every available type of business insurance. It also covers federal and state income taxes in detail.

Small Time Operator is also a workbook and includes a full year's worth of income and expenditure ledgers, year-end summaries, depreciation worksheets, credit and payroll ledgers. An entire section is devoted to explaining the why and how of bookkeeping including complete, step-by-step bookkeeping instructions.

Other chapters cover partnerships, corporations, hiring employees, dealing with the IRS, business locations, calculators and adding machines, financial analysis, and a lot of other information. The most interesting part of *Small Time Operator,* I think, is a collection of interviews, some of them quite amusing, with successful and not-so-successful businesspeople.

Small Time Operator was written by me, Bernard Kamoroff; I'm a 32-year-old certified public accountant with a practice in the Bay Area. This book was three years in the making. It comes out of my experience dur-

How to Start your own Small Business

ing the past nine years as a financial adviser and tax accountant for small businesses, businesses started from scratch by inexperienced people, and from operating two of my own small businesses. For a long time I've seen a need for a book like _Small Time Operator_, a book that will tell new businesspeople what they need to do--and not do--in language they can understand.

Small Time Operator costs $5.95 and will be available in local bookstores in November. Or you can obtain a copy by mail for $6.60 (which includes sales tax and shipping expenses) from _Bell Springs Publishing Company_, P.O. Box 322, Laytonville, California 95454.

A chapter from this book will be published in the next issue of _Briarpatch Review_.

saving shaving

I now shave with a brush and mug, thanks to a suggestion sent in by Bob Kahn of Lafayette, CA, last fall. It was a great Briarpatch suggestion. Simple living, since it's less dependent on technology, wastes fewer resources, is less expensive, and releases no aerosols into the air....and most Briarpatch of all: the warm brush and lather are fun. A note to you who haven't done it before--don't bother cleaning the brush after using it; leave it in the mug and you'll save soap.

--_Michael Phillips_

Cont'd. from page 165

The record was initially funded by my personal $1,000, which I borrowed from the bank. Expenses have quadrupled, mainly because we had to go to a double album (two records in the package) to contain all the story, and also we wanted a four-color cover, which was expensive. But we're proud that we have made the record exactly as we wanted. We expect to break even on the first 500 copies, then hopefully make a bit of money on the second 500. It's a nonprofit venture for me; all profits go to support JuneAppal, which is trying to get self-sufficient.

JuneAppal grew up as an offshoot of Appalshop, a documentary film cooperative in Whitesburg, KY. It's a co-op, run by young people and poor people in the Appalachians. It has seen many changes and growth--which will be described on television Nov. 19 in a 90-minute NET special called "The Appalshop Story."

Many volunteer hands worked on the record, and side four is given over to other story-tellers. Ancient Creek will be available by mail order direct from JuneAppal Records, Box 743, Whitesburg, KY 41858, for $8.00 plus 50 cents postage, or from the Whole Earth Truck Store.

****

Cont'd. from page 189

left hands, one above the other. Each person felt the energy rise to her hand. When the woman whose hand was on top felt the energy rise to that hand, they again tried to lift the subject, who was lifted high and effortlessly, this time.

This principle can be used to lift heavy in-animate objects. And if one is all alone, she can place one hand over the other eight times. It will still work.

We also talked about public relations, assertiveness and a way to clear our heads at the end of the day. It was a very energizing session.

Common Values

We had a lot of fun getting together, getting to know each other as Briars and as women with many common goals and values. We all agreed that in spite of the obstacles, the challenge of having one's own business is one of the most exciting adult games to play. We unanimously acknowledged the job of handling our businesses with the down-home simplicity we get from being associated with Briarpatch. Most of us are new at business and the lessons we learn from the Briarpatch way of doing business are simple enough for all of us to really get.

The meeting was relatively short, valuable and fun. Since we felt we had only touched the surface of this group's potential, we decided to meet the third Sunday evening each month at the various businesses. Open to Briarpatch members only.

Next WOMENERGY Meeting
Sunday, Nov.21, 7:30 P.M.
Carole Rae's Studio
151 Potrero, San Francisco

Distribution

Our distributors in the Bay Area are Serendipity Couriers and the Whole Earth Access Company. Andy Alpine drops off copies of the Review when he visits Briarpatch stores in the Bay Area, and other Briars distribute copies in likely places.

Stores in other parts of the country order ten or more copies at our standard discount of 50%. If you know stores you think would be interested, we'd be glad to send you, postage paid, ten or more copies for 50¢ each. Send payment with orders to: Briarpatch Review, 330 Ellis Street, San Francisco 94102, or call (415) 928-3960.

Costs

2,300 copies printed

Printing and production:	$ 570.01
Mailing:	66.98
Office expenses:	49.65
Miscellaneous:	40.00
	$ 726.64
Income since Spring issue:	$ 815.39

All labor donated.

BRIARPATCH REVIEW

CONTENTS

The Briarpatch Review is a product of the Briarpatch network: a group of people interested in simple living, openness, sharing, and learning how the world works through business.

This issue was put together by:

Kristin Anundsen   Annie Styron   Tamra
Michael Phillips   Kathy Mayer

Cover and special graphics: Jim Wintersteen

A Single Father in the Briarpatch

By Kristin Anundsen

Single father Charles Albert Parsons is a Briar who first heard of the Briarpatch through Rivendell, an alternative school his son Justin attended for three years, from the age of four-and-a-half. A number of Briars were and are involved in Rivendell, a three-year school that Charles Albert says is significantly different from public schools in that while public schools tend to restrict the child, Rivendell expands the experience the child is having.

Annie Styron and I visited Charles Albert and Justin at their comfortable, warm, rented house in the Glen Park section of San Francisco, where Charles Albert shared with us many of the feelings involved in being a lone parent. We would like to share these, in turn, with other Briars, particularly those who are also experiencing the problems and joys of single parenting. (The following article, by Salli Rasberry, is the personal account of a single mother.)

Choosing the right school was only one of the heavy decisions that had to be made--alone-- by Charles Albert, who is fiercely devoted to his son.

Now eight years old, Justin is a bright, independent, open young person who, when asked how he liked having a father for a mother, replied, "I like it better." Better than what? "Well, a lot of my friends have mothers but no fathers. I like this better."

Charles Albert says proudly that he "got Justin when he was nine months old." What he means is that he took over sole custody of his son at that time. Charles Albert's wife had divorced him for another man, with whom she planned to travel cross-country in a van. Justin was too young for that kind of trip, and his mother planned to leave him with a babysitter--but Charles Albert could have none of that. "I couldn't feature my son being with a babysitter while I was around the corner," he says. He took Justin himself and has had him ever since, although he still doesn't have legal custody, a state of affairs he refers to as "my sword of Damocles."

Thus it was that the newly single man, who had bought a motorcycle and was having a fine time dating ladies, took on a nine-month-old baby. "I decided it didn't have to change my patterns," says Charles Albert. Well, maybe not all his patterns, but it certainly did claim a good deal of his attention. Far from having regrets, Charles Albert says heartily that the experience has been "great--I'd recommend it."

While we talked with Charles Albert, Justin listened and contributed moderately to the conversation, when he wasn't busy creating his costume for Halloween. Like most kids, he made a couple of small tests of his father's indulgence and had the limits reinforced (Justin: "I can't see the lines to cut along." Charles Albert: "You can see well enough. If not, fake it." Justin: "Okay.") but for the most part the interaction between father and son seemed like a warm and respectful relation between two adults.

During our visit, Charles Albert offered the following perceptions of life as a single father of a son:

On child care:

"For the first month I had Justin I lived with my parents, but then I decided I couldn't live there any more, since my ideas of child-raising conflicted with my mother's. During that first month he got croup and sounded like he was going to die. I had to function in a way I never had to before. My mother didn't seem to know what to do, and neither did I, so I went down and called the hospital and told them to send an ambulance over. I realized that I had to do something, to move. That experience has stood me in good stead ever since. I took responsibility for Justin completely."

"I looked for a babysitter to take care of Justin while I was working. The first one we found turned out to be his babysitter for four years. We called her Auntie Gae, and she later became his godmother. She took care of as many as ten kids during the day--it was like a family, the ideal situation."

"Toilet training was the one thing I didn't know how to do and didn't particularly want to learn. So Gae trained him."

"It would have been ideal if I could have educated Justin myself, but that was impossible. Fortunately Rivendell allows maximum parent participation. Also, one of his teachers and I fell in love, and she became a surrogate mother. We broke up but she and Justin still see each other often."

"If I go to a party I usually take him with me because there are usually other kids there."

On women's attitudes:

"I've run into a lot of female chauvinism. Women don't believe I'm capable of taking care of a child by myself. They say, 'Well, how do you change his diapers?' (I say, 'How do you change diapers?') or 'Oh, do you cook?' At first I felt upset about these comments, but eventually they made me giggle."

"Women automatically assume I'm looking for a wife. 'He's a single father--obviously he needs me,' they think."

"I don't go out on many dates--women come to my home and participate in my family. I discovered that sometimes they come here to get laid. It makes me feel like a sex object."

"I've been fortunate in that the women I've been involved with were super. But once, a woman on our first date tried to get Justin to call her 'Mommy.'"

On mothering by the father:

"When I first got Justin, I decided that we were two guys who were going to live together and we would have to get along-- and I communicated that to him. He's my roommate."

"Most little babies are raised by women, and they're afraid of men. Justin was the opposite-- he liked men, especially men with beards because I had a beard-- but he was afraid of women."

"There's this thing I call the 'mother button,' which gets pushed when someone suggests that a kid's clothes are dirty or something. I used to get my mother button pushed a lot."

"I thought a lot about what I, as a single father, would need to provide my child. There were two main things: One was physical touching (or loving), which fathers don't usually do as much as mothers; I found out I loved it, and I still do. The

other was consistency. That was one reason I decided to stay with the same job. Now I know he's had the consistency and stability he needed--and I needed--and I feel free to move on."

"When he hurts his arm, say, I grab it real hard, and the pain of my grip makes him forget about the original pain in his arm. Then when I let go the pain is gone. A woman might 'kiss it and make it well,' but our method works for us."

"I **nev**er paid attention to what month or year he learned something. I didn't want to play that game. And he never went through what they call the 'terrible twos' because I wasn't expecting him to."

On responsibility:

"Once I got into it I found I loved it. I refer to this as my latest incarnation. His great-grandmother said to me, 'Charles, I think you're doing a wonderful job raising Justin.' I said, 'It's the other way around: he's raising me.'"

"Double parents have each other to check things out with; single parents don't. As a single parent I'm not willing or able to share responsibility for Justin, even though sometimes I'm longing to."

"Any woman who tried to manipulate some of the responsibility away from me got her teeth kicked in. It was like a reflex. Fortunately I run into that very, very seldom."

"If I got married again I wouldn't be marrying a mother for Justin, I'd be marrying somebody for me. And I would keep all the responsibility for Justin--I'd still be his single parent."

200

Relationship

By Salli Rasberry

Before my child was conceived I
knew that the adventure of
raising her would be my own.
The first year of my daughter's
life was very romantic and good
and I am grateful to my husband
David for sheltering us and for
his tenderness and strength and
for the music he gave to our
family. It was good to relax
and enjoy my baby nursing, to
bring her to our cozy bed; to
have the space of lazy days at
the ocean and nights of soft
guitar music and poetry. And
yes it was important to have the
support of a loving husband and
good friends.

But I was a restless person,
almost a girl myself, and
Fairyland was not what I wanted
for me or my girl-child. We
left San Francisco with one
suitcase and two large smiles.

She began to form sentences on
the hot white beaches of Mexico.

I followed my instincts, shedding
familial values like too many
clothes. Long-suppressed
feelings I recognized as my own
shone like polished stones and
I felt clean and good.

We moved on to play along beautiful Lake Charles in Boston and
with computers at M.I.T. I grew
self-conscious as others spoke of
children needing a father and
roots and the security of the
same bed each night. Sasha
learned to walk in New York City
and together with an unexpected
friend from California we shared
the tinsel of Christmas.

We rendezvoused with friends in
Luxembourg, explored the galleries
of Paris and her incredible
museums. Sasha ran between the
tables of numerous sidewalk cafes
while I lamely defended my
country to a group of table-
pounding African comrades. They
taught me French and politics.
We came home. I became a sheep
on any anti-establishment picket
line, my daughter riding high on
my shoulders, our banner of hope
for the new world we would build.

We set up house in the Haight
Ashbury with the help of various
Thrift Shop ladies and donations
from friends. We boogied. We
made our own music. We pulled
images from the cosmos. Wild
happy times laced with gentleness
and acid. We thought it was all
for free.

We grew careless with our precious
gift of youth and invited
strangers in with their tape
recorders and T.V. cameras who

raped us of our trust and of our
innocence. The Haight fast
became no place for children or
stoned moms.

We took to the road again,
heading north into Washington
to Tolstoy Farm. The country
was sweet and safe from exploit-
ers but impossible without more
help, so we came home to settle
where we could. The Fillmore
District was definitely a
bottom-of-the-barrel slum and
it was hard getting used to
sewer rats and the filth and
decay that was our neighborhood.
But the people! So full of
life! Nowhere had I experienced
such everyday exuberance, such
love for children. We drank a
lot of wine, dancing in clubs
and the back rooms of shoeshine
parlors. I learned to prepare
greens and pigs' tails. Discovered that being down was just
part of being up. Sasha grew
looser with her body, freer to
sample whatever life might offer.

We stayed many years in the
Fillmore through the riots and
the courageous work of the
Panthers, through redevelopment
and beginnings of a new black
pride. There came a time,
though, to move on to the
country, to come to terms with
our own culture, the one we
could no longer avoid.

Beautiful Freestone and a return
to Fairyland. Here we had
space to grow, the security of
a family. There was so much to
learn and I jumped right in
hurrying before it would all be
snatched from me. I shed the
city with my bra, allowing the
sun to brush my whole body, the
sauna to sweat me clean. Learning to garden, to formulate
theories, to raise sheep, to
write, to publish a book, to
share the raising of children
with a man. Dear Robert helping me to see my potential,
gently guiding me back to my
poetry, my music giving me
support to explore drawing.

202

It was very good and very high but it was too much all at once. Sasha was often angry at having to share me with so many other people; she wanted more of me and her own space back. I was used to doing things my way and I couldn't give it up...I hungered for psychic and physical space. When women all over the country began speaking their piece it became obvious that this was not a time for working things out with a man but for being alone for awhile, absorbing all the changes, risking being alone in the country. When our rented home was sold, Sasha and I moved into our tipi in Bodega, where we have settled.

I grew up with my daughter; it's hard to remember what life was like before she was born. I wanted for her what I wanted for myself. She listens to my conversations, absorbing, trying to figure out what being grown up is all about.

I live in a cabin now with a man who understands where I am coming from and the close bond between me and Sasha. We all three give each other lots of space, knowing it's crucial to maintain separateness, our individuality. Sasha shares with me her fantasies of having a career and her own apartment filled with cats and plants, of having her own car. I have daydreams of what it will be like not being responsible for anyone but myself. She and I are moving slowly apart, re-forming the patterns of our relationship. Sometimes we scream and stamp our feet in frustration, often we are awkward, each dependent on the other in ways we barely realize. There are many close, special times too and I am happy that my main sharing was not with a person I called "Husband" but with my daughter.

203

SAN FRANCISCO

bold step

By *Kristin Anundsen*

Marc and Carol in kitchen

Since its founding in May of 1970, the San Francisco Ecology Center has, as its current spokesperson Marc Kasky puts it, "taken a direction strongly influenced by whoever is working here." But it was also strongly influenced by whoever was funding it--a number of foundations plus the board of directors. As of December 1, 1975, the Center has become independent of grants, self-supporting in the sense that those who are involved in it first-hand are the only ones contributing to its livelihood (that's right livelihood, of course).

The decision to cut loose from grants will probably result in "a few tight months," says Marc. "But it's what we want to do. Now we'll have the freedom to be what we want to be, and to move in different directions when we feel the urge to move. Change is happening faster and faster these days, and the Ecology Center's function will be able to change faster too if we don't have to keep a year-long commitment to a foundation. Just the decision to do this has resulted in a cleaner feeling about the place. We won't have to worry about ripping off some foundation by doing something different from what that foundation had in mind."

He adds, "The Briarpatch was our inspiration when we were making this decision. The Briarpatch is a model of doing what you want to do rather than focusing on how to generate income."

And what the San Francisco Ecology Center wants to do is currently experiencing a new incarnation.

204

ECOLOGY CENTER

into self-determination

Evolution

The Center was started by
a group of citizens concerned
with the need for increased
environmental awareness and
action. It had two main
functions then: advocacy
and celebration. Advocacy
consisted of publicly em-
phasizing the ecological
point of view before local
and regional agencies; celebration was an observation
of the solstices and equi-
noxes, in order to heighten
awareness of the natural
world. Besides these two
major functions, the Center
conducted research on energy

and land use, held news conferences for Bay Area media,
sponsored an "Ecology of the
City" class, and maintained
a liaison with San Francisco's public school system
and community groups.

Initial organizer Gil Bailie
was director until 1973,
the year in which the Ecology
Center was propelled into
public awareness via its suit
to prevent the expansion of
the San Francisco airport.
(The suit finally lost in
higher court.) The advocacy
function was continued under
the new director, lawyer
Charles Starbuck, but the
celebrations were phased out.
In September 1974 Vince Bacon
took over as director, and
the Center began to reflect
his interests: environmental
impact statements and the environmental review process.

From about 1973 to 1975,
the Ecology Center was relatively quiescent, sponsoring
few activities that would draw
people into its activities or
its storefront. A soup kitchen was started, but had to

close down in a few months because the Board of Health ruled that its facilities were inadequate--it had only a refrigerator and hot plates, no stove or sink. However, the Center, as a nonprofit organization, continued to serve as a channel for grant-funded projects.

Some of the grants were general but most were for specific activities such as an environmental education series, press conferences on aerosol cans, film series, etc. The Center was a funding channel for groups as well as individuals; among these groups were the Living Creatures Association and a group proposing to refoliate Alcatraz.

WHEAT IN THE STREET

From time to time, attempts were made to help the Center become self-supporting. Once it was partly a bookstore (the San Francisco Ecology Center and Sunflower Bookstore) and once it was partly an art gallery, selling prints and keeping a percentage of the profits. But funding from foundations was still the major source of revenue, and if there was a gap in the funding cycle, members of the board of directors would make contributions out of their own pockets. On average, it has cost about $20,000-$25,000 annually to operate the Center.

Then, in May of 1975, the Center's focus shifted again as Marc Kasky took over as director. One of the changes Marc insisted on was that he was not to be the director. "It's ridiculous to have one director when everyone has equal responsibility," explains Marc. "We felt that authority was a deadly concept. We were all doing what we're good at, so it would be silly for one of us to be telling the others what to do." The other Ecology Center principals-- Carolyn Schaffer, Erica Fielder, and Carol Brendlinger --are now considered "co-directors" along with Marc. He does, however, put in more hours than the others, and

the major responsibility
for determining the Center's
direction is his.

Former directors Gil Bailie,
Vince Bacon, and Charlie
Starbuck remain involved with
the Center, but in many ways
the place now reflects Marc's
interests, which he describes
as "quality of life, nutrition, understanding the city,
education, simple living."
He wants the place to become
a "living room" where ideas
and sometimes music can be
shared, as well as a clearing
house for information.

The Center's location, at 13
Columbus Street, on the fringe
of San Francisco's financial
district, attracted a number
of drop-ins--I was one of
them--whom Marc greeted and
drew into conversation about
the Center. Gradually a community of interest grew, and
people who had stopped hanging
out at the Ecology Center began to return. The soup kitchen was revived, with the

proper facilities and the
culinary output of chef Carol
Brendlinger. A lunch-speaker
program was started, so that
visitors can now exchange information while they eat.

The Turning Point

One of the Center's programs,
which had been funded by the
San Francisco Foundation with
a matching grant from the
Gerbode Foundation, was an
educational program called
"Ecology for City Kids," conducted through the public
schools by Carolyn Shaffer
and Erica Fielder. "We had
the grant for the next year,"
says Marc, "and we were writing major proposals to get
other grants. Then Carolyn
and Erica came back from a
vacation and said they had
decided not to repeat the
Ecology for City Kids program--
it just wasn't what they
wanted to do. Suddenly we
realized that we were tailor-
ing proposals to what foundations wanted to do rather
than doing what we wanted.
We were compromising our own
interests to get money to
keep going."

So the Ecology Center turned
down the San Francisco Foundation grant. About that
time the board of directors,
which consists of naturalists,
lawyers, and business people,
decided that the time had

come for the Center to become self-supporting.

Previous grants have now expired, and the Ecology Center is on its own, for better or worse.

So where is its revenue coming from? It's coming from people who are using the Center. One recent addition to the Center's family is the New Games Foundation, a Briarpatch organization that promotes non-competitive recreation and play. New Games now maintains space in the Center's offices, contributing $200 a month to the $450 rent, and Marc is involved in its activities.

The soup kitchen, which serves a soup/salad/sandwich lunch every day for $1.75 (all you can eat), has become so successful that it now contributes another $100. Various other groups that use the Center—such as the Street Artists Guild, the Media Alliance, the West Coast People's Commune, and the Institute of Man and Nature—contribute funds also. There is still an opportunity for one or perhaps two more groups to pay $50-$100 a month for the use of a desk and phone at the Center.

The Living Room

Not everyone who uses the Center contributes financially,

though. On one of my recent visits there I encountered Mycall Sunu of the Universing Center in Eugene, Oregon, which is into neighborhooding, ecology, healing, and so on. Although his organization does have a San Francisco office, he was using the Ecology Center's space that day because "there's energy here." An American Indian group used the Center without charge to hold a press conference. As Marc puts it, "The place needs to be used. It's enriched by everything that happens here."

The Center's advocacy posture is now a thing of the past. Its interests have shifted from dealing with the environment as an external thing to including transformation of individuals through increased awareness and communication. The emotional presence of such essences as Findhorn— a semi-spiritual community in Scotland that is considered an "energy center"—will undoubtedly help shape the Center's future. Carolyn and Erica visited Findhorn last summer and have conducted a number of discussions and film programs on it. Marc and the others hope that, eventually, 13 Columbus Street in San Francisco will become a sort of energy center in its own right.

"The place exists because the people using it are contributing to it," he says. "We want it to continue that way. Now I need to find a way to be self-sufficient; but I'm not worried about myself or the Center. I'm willing to wait and see what happens."

Once upon a time there was a strong interest in creating a soup kitchen/environmental luncheon program at the Ecology Center. In fact, a lunch program had actually been started, but the Board of Health had stepped in in an effort to protect the public from themselves and told us we had to close down. We needed a legitimately equipped, regulation kitchen or something approaching that. What was lacking, of course, was the money, the equipment, and someone to put it all together. The staff went to the Pygmy Forest Ecological Staircase for a weekend of discussion and meditation. They realized they needed a carpenter, an electrician, and a plumber, as well as a triple aluminum sink. At one point during the weekend everyone went for a walk, except Gil Bailie, who stayed behind at the house. There soon came a knock at the door, and a man appeared. He said he had picked up a hitchhiker who had told him about the house and the Center and what kinds of things were going on, and asked if he could help in any way. Gil explained that what they most needed was a carpenter, a plumber, and an electrician. The man said, "Well, I'm a carpenter and a plumber and an electrician." Gil said, "We also need a triple aluminum sink for a kitchen we're trying to put together." The man said, "Well, I have a triple aluminum sink in my garage." A few weeks later the Ecology Center had a real, live, regulation kitchen that to this day is the heart of what happens there.

--Marc Kasky

209

wins in the bay area
briarpatch network

It's been a few good months for the Network and I thought I'd
mention a few of the specific "wins" or nice happenings:

-David Reardon produced a record called "Wilderness America/
Celebration of the Land." This album of original music by
David, Iasos, some whales, and foxes was the fruition of
many months of work co-sponsored by seven environmental groups
(Sierra Club, Friends of the Sea Otter, etc.). The proceeds of
the record will be used to help preserve and protect the en-
vironment. Copies from record stores or the Ecology Center in
San Francisco. $3.98 each.

-Michael Toms and the New Dimensions family presented Dr.
Frederick Leboyer, author of Birth Without Violence, to sell-
out crowds in San Francisco's Masonic Auditorium on December
6th and 7th. Some of the proceeds of the lecture will be used
for the Holistic Childbirth Institute.

-Lou Durham held a successful weekend conference on communal
living attended by more than 50 communal households.

-Pat Farrington of the New Games Foundation was hired as a consultant to the Australian Ministry of Education. Pat is now
in Australia for three months setting up New Games for kangar-
oos and koala bears.

-Andrew Fluegelman and Headlands Press published the San Francisco
Bay Guardian guide, Free and Easy, now in its third printing.

-Dick Raymond and One More Company, Inc., after months of research and testing, have come out with "Shoe Patch," an adhesive
liquid that you "squeeze out of a tube and spread like peanut
butter over worn spots, tears, and holes in your shoes and
sneakers" and much more. (See page 220 for a story.)

-Gary Warne and Oz of Circus of the Soul Bookstore and the San
Francisco Roommate Referral Service have created a Friday Pie-
Throwing Club. The culmination of years of creation and fan-
tasy, it stipulates that Club members must be prepared to
receive a pie in the face at any time on Fridays from fellow
members. It costs 25¢ a week and on Mondays a blind lottery
is held to determine the thrower and victim. For all but the
thrower, the ultimate in paranoia.

-Raskinflakkers, ice cream dispensary extraordinaire, after
nine months under new management, became proof that one Briar
selling his business to another Briar and saying that it was
a fair deal -- was a fair deal and more.

-The Communiversity, maintaining its standards of a truly free
and self-supporting university, "educated" 400 students during
its fall semester.

-"A" and Steve of Rivendell School got married in the Shakes-
peare Garden of Golden Gate Park on December 20th.

-Jan Tangen and the Family Light Music School held an incredibly
successful and well-attended Jazz Festival in September.

..... and then there was the Briarpatch Bay Area Christmas
Party: hard-driving boogie, lots of good pot-luck food, and
lots of room to dance, thanks to the band "Creation" and Bonnie
and Jack's Farm.

-Andy Alpine

211

Japanese
Business Lesson

By Michael Phillips

Large Japanese corporations have many interesting qualities--such as lifetime employment and management by consensus--that have been described in business journals. However, the operating methods of most of these corporations do not appear easily transferable to our culture, especially Briarpatch culture. We wondered what we could learn from smaller Japanese firms, so we interviewed Paul, a Zen priest who recently spent five and a half years in Japan as an apprentice temple carpenter. Paul worked for three different companies with four to 10 employees each. I have paraphrased Paul's language in the following summaries:

Teaching

To teach me how to use the Japanese plane, which is a very delicate instrument, my co-workers gave me the worst possible boards and told me to plane them. I worked for over a month, fucking up all along the way. They'd say, "That's really lousy" and tell me to go back and work more, with no help. I did about half the job in that time; then when I was off and the rest of the crew was in a hurry to finish, one man completed the job in two days. Learning is by trying, watching, finding out for yourself. Often, in Japan, the better you are doing the more you are criticized. The Japanese experience is that feelings of overconfidence hold you back from learning more.

The companies I worked for, even though they were small,

212

were not concerned with efficiency in the American sense;
learning and skill were paramount. They accept what a
person is. A fast person is
expected to be fast, and a slow
person is expected to be slow.
This accommodation to people
is part of what makes consensus
possible.

Consensus

There was consensus on everything. Since we traveled to
jobs and lived together while
working on the sites, even the
time and place where we ate
every meal was decided by
consensus. There is a proper
way to do almost everything,
and as long as you do it that
way there's very little friction.
When someone had strong feelings about something the group
went along with it. On occa-
sion I expressed a desire to
eat at a particular restaurant
and after some discussion we
would all go.

Two things seem to make this
consensus possible: First,
there is little or no alco-
holism in Japan but we would
occasionally get drunk together
and at that time anyone could
say anything to anyone else.
The next day it was forgotten
forever since "he was drunk."
Also, the Japanese fight
among themselves to be the
one who does the dirty work--

such as cleaning the bathroom
or unloading something. It's
a little like the way American
businessmen clamor to pay the
lunch bill.

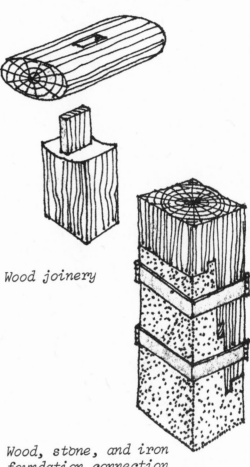

Wood joinery

*Wood, stone, and iron
foundation connection*

Work Habits

The Japanese are a nonverbal
body culture to such an extent
that the way they work together
seems to us to be based on ESP.
To that extent it isn't adapt-

213

able to our businesses. The distinguishing quality of Japanese work is the extreme precision in timing, which leads to smoothness of work flow. Tools are in the right place and the material is in the right spot at the precise time it should be...and every action feeds into the next action.

The depth of Japanese tradition and their view of the "proper" way to do everything are so pervasive in all of their detailed daily actions that they spend almost no "down time" thinking about what to do next. We Americans seem to waste a lot of time stopping and thinking, when we could be working. If our planning and processes fit together, much of our work might be better and more rewarding.

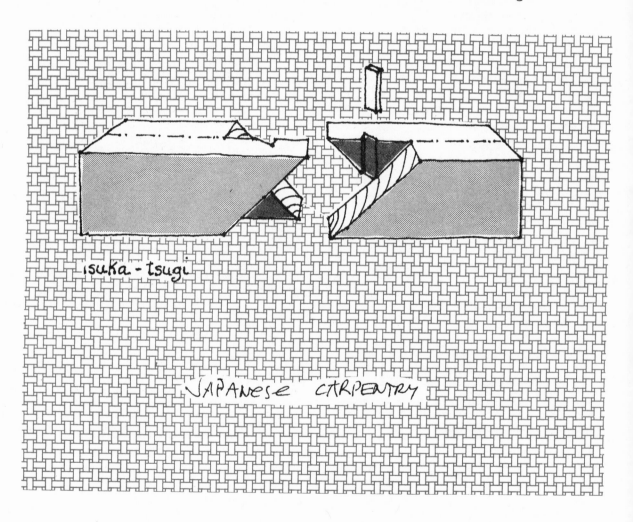

isuka - tsugi

JAPANESE CARPENTRY

A Real Publishing 'House'

By Kathy Mayer

Well-Being is a natural-healing magazine that focuses on healing the whole person. Distributed nationally, mostly through natural food stores, it offers down-to-earth information on staying healthy and balanced. In six issues, over a period of 10 months, Well-Being's circulation has jumped from 2,500 to 20,000.

Well-Being staff members work in a sunlit, quietly busy house in San Diego. The garage is the printing and shipping room. The largest bedroom is editorial and advertising space. The basement houses the bindery and darkroom. The dining room is the subscription and distribution center. Up until recently the living room wasn't used for work, but now it's the publisher's office and periodically the subscription mailing room. The kitchen, bathroom, and patio are occasionally used for business conferences.

We interviewed Well-Being's editor, Barbara Salat, and publisher, David Copperfield, who are also husband and wife, to exchange information about

publishing magazines and gain insights for fellow Briars. They told us: "We'd advise others to start out as small as they can and to grow only as quickly as they need to-- if you have something that's good, you'll grow quickly

enough. By moving slowly you allow opportunities to come forward, like a good deal on a new press, giant savings on paper, unasked-for loans from generous friends. Also, having less money in the beginning can save you from large and embarrassing mistakes."

A year and a half ago, Barbara and David were distributing

215

herbs and natural products in San Diego County. Realizing how much education was needed about herbs, foods, and healing systems, they put out a small newsletter in their spare time. This newsletter grew into the magazine, and the first issue of Well-Being was printed with income from the distribution company. Then, realizing that selling herbs and also writing about them might seem like a conflict of interest, Barbara and David decided to commit themselves solely to publishing Well-Being. They traded the distribution company to a friend who owns a natural foods restaurant. They keep a system of barter with the restaurant, exchanging advertising for food credit at wholesale food prices.

Growing

Well-Being has added new people one at a time as they were needed. This helped each person find the job that suited him or her best. In the beginning Barbara, David, and Joshua (welcome first addition to their staff) had to be multi-talented, doing all the jobs that were necessary. This created more pressure than they would have preferred, but they looked on it as a growth experience. In fact, the whole of Well-Being's staff, which now numbers six full-time people, looks at putting together a magazine as an experience in personal growth

and working together. A weekly "sharing meeting" is held as a time for "being honest with each other." As David explains, "The format is based on each expressing how we've been doing personally in the past week and sharing that with the whole group. If we've been having trouble with each other, or not taking time to enjoy each other enough, it's a time for correcting these 'unclarities' or 'deficiencies.'"

Both David and Barbara have struggled with the fact that being editor and publisher means making decisions for others. Prayer, they say, helps them come to terms with those positions of "power," so that they remain conscious of other people's feelings rather than misusing that power. Although most of the important business decisions are made by two or three people—because the others are very new or uncommitted—there is a weekly business meeting where everyone makes suggestions, hears plans, and gives feedback concerning the work.

Old Resistances

Barbara and David had hoped to have a business free of the "old encumbrances" of deadlines, time cards, and five-day-a-week schedules. But they've seen these resistances break down.

In the beginning there were no deadlines. They did the work as fast as they could and watched their pace. It took an average of six to 10 weeks to put out an issue. They decided to aim for the fastest time and hoped they'd get more efficient-- realizing that if an issue was not out in six weeks, all expenses, like rent and utilities, came up twice an issue instead of once and a half. (They still have trouble making deadlines but it's gradually getting easier.)

Time cards increased awareness and helped efficiency and planning. The staff would often feel they had worked 10 to 12 hours and after checking the cards found it was five or six. Time cards also help to break down the cost of production into its various elements, thereby showing everyone where time might be saved by hiring "professionals" from the outside. The staff also found that working seven days a week was not a good idea, so they force themselves to take weekends off

and try not to worry about "business."

Advertising

Advertisements were another predicament. Barbara's first reaction to the idea was "We're selling out," until she realized that aside from assuring the continuation of the magazine, advertising could help small businesses and promote worthwhile products.

Well-Being is acquainted in some way with most of its advertisers. Although Barbara doesn't personally recommend every product, she'd leave it out of the magazine

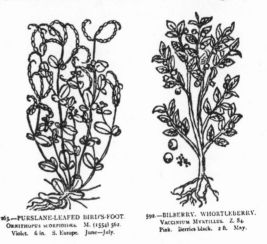

263.—PURSLANE-LEAFED BIRD'S-FOOT. ORNITHOPUS SCORPIOIDES. M. (1554) 562. Violet. 6 in. S. Europe. June—July.

592.—BILBERRY. WHORTLEBERRY. VACCINIUM MYRTILLUS. Z. 84. Pink. Berries black. 2 ft. May.

if she felt it were harmful or questionable. She would like to get national advertisers like book companies and large organic-product companies, but has heard that most of them don't want to advertise in a magazine as home-spun and unslick as theirs. She plans to alert that group of advertisers to the fact that "people are responding to a journal that says you can do it yourself, produced by a staff that says look--we're doing it ourselves."

David in the herb garden

Money

Well-Being sought bookkeeping advice from an experienced businessperson after the first issue. David also looked at the bookkeeping systems of two other publications, one large and one small, and developed a system tailored to Well-Being's own size. Account cards are kept for all barter arrangements, distributors, and advertisers. Methodically kept books have shown where the company is in a very vivid way and have also helped

its credibility.

Loan money is recorded in the back of the checkbook ledger and used only as a capital outlay account. It's not used for salaries, although money may be borrowed from the account for salaries or for other reasons. The first $1,500 loan bought a press, rented a forklift, moved the press, and built a light table.

All members of Well-Being make $1.50 an hour. When the business is stable enough the rate will go to $2.50. At 40 hours a week, that will be $400 a month--an "ecological wage," according to David. It's enough for shared

Marianne and Chrystee moving magazines

Barbara typing copy

a personal savings account called "Money in the Bank." Individuals could withdraw money from this account for traveling or when they leave the company. A portion of the money could also be used by the company, since individuals wouldn't be withdrawing it all at once. There is another account called "Raincheck," with checks marked "non-negotiable." If there's not enough money in Well-Being's regular cash account, an individual receives part of his or her pay as a raincheck which can be cashed in as funds become available.

rent, board, gas, visits to a doctor or dentist, an occasional movie, book, or dinner out; but it doesn't allow for much impulsive/compulsive buying. Part of that $2.50 might go into

Despite their low pay, the members of Well-Being have a way of feeling abundant. David and Barbara have adopted the old law of personal tithing (10% of one's wages to God). According to David, "no matter what you make, when you take 10% off the top you automatically feel good, as though you have enough to give away."

FOR CITY BRIARS

A bunch of people in Ohio are planning to publish a magazine called doing it! A Magazine of Practical Alternatives for Humanizing City Life. They'll try to avoid rhetoric and stick to stories that describe just what people are actually doing to make some human space around themselves, whether they are embarking on their right livelihood or joining a living collective or merely forming a food co-op, or any points in between. They intend to concentrate on the city scene because, despite its undeniable seductiveness, returning to the land is not a possible alternative for most people. If you're interested in finding a way out of the maelstrom, write to Jaques, Ruth, Jenny, Art, Dvora, Carl, Curt, or Judy, or simply to doing it! P.O. Box 303, Worthington, Ohio 43085.

One More Company

New in the patch is One More Company, Inc. of Menlo Park, California. Its first product, ("there'll always be one more," they say) is Shoe Patch, a substance that squeezes from a tube, spreads like peanut butter and will restore the holes, worn places and usefulness of anyone's old, favorite shoes.

The organizers of One More Company are drawn mainly from the ranks of Portola Institute (which published the first "Whole Earth Catalog") and they are scrutinizing every business decision to insure that Briarpatch principles are adhered to as firmly as their Shoe Patch sticks to tennie soles. They even have in their company minutes that at all times the customers have privileges on a par with investors, lenders or employees, since the customer's money is the major source of any company's funding. Dick Raymond, the Company's president, says, "We want the customers to know what we're doing and how we're doing it--even if we do poorly." So their corporate records are open to customers, and excerpts of various memos (there will also always

be one more memo), minutes of meetings and financial reports are available in booklet form (ask for "The Open File", price 50¢, free to Review subscribers).

In accordance with Briarpatch principles of simple living, wages are modest and dividends (if any) to stockholders will be modest. If profits accumulate, One More Company plans to donate as much as possible to help other Briarpatch enterprises, and furthermore to lower the price of the product whenever it can be done.

To distribute Shoe Patch, One More Company is emphasizing direct mail and also hopes to have it in "Briarpatchy" stores. Kay Rawlings, a director, points out that "Shoe Patch will undoubtedly find its way into non-Briarpatch stores, but in all cases we will consider that our alliances must be carefully selected. And any store which handles Shoe Patch will be given a strong indoctrination into Briarpatch ways of thinking."

The company has 12 stockholders, who invested roughly $1,000 apiece (Dick Raymond put in more).

Other funds were scrounged from a bank loan, guaranteed by several of the stockholders. The directors are Richard Raymond, Kay Rawlings, Michael Phillips, and Steve Goldman, all of whom play active roles in setting policy, writing ads, and even stuffing the tubes into the mailing cartons.

A visible expression of Briarpatch ideas is the "Raparound", a 12-page mini-magazine that accompanies each tube of Shoe Patch. It tells about the company and the origin of the product, and has write-ups about Briarpatch ideas and products.

As explained by Arthur Hastings (a communications Ph.D. who acts as One More's writing coach), "In the 'Raparound' we want to reveal a bit of ourselves...not just talk about the product's uses, but do a bit of show and tell about our personalities and our motives, and admit publicly that we all have a sense of humor. Also, though customers are buying Shoe Patch to patch their shoes, we would like them to get ideas and information about

a way of life as well."

Shoe Patch comes in a reusable cardboard canister and costs $3.25 (plus 20¢ sales tax). If you want to get some or inquire about ordering it for resale, the address is:

One More Company, Inc.
540 Santa Cruz Avenue
Menlo Park, CA 94025

Excerpt from "Raparound"

REUSE OUR CARTON!

It wasn't easy selecting a container for mailing and displaying Shoe Patch, since our primary considerations were that the container be not only inexpensive and strong but be made from recycled materials and even be reusable. We hope we have chosen a handsome and useful carton and we think of it as an additional service to our customers.

We asked Susan, one of our staff, to name some things that the container could be used for, and she immediately came up with these:

As a container for nails, spices, hairpins, knickknacks, candies, jewelry, seeds, toothbrushes, artificial flowers, pens and pencils, nuts and bolts.

You can probably find many more things to put in it. Susan suggests covering it with contact sensitive paper. Send us your suggestions (see the suggestion box) and we will report them in the next revision of RAParound.

business and pleasure

After collating and stapling the Fall _Briarpatch Review_, we all had lunch on the roof, where there's a small garden.

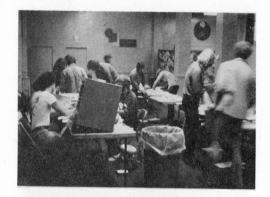

A Bay Area Pot-luck, one of the regular monthly get-togethers, was held at Nick and Flash's home/studio. Photos are by Salli Rasberry. Andy Alpine is in the middle of photo on lower left.

SUBSCRIBE

You KNOW whether you are a Briar. The Briarpatch Review is
intended to be the membership magazine for Briars. It is sent
to everyone who actively participates in the Briarpatch. The
Briarpatch doesn't have dues; people are members because they
participate! Some tithe, some barter their services, and some
carry on the local administration....Are you a Briar? are you
trying to live on less, finding ways to share your resources
with others? If you are, we will send you the Briarpatch
Review. What we would like in return is your participation
in the magazine. There are at least four ways to be on our
mailing list: (1) send a gift of $5.00 to cover our estimated
annual costs; (2) send us articles; (3) send letters on local
Briarpatch gossip; (4) help on the production. Check an
option or two below; send in the coupon...let us know.

Please send me the Briarpatch Review.	Please send a gift sub-scription to:
Name.......................	Name.......................
Address....................	Address....................
City.......................	City.......................
State & Zip................	State & Zip................
⭐ Enclosed is $5 for a year.	Let them know it's a gift from me.
⭐ Enclosed is an article I have written.	⭐ Enclosed is $5 for a year.
⭐ Enclosed is some local Briarpatch gossip; more will be coming.	Send this form to: Briarpatch Review 330 Ellis St. San Francisco, CA 94102
⭐ I'll be there to help put together the next issue.	

223

SOME ETHICAL QUESTIONS ABOUT USING
UNEMPLOYMENT INSURANCE

By Michael Phillips

Many of us have been discussing the ethical questions involved in taking unemployment insurance while we "find out about ourselves," find our right livelihood, learn to live simply, and prepare to start our own businesses. In some cases it borders on the illegal to accept the unemployment payment unless you are actively seeking a conventional 40-hour job.

How About You?

SHOULD YOU DO IT? I can't answer the ethical question for you in this article. It's a personal matter. I raise it so we can discuss it openly. It's important because many of my friends have used unemployment insurance to help them find their right livelihood.

Also, we often find that the unemployment insurance question is a good one for opening a discussion of a whole range of issues surrounding simple living and Briarpatch business.

Learning to "Live on Less" on Unemployment

A number of people I know use unemployment insurance as a transition fund that allows them to go from a stable 40-hour-a-week, high-paying job to the free-wheeling irregular work they want, at a low income with a Briarpatch lifestyle. I can't say whether accepting the unemployment money is desirable or not; I do know that the 65 weeks of free time has allowed many of my friends to make changes in their lives--changes that have been wonderful for them.

Steve was spending $1,000 a month before he got himself laid off from a high-paying institutional job as a psychologist. He did little or nothing for eight months, then started the Network Coffee House and work on the

New World Fair. Now he's doing what he wants and spending less than $350 a month. Bob and Eileen both got laid off from their well-paying jobs; they had been spending over $1,500 a month. While on unemployment they worked on a variety of nonprofit projects, had a child, and, as the unemployment insurance was running out, finally got their own small publishing company on its feet. They sell their books (which are very limited editions) on **a person-to-**

person basis and are able to live simply and comfortably on the net revenue of under $500 a month.

Simple Living Is A New Concept

The extraordinary part of these stories and the exciting thing about the Briarpatch is that we are people who are intentionally learning to live simpler lives, to consume less, and to have fewer and fewer possessions. Living on less is not something we were taught by our parents,

by our schools, or by TV. It is something that is still very alien to many of our longtime friends and most of our neighbors. It is not even a concept included in the structure of unemployment insurance, which expects recipients to look for stable, well-paying jobs in their "old" line of work.

Our Old Myths

There are very few stories in American mythology about living on less. Most heroes are people who acquired power (Stonewall Jackson, Teddy Roosevelt, Captain Ahab) or success, usually financial (Thomas Edison, Henry Ford, Babe Ruth), or notoriety (Jesse James, Wyatt Earp, P.T. Barnum). There are very few who are heroes because they found pleasure in their work and lived simply. The two exceptions are Johnny Appleseed, who seems to have crept into our history as some sort of a nut (he spent his life planting apple trees and being taken care of by the people he met along the way), and Henry Thoreau, who lived simply for a while and wrote about it. The only respected American models of simple living are ministers, priests, and nuns who take vows of poverty.

Our New Goals

So why do we want to live on less, make do with fewer possessions, and live by sharing with others? Some of us do it for political reasons: we believe it is necessary to use fewer resources if the world is to survive. Most of us do it because living on less is rewarding in itself--we love it.

The Briarpatch is created by and for people who want to live simply. Our small businesses can charge less because we want

Barbara Shelley

less income for ourselves. Our services can be better because our enjoyment comes from our work; we are not working to make money in order to do something else. Our work is what we want to do, and we design it to be that way. It's our hours, our location, our own environment, and our source of enjoyment.

Simple Living For Its Own Sake

For me, simple living is not a specific dollar income level (it might be $200 for a single person making and selling cabinets in a country home, or $1,300 for a family running a mail-order business in the city); it's a state of mind that constantly looks for ways to use less and seeks joy out of every act. I love to walk

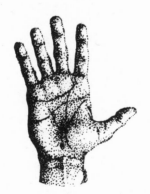

226

instead of ride, smelling the
stores I pass, watching people's
faces. I love to sew up the
holes in my own socks and bite
the thread off, stitch leather
trim on the sleeves of my coat
so it'll last longer, and take
cuttings from plants to start
new ones. I prefer finding
beach stones for my mantel,
carving small sculptures instead of buying decorations,
and sending handmade gifts to
my friends. I prefer bicycle
riding with my kids on our old
bicycles that we fix ourselves.
These values carry over to
work, play, and friends.

Getting Off The System

How does all this relate to
the ethical questions surrounding unemployment insurance?
The classical position would
be that unemployment insurance
is only for those actively
seeking employment in the field
they last worked in. The argument we hear these days among
Briars is that we are finding
new ways of getting off the
unemployment "system" <u>altogether</u>,
of ending our dependence on the
world of 40-hour-a-week salaried
jobs. We are creating a new
system of values that will take
us completely out of the world
of unemployment insurance and
lead us to self-sufficiency in
a community of sharing. To me,
it seems that we are presenting
the American culture and our

friends with an alternative to
avarice and competition, an
alternative that doesn't yet
fit in with the standard institutions of today.

We're Just Leading The Way Again

So, sometimes the way we handle
the ethical questions about
taking unemployment insurance
parallels similar choices we
made about the anti-marijuana
and anti-psychedelics laws a
decade ago (we ignored the laws)
and currently, the way we view
sex between consenting adults
(we ignore the law). It turns
out that we are ahead of our
time, so we are outlaws until
society starts copying us.

Simple Living

AFSC Project

The Simple Living Project developed by the American Friends Service Committee has been our practical and philosophical touchstone as well as the inspiration for our Simple Living Department. AFSC's "anti-consumerism" efforts have taken many forms, the core of which is their publication, <u>Taking Charge</u>, a process packet to use as a handbook in learning to live simply. Here are some excerpts:

AFSC's David Hartsough employs Briar technique: scavenging

QUERIES:

1. Which of the things that I own promote activity, self-reliance and involvement? Which promote passivity and dependence on major socio-economic institutions?

2. How many things do I own which cost over $200.00 (the per capita annual income of the poorest third of the world's population)?

3. Are my consumption patterns basically satisfying or basically burdensome?

4. To what extent am I tied to my present job and life style by the requirements of installment payments, maintenance and repair cost, and the expectations of others?

5. Do I consider the effect of my consumption patterns on the earth and the people with whom I share it?

228

WHAT YOU CAN DO:

1. List the goods and services on which you lifestyle depends. Of these, which were not in use 75 years ago? Which make you dependent on centralized sources of energy, water, food, spare parts and the like?

2. For a period of two weeks or so really pay attention to the advertising to which you are exposed. What is it telling you about what you are as a human being? How does it influence your goals and desires? Those of your children?

WHY COMMUNITY?

1. Are we seeking closer, more meaningful relationships with other people?

2. Do we feel that for our own support and personal growth, we need a larger group than our own immediate family as a support community?

3. Are we feeling with the rush of inflation and the ever growing "need" to work more to buy the "necessities" of life and building a living community could perhaps help us cut back considerably on our economic needs and thus free us to do what we really want to do with our lives?

WHAT YOU CAN DO:

1. Assess the support and security you now receive from insurance policies, savings accounts, investments, family ties, and other "security blankets." Compare the feeling of security you feel as a result of institutions with the feeling of security you feel as a member of a family or community.

2. Enjoy a series of potluck dinners with people who share your values and who desire to live in a more closely-knit community. At these gatherings discuss:
-What kind of community is right for you--spiritually, communally, geographically?
-What do you hope to gain from your envisioned community?
-Which kind of community would best satisfy your needs?
-How can you begin building that community?

3. Start a resource and skills exchange.

TAKING CHARGE: a process packet for Simple Living

from: American Friends Service
       Committee Bookstore
       2160 Lake Street
       San Francisco, CA 94121

single copies postpaid $1.25.

229

WE BARTER FOR LAUGHS

GET A FREE ROOM OR A FREE BOOK
IF YOU CAN MAKE US LAUGH......

San Francisco
Roommate Referral Service
phone: 564-6888

Circus of the Soul
Used Book Store

451 Judah near 10th Avenue
San Francisco, CA 94122

Pamphlets

The following pamphlets are
available from the Briarpatch
Review:

2nd Issue:	Farm Charter....$1.00
	Automatic
	Human Jukebox...$ .50
3rd Issue:	Auto Repair
	Co-op Guide.....$1.00
4th Issue:	Notes from One
	More Company....$ .50

FREE to members/subscribers

Ad Award

Each issue we provide the advertising space above to an outstanding business we select from the
Briarpatch and give them $25.00.
(We reward our advertisers.) This
month its Oz's ROOMMATE REFERRAL
SERVICE and Gary Warne's CIRCUS
OF THE SOUL USED BOOK STORE, who
share the same store front. Business has been so good for Oz, he's
got more customers looking for
roommates than he wants to handle
and he doesn't want to raise his
prices ($6.00 per person). So
he tries to make his customers
laugh with jumping snakes, fire-
crackers, flying planes, and a
rubber chicken that falls from
the ceiling. Result, he has fun
every day and the customers who
enjoy his shenanigans make good
roommates.

Costs

2,000 copies printed

Printing:	$385.
Office expenses:	58.
Advertising award:	25.
Mailing costs:	169.
Total	$637.

Income since Fall
        issue: $975.

All labor donated.

Five or more copies of the Review
are available to individuals and
retailers for 70¢ each. Send
orders with payment (postage paid)
to the Briarpatch Review, 330
Ellis Street, San Francisco 94102.

230

Messages from the Briarpatch

One of the most rewarding aspects of publishing the Briarpatch Review is getting letters from Briars. Our readers write to us like friends--telling us how they feel and what they're doing--and the letters give such a warm feeling of community that reading one is like getting a hug. And of course, these Briars are talking to each other as well as to us, giving valuable information and support. That's what the Review is all about: communication, communion....We need these responses to know whether we're meeting your needs and how we can make the Review truly relevant to Briarpatch living.

BRIAR IN B.C.

The Review is an inspiration and important source for right living. I can offer help with information about day care for children (where I am now) including creative programs, design, business (though mostly relevant to local British Columbia situations). I'm not sure how day care has developed down there, but would be interested in what is happening, what sorts of environments are available for children as alternatives to home-school situations.

Looking forward--I would like to organize a small, portable, sawmilling/lumber-producing business in the Gulf-Vancouver Island area. Has anyone done similar? Any information concerning accounting or business procedures appropriate to us would be greatly appreciated.

About "Couples and Money" (Fall '75): about four months ago, Sandra and I set up ways to handle money that are so much like your article, I was surprised to read it months later. After having our monies vaguely "together," joint accounts, etc. we set up individual accounts for our own, different needs. We began paying our own way when we go out and keeping track of common expenses in a book that is totaled monthly. We settle any difference in amount spent then, so we equally share expenses. This seemed a hassle at first, but now it's so simple we think nothing of it. It has made our economic relationship and life in general smoother. It has also provided a new openness about another part of our lives.

We have an identical agreement about "the one with more money provides capital," with respect to our truck and other "big" things like chainsaws, major tools, furniture, etc. This too has been a new and very satisfying experience. Here's some $ for more subscription this year.

Thomas Hall
134 Michigan St.
Victoria, B.C.,
    Canada V8VIRI

NEW PEOPLE

There's a buck somewhere in this envelope for the word on Briarpatch. Sounds like the Wall Street Journal of the new people--great!!

Leon V. Messier
P.O. Box 1084
Los Gatos, CA 95030

EXCHANGES

If anyone there needs a massage, call me, and I'll come work on necks and shoulders at press time, labor donated!

Especially appreciated your notes on couples and money. One way I'm working on now, with one man, is: since he's employed and I'm not (in the $ sense), I give him credit coupons for when he treats me (to lectures, films, etc.) and at $10 worth he gets a massage. We don't eat out at all, but mostly at my place, and he brings the salad things. When we eat at his place, I bring something. But there is something out of balance about it...he's not really comfortable with this new way (or perhaps it's my discomfort). Money makes things easier (finalized). I definitely agree about the implications of "being paid for." I gave my attention to another person (man) while we went camping, and the man I went with complained that since he'd paid the entrance fee, I should be with him only!

Re the Simple Living Dept.: I appreciate recipes. I am working now on a cookbook (no title yet). The recipes have as criteria: meatless, minimum of cooking (saving on energy), simple (i.e., proper food combinations).

Sunshine H. Appleby
Pt. Reyes Station
CA 94956

ANYONE IN MICHIGAN?

My husband and I have always believed in and tried to live by some rather basic concepts. To some extent we have succeeded but now we are faced with the fact that in order to survive psychologically or financially as humans we are going to have to adopt a totally new life style.

We have a large, healthy, and energetic family. We tend to constitute a small community all by ourselves. We feel there is little we can't do for ourselves given an honest chance

and some intelligent guidelines. We also feel there is much we can (and do) contribute to others. How do we go about establishing a beachhead based on actual human needs rather than material desires?

Do we do it on our own here? Are there like-minded people here in Michigan?

Elaine (& Charles)
Roberts
125 Saginaw St.
Byron, MI 48418

SOMETHING TO SUPPORT

I've felt besieged today by the tons of requests for donations, support, guilt dues, life blood, an ounce of flesh... gasp, fgf! Who knows what to do with all of those harpies? They're not speakin' to my heart.

Then along came this copy of Briarpatch into my hands (I've seen it hanging around for a month, but only just now read it!) and resolved all this for me. Now here's something I can support.

You're the god-damndest, raggedy-assed bunch I've heard in a long while and I like it. After all, I'm with ya.

Jeff Dick
c/o Sam Ely
Box 116
Brunswick, ME 04011

233

BRIARPATCH REVIEW

Tofu Business

Small Time Operator

Open Book Accounting

Brer Rabbit Speaks

Yurok Story

Womenergy

Fun in Business

Table of Contents

This issue was put together by Kris Anundsen, Mary Cunov,
Tom Hargadon, Greg Hastings, Deon Kaner, Michael Phillips,
Chris Popp, Steve Phillips, & Diane Keenan.

Art and Photo Credits:

Cover drawing adapted by Deon Kaner;
Larry Needleman, New Games Foundation,
Wind Bell Publications, Charles Albert Parsons,
Greg Hastings, Michael Phillips, Steve Phillips,
Mary Cunov, Deon Kaner, Ray Cook.

*The Briarpatch Review is a journal of the Briarpatch Network:
a group of people interested in simple living, openness,
sharing, and learning how the world works through business.
It is published every three months at 330 Ellis Street, San
Francisco, CA 94102; Tel. (415) 928-3960. Subscription rates
are $5 per year (add $2 outside U.S.); supporting membership
$25. Single issues and back copies are $1.25 postpaid. We
welcome feedback and stories about your own Briarpatch.*

The TOFU KIT Story

By Larry Needleman

I remember sometime last spring, April or May I think, deciding that it was time. I wanted to create a situation that utilized my food karma and experience, but that wasn't a quick burnout like a restaurant, and was healthy and made sense world economically--one that would provide unlimited personal and spiritual growth and was a service.

I remembered something Stephen Gaskin had said about the Universe not giving juice to someone who was complaining because they obviously didn't need any, so I committed myself to positive thinking and positive action. I began fasting a lot, meditating, praying and concentrating regularly, taking my jogging seriously and generally just putting out good energy. About a month into this I remember saying, "O.K., Lord, I'm ready, lay it on me." And that week the Tofu Kit was born.

Inspiration

I had just received test results from a physical exam, saying I was in fine shape but my cholesterol was too high. That day, as I remember, I saw a copy of The Book of Tofu by Bill Shurtleff and Akiko Aoyagi. It blew me wide open. I'd used tofu like any other good, miso-soup-loving hippie, but hadn't connected heavily with the bland, unappealing white cake. But the book gave marvelous ways to use this new-found "friendly" food and pointed out how shifting from meat to tofu could have a direct effect, helping feed people elsewhere.

Some 300 pages and 500 recipes later I came to the book's last page, "Sending Tofu to the Four Directions," an inspirational page that said, "Do it!" So I did.

Three of us were sitting around a wood stove in Sonoma County talking about tofu and tofu making, when the word "kit" popped up. It rang the bell. I immediately began researching and developing the kit the very next day and have continued work on it daily since then. This is my first venture into the manufacturing world.

Connection

When the kit was about 3/4 of the way to market, Bill and Akiko arrived from Japan and Bill called me to say he'd heard from Westbrae Natural Foods that I was working on a tofu kit. I was really excited. He invited me to share food, films, and tales of tofu with him and asked me to bring the kit. What a connection! That meeting, one of several, tuned up and accelerated the kit. We talked of and planned many projects together, and then around midnight on the first of October, I bid Bill and Akiko goodbye as they began a four-month speaking tour.

Bill left me with instructions to meet with The Farm Food Co. people in San Rafael, CA. and to begin organizing a school to share the technology and equipment of small-shop tofu making with the hundreds of people in this country who were waiting for it; I left him with 200 Tofu Kits and a sales rep. agreement.

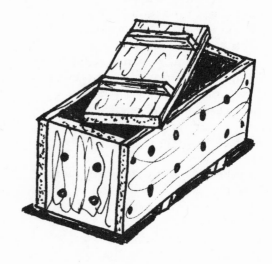

Orders started pouring in for Tofu Kits, but production wasn't pouring out. By then it was obvious that commuting from Occidental, CA to the Bay Area three or four days a week wasn't getting the job done, so for the first time in 7½ years, I relocated in an urban area, Corte Madera, CA.

238

Production

Developing the Tofu Kit meant
testing eight or ten different
kinds of wood for durability and
toxicity and ways of joining
the wood so that the settling
box could withstand the hot
liquid, cold liquid, and drying
each time tofu was made. I
arrive at Philippine mahogany,
joined by silicon-bronze boat-
building nails. We added a
gluing step to the joints,
which gave us a good strong
box. (The kit also contains
a muslin pressing sack, a
three-ounce packet of natural
nigari--solidifier--and a
16-page instruction and recipe
booklet.) Each of the items
in the kid, plus the poly-
ethylene shrink packaging, took

months to develop and test, but
now my second production plant,
Westcom Industries in Richmond,
CA, a handicapped factory and
work training center, is producing 150-200 fine quality
kits per day.

For those who aren't familiar
with the process of tofu making,
it takes about an hour, including
cleaning up. It consists of
grinding soybeans, which have
been soaked overnight, adding
them to water boiling in a pot,
straining the mixture through a
sack, and simmering the strained
liquid for seven minutes; then,
after a three-step (six-minute)
curdling process the curds are
ladled into the settling box
for 15 minutes of pressing into
a cake of tofu.

The difference between storebought tofu and homemade tofu is
as stark as the difference between
storebought bread and homemade
bread. The kit retails for
$11.95 and is available to Briars
wholesale.

Education

The tofu school is slowly coming together. The term will probably be about three weeks long. Enrollment will be limited to approximately ten students per term. The facility will be the tofu shop and soy dairy at the Farm Food Co. Classes in how to start and stay in business will be taught by Charles Albert Parsons and Michael Phillips of the Briarpatch. The actual tofu, and other soy dairy product, instruction will take place in the dairy, with classes given upstairs. There's a residential hotel adjacent to The Farm, that they run, and out-of-towners who need a place to stay can stay there. We're developing an equipment company to supply people with what they'll need to start their own shops.

Anyone who wants to share tofu knowledge, please get in touch with me at The Learning Tree, P.O. Box 829, Corte Madera, CA 94925.

How to Save Time and Money
by Not Becoming an Employer

By Bernard Kamoroff

BOSS.
THE CLEVER LEATHER COMPANY.

OWNER.
THE MORE CLEVER THAN EVER
LEATHER COMPANY

*This article is condensed
from a chapter in the author's
book, Small Time Operator.*

Hiring employees will just about
double the amount of your paperwork. As an employer, you must
keep separate payroll records
for each employee, withhold
federal income and Social
Security taxes, withhold state
income and possible state
disability taxes, prepare
quarterly and year-end payroll tax returns, pay em-
ployer's portion of Social
Security taxes and unemployment taxes, purchase workers'
compensation insurance, and
prepare year-end earnings
statements for each employee.
It's been estimated that the
employer's taxes, workers'
comp insurance, and paperwork
will cost you an additional
thirty percent of your payroll.

In other words, if you pay
a wage of $3.00 per hour,
it's really costing you about
$3.90 per hour!

Businesses hiring employees
are also more closely con-
trolled and regulated than one-
person businesses. Federal
and state governments demand
prompt payroll tax returns and
require strict adherence to employment laws. If you are late
filing your income tax return,
it might easily be six months
or more before you even hear
from the government, and then
it will just be a letter of
inquiry or a bill.

If, however, you are late
filing your quarterly payroll
tax return, in just a few weeks
you could find your business
under lock and key and your bank
account impounded.

Who are employees? From the
Internal Revenue Service:
"Everyone who performs services subject to the will and
control of an employer both as
to what shall be done and how
it shall be done, is an employee.
It does not matter that the
employer permits the employee
considerable discretion and
freedom of action, if the
employer has the legal right
to control both the method
and the result of the services.
Though not always applicable,
some of the characteristics
of the term 'employee' are
that the employer has the
right to discharge him and
furnishes him with tools
and a place to work."

In addition, the following
people are also considered
employees by the Internal
Revenue Service (called
"statutory employees") regardless of the circumstances:
commission truck drivers
distributing certain food
products or laundry; full-
time life insurance sales
people; home workers such
as maids or cooks; and full-
time travelling sales people.

Some businesses such as restaurants and larger retail
stores must have employees:
there is no getting around
it. You can't possibly do
all the work yourself, and
the people you hire - dish-
washers, waitresses, clerks
definitely fall within the
legal definition of "em-
ployee."

Certain small businesses,
especially crafts and repair
shops, can sometimes get outside help without hiring employees. These shops often
hire "outside contractors,"
people like you, in business
for themselves, people who
sell their services to you.
When you hire an outside contractor, you pay the con-
tractor his fee in full. You
do not withhold taxes, pay
employment taxes, or file payroll tax returns.

What's an Outside Contractor?

Here are two hypothetical examples to illustrate employees vs. non-employees:

Example I: The Clever Leather
Belt Company (that's you)
needs help making belts. You
want someone to cut the leather
into 2"-wide strips so you can
devote your talent to the design work. You hire your buddy
for $2.50 an hour, sit him down
in your shop, and tell him to
cut out 250 2"-wide belts, each
three feet long.

The Clever Leather Company has
just become a bona-bide employer.
When you pay your friend, you
must withold income and Social
Security taxes, send the withheld
taxes to the government, pay
employer Social Security and
unemployment taxes, maintain payroll ledgers, prepare earnings
statements at year-end. Ugh.

Example II: The More-Clever-
Than-Ever Leather Compaay
(that's me) needs help making
belts. I want someone to
cut the leather into 2"-wide
strips so I can devote my
talent to the design work. I
call up the Leather Cutting
Company (that's my buddy) and
order up 250 of his standard
2"-wide, 3"-long belts. The
Leather Cutting Company produces the belts on its own
work schedule and delivers the
completed order to me. The
More-Clever-Than-Ever Leather
company just conducted business with an outside contractor.
More-Clever-Than-Ever Leather
wrote a check for the full
amount billed and recorded
it in the expenditure ledger.

Legal Guidelines

Seriously, it is important that you carefully determine the legal status of your hired help. A person who falls within the definition of an employee <u>is</u> an employee no matter what you call him. Says the IRS: "If the relationship of employer and employee exists, the description of the relationship by the parties as anything other than that of employer and employee is immaterial. It does not matter that the employee is designated as a partner, coadventurer, agent, or independent contractor. Nor does it matter how the payments are measured, or how they are paid, or what they are called; nor whether the individual is employed full or part time." The IRS puts out a free publication. <u>Circular E - Employer's Tax Guide</u> (Publication #15), which includes all of their definitions and guidelines. When in doubt about the status of your "employee," you may request a ruling from the IRS on form #SS-8.

If you hire outside contractors, there is one extra bit of paperwork that you must do at year-end. For each person to whom you paid $600 or more during the year, you must file a federal form #1099, "Statement of Miscellanous Earnings." The form shows the contractor's name and address, Social Security number, and amount paid. One copy goes to the Internal Revenue Service and another copy to the contractor. You will not have to keep extra records or pay any extra taxes.

244

Continued:
The Ecology Center —
A SUCCESS STORY

by Marc Kasky

At the San Francisco Ecology Center, we have always talked about the importance of becoming financially independent of foundation grants for our continued existence. However, we have always had just enough determination to write grant proposals (and get them funded), just enough support from a very generous and committed core on our Board of Directors, and just enough surprise windfalls to permit us the luxury of talking about financial independence without having to actually achieve it.

Well, it was reported last winter in the <u>Briarpatch Review</u> that the Ecology Center had taken a "bold step into self-determination"; that not only were we not going to look for foundation grants, but we were actually going to turn down two

that we had recently been awarded. It certainly sounded bold, and we were inspired by the image of assuming full responsibility among ourselves for the future of the Center. We felt that after six years, it would be interesting, at the very least, to see what would happen to the Center if it was without the guarantee of continued "life" provided by a combination of $5,000-$12,000 grants.

These proposals were assuring us that our overhead was being met, as were our salaries and program expenses. What they did not assure us, however, was that what we were doing had importance to anyone besides the foundations and ourselves. It sounded like the perfect time to do two significant things first, find out what we would do in-

Rain please

Trimming the Budget

First, we took a good hard look at our monthly operating expenses. They provided an excellent example of how fiscally careless a project can get when it has the "security" that foundation grants provide.

```
rent-------$450
phone------ 125
answering
service---- 20
utilities-- 45
garbage---- 18
miscel-
laneous---- 25
postage &
printing--- 30
```

TOTAL------$713

This, of course, excludes salaries. We had made the decision that this was a separate issue, and that we would not make it a condition that the Ecology Center would have to support us for it to continue to exist.

We decided to attack what we saw as the variables (fat) in this expense budget.

The Phone--Well, we had three phones, three numbers, buttons, lights, bells, an answering service; in short, we had bought the whole package from Ma Bell. Slowly we chipped away: two numbers;

individually or collectively if we were not beholden to a grant proposal description of our livelihood; and second, to discover where the money would come from to maintain our home at 13 Columbus Ave., a place to which we had become increasingly attached. What follows describes how we have generated the income not only to keep the doors open, and maintain a consistent level of activity here, but actually to operate in the black for the past six months with no foundation grants. We hope it will suggest some ideas which may be helpful to other groups that have faced similar problems.

two phones; no lights or buttons; one number. With this our phone bill dropped to $60. Then the flash--who needs a phone, who wants a phone, how were we using it, and how was it using us? We decided to have Ma Bell come and take the whole thing out, and give us a pay phone which costs us $8.33 per month. Just like that we needed to raise $137 less each month. Equally important, it frees us from dealing with the accumulated issues of six years, and allowed us with only minor inconvenience to move forward with whatever it is we will be doing.

Rent--We decided to appeal our landlord's reasonable side. We expressed our appreciation for the way he had kept our rent constant at $450 for five years; how we were happy with the relationship; how we loved the location, and were very strongly identified with it. We said that if we ever had to move we would probably choose to close up rather than start fresh in a new location. Most important, we stated our strong desire to

establish and maintain fiscal responsibility, to pay our bills on time and live within our means. We said that in order to help us do all this, and until we were in a stronger financial position, we would like to request that our rent be reduced from $450 to $350 per month. The landlord respected our approach, was also happy with the relationship, and yes, would be pleased to reduce our rent by $100 per month.

Miscellaneous--I've yet to see a "miscellaneous" budget that didn't have so much fluff in it you could hardly find the substance. We determined we would need $100 per year for plumbing, electrical work, and repair. That's $8.50 per month.

Postage and Printing--Here we had accumulated a mailing list that was, I'm sure, less reliable that the Democratic voter registration lists in some Chicago wards. What could we do? We sent out our monthly mailing, indicating that anyone who wanted to remain on the list should respond with $1 to cover all costs for one year. Not only is our mailing list down from approximately 650 to approximately 200, but all the people on it are interested in being on it. In addition, it now pays for itself.

248

Utilities--We put all our lights on individual switches rather than a master switch which would light the whole place up, and as a result, have knocked at least $5 per month off our bill. Now we found ourselves having to raise $424 per month to keep the Center alive, rather than $713. We were happy about that. But with no grants, we had to figure out where even this reduced amount was going to come from.

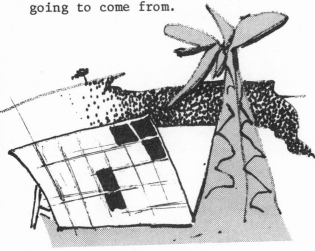

Capitalizing on Assets

First, we looked at our assets: a great location, a warm and comfortable place, a number of friends (some of whom were using the Center for monthly meetings, classes, and various other purposes), and the Briarpatch Network. We decided to try to put together, in some modest way, a collection of groups who could share the space with us, pay part of the operating expenses, and bring with them the kind of activity that would help enrich the Center during this period of transition. We invited the New Games Foundation in, the Media Alliance, PACE (a coastal protection group), and the California Institute of Man in Nature. We chose groups we felt would be compatible, and from whom some new direction might develop for the Center. We charged them based on ability-to-pay rather than the space they used (the group paying the most actually uses very little space), and were able to generate $325 per month from these four groups.

Carol Brendlinger and I committed ourselves to a minimum of $50 per month to be raised by producing twice-monthly gourmet, ethnic dinners to which we invite 25 people, and at which we have guests who discuss topics like animal migrations or the ecology of the city, perform Balinese shadow plays, or present interesting media events.

249

We sold a $15-per-month "life insurance policy" to one friend who felt that his well-being was significantly enhanced as long as the Center was operating. We also got a $50-per-month pledge from one board member who totally supported our actions and motives. This brought our monthly income to $440. To this we have added the following:

We sell records on the Bio-Centennial Records label, and share in the profits ($5-$10 per month).

We sell Earthgifts for the California Institute of Man in Nature, and get 25% of the profits, the rest going towards the development of a Cross-California Trail ($5-$10 per month, more at Christmas).

We have rented the Center to groups who meet here for weekend workshops or evening classes, groups ranging from the Women's Democratic Caucus to the Vegetarian Society, a group doing community service work to a group doing dream workshops. Again, this is always based on ability-to-pay.

We let people know that we were becoming self-supporting, and they responded to the opportunity to help a group that wasn't perpetually complaining about where their next dollar was coming from.

We sell the Briarpatch Review, literature for the Vegetarian Society, and our own Ecology for City Kids book.

We did an annual membership drive, and emphasized our new intentions.

We have encouraged people who have come to us with ideas they would like to get funding for (ideas which we, too, support) to apply for grants through the Ecology Center, and to include a monthly overhead figure for rent and services from the Center.

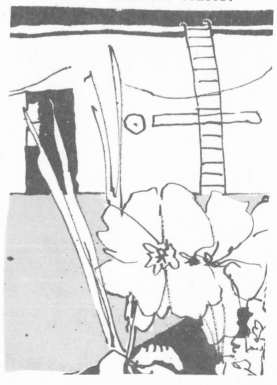

I don't want to suggest that everything we have tried has succeeded. We have had our financial failures as well, and time was when we considered a fund-raising venture successful if we broke even (even then our success rate was pretty poor). But now, without grants, with a reduced budget, and with a diversified base of support, we have achieved a high degree of financial security. We feel able to take an unpressured look at what we would like to do here.

We are in the process of doing some remodelling and repairing of the Center (made possible by our surplus income), and may even look for foundation support when we find out what we would like to do next. However, we will never again depend on grants for security.

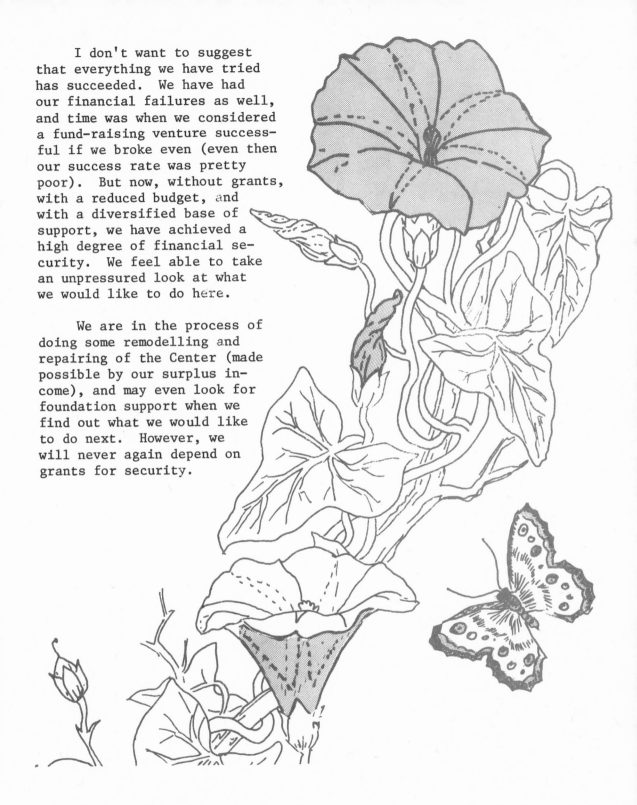

OPEN BOOKS: Keystone of the Briarpatch Network

By Michael Phillips and Kristin Anundsen

Business is essentially a mysterious thing. In most cases, when a business is successful or unsuccessful, no one can tell you precisely why. It may have been the location, the match between type of business and current need, the ads and logo, the distributor... almost anything. Relationships among all these aspects and many more are complex and usually far from obvious. There is only one language in which business speaks to us - only one indicator that is concrete: money. The only place to look for signals is the company's books.

Many companies want to keep their books secret. That is not the Briarpatch way of doing things. Openness is a keystone of Briarpatch operations, for it promotes community and learning, two other Briarpatch values. Openness leads to trust, responsibility, new ideas, greater awareness. It promotes better relationships with customers or creditors as well as with other people who are in similar businesses.

The Originator

The first Briar business to initiate the "open books" policy was the Whole Earth Catalog. In each issue, Stewart Brand published a financial statement. He figured that since the Catalog was supposed to describe tools that help people run their lives better, and learning about finances is an important tool, a statement about the financial condition of the Catalog itself would be appropriate. He had another motive as well: he wanted other people to learn how to start publications like his own so he wouldn't have to keep doing the Catalog forever. The CoEvolution Quarterly, also run by Stewart Brand, does the same thing, and so does Briarpatch Review. The Review editors want to show how inexpensively a journal can be put out, so others will be encouraged to publish their own.

Many Briar businesses have brief financial statements posted on their walls so all customers can see why the goods or services cost what they cost. Complete financial statements are available to anyone who wants to see them - including people who want to start the same kind of business.

Competitors

The idea of being open even with potential competitors is a little hard for some people to get used to. One business, a natural cosmetics store, had joined the Briarpatch and was

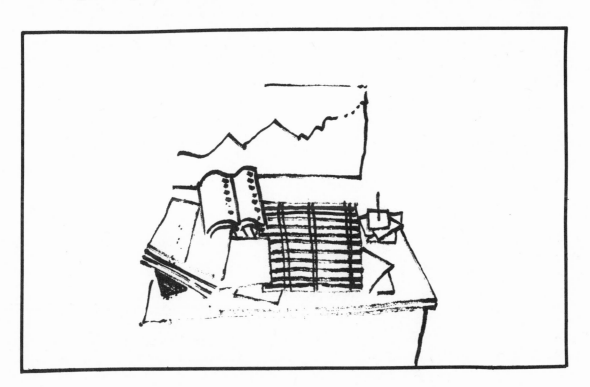

enjoying the benefits of belonging to it. Then another
cosmetics store joined the network and needed information
about rents and so forth.
Briarpatch coordinator Andy
Alpine asked the first store to
share its financial records.
To his shock, the proprietors
refused. (Closed books is an
insult within the Briarpatch.)
Eventually, the first store
dropped out of the network because the proprietors couldn't
embrace the Briar values.

In another business, there
were three partners; two were
very open but the third
wanted to keep all information proprietary. When Mike
Phillips and Andy Alpine
visited this business to give
financial advice they didn't
want to deal in abstractions,
so they asked to see the books.
The third partner was exceed-
ingly reluctant to divulge any

information, and the other two
had to spend a lot of time
convincing him of the importance of being open. They were
successful, and the relationship among the partners significantly improved as a result of the mutual discussion
of goals.

But isn't it dangerous to share
with competitors? Briars
don't think so. Information,
as Mike Phillips pointed out
in an earlier Review article,
has a unique quality - its
value increases with its
abundance. For example, the
more telephones that are
connected to a switchboard the
more valuable each telephone
is. If I give information to
you, both of us are better
off. Keeping our financial
records open helps other
people to start low-cost businesses where we and our
friends can buy, and openness lets other people help

with advice and suggestions. Sharing of information often leads also to sharing of material things such as trucks, houses, and tools.

Involving Customers

Openness helped one Briar-patch member, Howard Sutherland, keep his business going. Howard, who publishes a bicycle home-repair manual, was having financial problems -- he didn't have enough money to publish a second edition. He considered taking on advertising, but was reluctant to do so because manufacturers' ads might compromise the advice and guidance given in the manual. Finally he called a meeting of his customers, showed them his books, and frankly told them his problem. What he wanted was advice on whether to take ads; what he got was the advice - "No!" - plus financial help: several of the customers offered to co-sign a loan. Howard accepted one of these offers. The financial support was crucial - and the emotional support was an important, if unmeasurable, factor too.

The "open books" policy has made proprietors aware of their accountability to customers, clients, colleagues, and themselves. Open books indicates a personal vulnerability that makes manipulations impossible, and if you are not manipulating others, you can have closer and more productive relationships with them.

Greed and secrecy have got many traditional businesses - and governments - into trouble. Briars say that greed and secrecy have no place in the kind of business environment we want.

WOMENERGY

By Deon Kaner

*This is the second in a series of articles by and about
Briar women.*

I attended a Harvest Pot-Luck Gathering for women at Bonnie
Sherk's Farm, which is located immediately adjacent to the
freeway stacks in San Francisco. (See Briarpatch Review,
Summer, 1976.) There were 30 or more women present and the
energy was quiet and high. The program was led by Laughing
Bird and Dyveke Spino. Dyveke was recently written up in
the San Francisco Chronicle for the physical fitness work
she has done with Olympics trainees and the work she is now
doing in the Bay Area, mostly with women. Laughing Bird
is a "master" at ceremonies.   They led us through a
series of breathings, chants, movements, runnings, sharings,
offerings, music, quiet.

What I was most impressed with was the contrast of the
duality of energy that was being evoked in all of us, and
synergized in proportion to the number of us, so that each
of us had a piece of it to leave with at the end of the
evening. How important it seemed to me, especially for
women who are in business, to have the opportunity to
gather together and collectively get in touch with the
Source in each of us and share that. Being in business
and doing business calls for a very active, Yang, kind of
energy. It feels equally important for women to renew
our Spiritual, soft, Yin energy in order to stay in
balance.

How wonderful it was to be in the country, yet so much in
the city that we could see the traffic on the freeway just
outside the softly curtained windows, and to share those
parts of ourselves which usually get put into our work but
all too often don't get acknowledged.

A YUROK STORY *

by Harry Roberts

Harry Roberts is a Yurok Indian, deeply immersed in the Indian Knowledge and way of the natural elements, plants, soil, sunlight, and air. He is also a Western university trained agronomist with a lifetime experience on the California Coast, including developing seed stock, nurseries, and even working the Zen Center's Green Gulch as a cowboy forty years ago.

He has been going to Green Gulch for extended visits, teaching and helping them to know the land. The following story is one of a collection, eventually to be published as a book, about the way of the Yurok people.

My uncle was sitting in the morning sun in front of his house fixing the feathers on the long headdress wands for the brush dance. He had made a pot of sturgeon glue and was very carefully smoothing the feathers down and gluing new feathers in where the old ones were damaged or torn loose. He was working very carefully and slowly for this was very fine, difficult work to do.

I looked over one of the wands that he was repairing and I could barely see where the feathers were damaged. I told him that I didn't think that he had to repair that one as I could barely find the damage. My uncle just looked at me for a while, and then he asked me what it was that the wand I held in my hand was. And I said that it was a brush dance headdress wand. My uncle waited a while and then asked me what it was for, and I told him that it was for wearing in your headdress when you danced the brush dance. And that since one danced at night no one could see that it was very slightly damaged. He looked at me some more, and finally he said, "But I know."

We sat in the sun and I helped him fix the headdress. After a while he said that it was about time that I should begin to study to be a man. He would start asking me the questions that a man must be able to answer so that I could understand the law.

I asked my uncle what was so hard to understand about the law. It seemed very simple to me because there was but one law and that was merely "Be true to thyself."

My uncle asked me, "If you understand the law, why do you not understand why I am fixing my headdress wands?" This I could not answer.

So he said to me, "Let us start over again. What is it that you are holding in your hand?" I answered, "A headdress wand." My uncle made no answer. He quietly kept on repairing his headdress. After he had finished he put the headdress away and went to work chopping wood for his fire. When he had finished his wood he got out his dip net and mended it and started down to the beach to see if he could catch some fish for breakfast. He still spoke not a word to me. I asked him if I could go fishing with him. He merely looked at me and said nothing. I could not understand why he wouldn't speak to me. Finally I asked him what was the matter. Had I offended him? He smiled and said no, that it was he who had not wished to offend me by interrupting my thoughts before I had finished answering the question.

I said, "But I answered the question. I told you what it was." He just looked at me some more and said nothing.

So I thought and thought and thought. Finally I told him, "It is a headdress wand for the last night of the brush dance." He looked at me and slightly smiled and said "Unh," by which I knew that he meant yes, that's a little better, it will do as a start; now let's get after the answer. So I said, "It is to show how rich you are because it is the best and most expensive of all of the headdress wands on the river." Whereupon my uncle looked upon me with disgust and said, "I thought that you wished to be a man. Why don't you start to think like one?" After having so expressed himself, he left and went fishing, and not one more word was addressed to me that day.

The next morning my uncle was again sitting in the sun in front of his house. This time he was making some bone arrow points. He had been soaking the bone for several weeks in the creek and it was nice and soft and just right for cutting into shape. I sat beside him to watch how he carved the bone and to see how he cut with the grain so as to cut more easily.

Finally he looked at me and said "Well?"

This was very bad for me. For elder uncle only spoke this way when he was very, very angry. I had seen big grownup persons cast their eyes aside and blush when he so addressed them in council meeting. I had even seen important men leave the council and start out on long pilgrimages to the high places when so addressed.

I was only a small boy, and so I just cried and ran and cuddled up to my dog and told my dog how hard it was for a little boy to have such a great man for an uncle. And my dog understood and licked my face all over, and especially my ears.

Presently my uncle came to me and inquired if my ears were now clean enough to listen with, and did I still wish to be a man?

I said, Oh yes, I did.

My uncle said that since I was such a little boy he would help me a little more. So I should tell him again what it was that the brush dance wand was. This time I told him that it was the wand which one wore in his headdress on the last night of the brush dance for the final curing of a sickness in the person for whom the dance was being held.

My uncle smiled and said that that was a little better, but what was the brush dance really all about anyway? I said that it was to drive out the evil spirits which were making the person sick. Uncle looked at me and shook his head. He said, "You sound like a superstitious old woman. I shall be kind to you this time and tell you all about it."

So he spoke: "When a person is sick of a sickness which people cannot see, it is then that for that person we hold a brush dance. In the brush dance we sing fun songs and make jokes to let that person know that there is fun in the world. While everyone dances around the sick person, the doctor talks to the patient about what it is that troubles him. When that person sees that he is surrounded by friends who are singing happy songs to make him feel better, then he feels that it is that people care for him. He feels safe and tells the doctor what it is that bothers him, and the doctor tells the patient what he can do about his troubles.

"On the last night of the dance everyone brings out their very best costumes. These costumes represent hundreds of hours of very careful work. They are made of the rarest and most difficult to obtain materials. They have been kept in absolutely perfect condition. Never does a costume ever show any wear or that it has been used before. Everything is perfect. These costumes are the most beautiful things that an Indian can make. Thus when one dances before the sick person in this costume it means that the dancer has cared enough for the patient to go to all of that trouble in the hope that he can help the patient.

"Now. How could I respect myself if I only went halfway, or three quarters of the way to help someone? If I'm not going to help all of the way, it is better that I don't go to that dance at all. So when I make a brush dance the patient knows that I am all of the way for him. Then he feels reassured and will quite likely get well.

259

"This is what the brush dance wands represent. This is the way to be true to yourself. Now let us see if you can think like a man the next time we have a question."

Then it was that I saw that the law was not quite as simple as it appeared. Thus it was that I realized that to be a man meant to be proud to yourself in everything; you could never be less than all of yourself without breaking the law.

When I finally understood what a person who entered a brush dance was doing, I then wanted to know just what the dance meant. Why it was danced the way it was danced. I asked why the dancers did not all dance up and down in unison.

This is what my uncle said: "The dancers do not all go up and down together because the world is like a canoe. If everyone leans to one side of the boat together, and to the other side together, they rock the boat and pretty soon it turns over."

I asked what the solo dancers were doing when they jumped in the middle and acted so strangely. He said, "Don't you remember the story of how, when the world was reborn, creation appointed the giant woodpecker to go around the world and report to him how things were going? So in this dance men who have pure spirit jump in the middle and jerk their heads back and forth like a woodpecker and spread their arms and fly around and sing the woodpecker song and everyone wears woodpecker scalps and heads. This is to remind the great woodpecker spirit that there is someone who is sick and he should go and report it to Creation so that Creation will lend his strength to the doctor so that the sick person or child can get well."

Brer Rabbit Speaks

By C. A. Parsons

Briar meeting

...So here's Brer Rabbit a-settin' in his hole by the log fire hoping for some of the rain and thinking about the Briars...

Lots of planning--the Network held two meetings this winter. One to discuss the coming year and what was wanted for activities and services in '77. The other was to ponder the future of <u>The Briarpatch Review</u>.

Maybe their should be a word about how we hold a Briarpatch meeting. Briars don't seem to like meetings much. We've all done that and it wasn't much fun. So, when the time comes for input from the network, a random sample is run on Mike's trusty calculator and fifteen or so Briars are invited to convene and consider a topic. The lively exchanges and thoughtful diverse perspectives provide ample direction for continuing the flow. (The compensations of a hot tub, a handsome fire, and apple pie with honey ice cream ain't bad, either)

The local Network is feeling the pressure of 180 member businesses, and, even with two coordinators, a resultant loss of personal contact. The old way would be to organize but we want to remain a network, not an organization. There seems to be a fundamental and subtle difference there.

From the first gathering, the answer came through loud and clear, "more parties!" Since this is where most networking gets done, five businesses around the Bay Area with facilities large enough to hold our growing numbers were selected and we'll invite a few similarly oriented enterprises within the Network to display and demonstrate their wares to promote more inter-understanding of what we're doing. That should get things jumpin' in fine fashion in the next few months.

Also, "more coordination" was mentioned. By that was meant the creation of projects for the Network so Briars who want to can more fully participate in the functions of our community. The upcoming production of the new cross-referenced edition of the Briarpatch Network Directory is an example of a project which needs more hands.

A couple of weeks later another random sample came together and considered the timely tome you are now perusing. The Briarpatch Review has been produced totally by volunteers for over two years and the energy is beginning to stretch a little thin. It was felt that a more viable direction and the maintenance of the quality and the unique perspective of the Review could be achieved by expanding and increasing the effectiveness of our distribution operation, generating a sufficient income to pay a staff (initially an editor and a distribution manager). Another suggestion was to ask readers to donate their copies when they are finished with them to their local libraries as they are a good source of sustaining subscriptions. Also, the question of advertising in the Review by Briarpatch Network businesses was discussed. No decisions were made and we're open to the comments of all Briars, if you are in the Network or not. (Which is why it got writ here.)

...So here's Brer Rabbit rarin' back on his haunches thinkin', "That oughta stir the pot", and thinking about the Networking going on (call Charles Albert on Mondays and Tuesdays, and Bahauddin (formerly Andy) on Thursdays and Fridays at 731-8743 and 647-1120 respectively) and the consulting with Network businesses on Wednesdays when those two rascals and their stalwart compatriot, Michael Phillips jump into the patch to play with their friends...and he blows out the lamp and pokes the coals and...

262

Fun In Business

By Kristen Anundsen & Michael Phillips

Historically, in cultures not so specialized as ours, fun has been an important part of the business scene. Even now, in some parts of Africa, among the thousands of people in the marketplace are clowns, jugglers, singers, and comedians. The marketplace is one place to come for fun.

In the Briarpatch, this tradition has survived--or resurfaced. Briars take a wholistic approach to Right Livelihood. They want to integrate their lives so that all the necessary elements of living áre part of their business as well as non-business activities. Naturally, one of those necessary elements is fun, so fun is integrated into business.

Another reason fun is so important is that it is part of the way we learn. Games are models of the world; They allow us to look at ourselves from new perspectives. They let us express ourselves in new ways. We can get excited and we can let our emotions escape in harmless and enjoyable ways. Fun is part of the Briarpatch art.

Sometimes fun is added to daily work activities. The CoEvolution Quarterly, for example, has a volleyball court next to its office building, and everyone takes volley ball breaks during the day. At the San Francisco Roommate Referral Service, run by Oz Koosed, so much fun has been added that it now characterizes the business. Roommate Referral could be a rather somber business, since its clients are people who are making a transition in their lives and come in with a certain amount of anxiety. They fill out forms indicating what kind of roommate they are looking for and poring through other forms to see if they can find a match. There is no particular reason to communicate in a lighthearted manner... no reason except for Oz himself. He has added games

263

and gimmicks designed to
startle people out of their
blahs. Sometimes he turns
his chair around and a firecracker goes off. If there
is no response from the client, a rubber chicken
may fall from the ceiling
or a set of teeth may
go clacking across the desk.
Oz and his cohort Gary
Warne, whose Circus of the
Soul Used Book Store used
to share a storefront with
Oz's business, even ad-
vertised "a free room or
a free book if you can make
us laugh." Gary also gave
extra books to anyone who
came into the store in costume. Their storefront
was a sort of drop-in-
center with "work" hours
not separated from "fun"
hours.

One reason Briar busi-
nesses can incorporate fun
so easily is their choice of
location. Briars tend to
have their own storefronts
or service centers rather
than being holed up in big
downtown office buildings
where behavior codes influence the way people express
themselves. Another reason
fun is possible is the pace
of Briarpatch businesses.

It's a very human pace most
of the time. People who run
the businesses take time to
talk to clients and customers because they want to--
that's what turns them on
about being in business.
If you take "making a lot
of money" off the list of
reasons for being in business you can pretty eas-
ily replace it with "fun,"
since you then have time to
enjoy yourself by interacting
with others.

When Andy Alpine, Charles
Albert Parsons and Mike Phillips visit Briarpatch businesses to offer financial advice, they arrange to have
some fun in the process. This
is easy to manage because some
of the businesses are in the
"enjoyment business" themselves. If the business is a
sauna shop, the proprietors
and the financial consul-
tants chat in the sauna. Trying out biofeedback devices
was part of another consulting
visit. Some Briar busi-
nesses have hot tubs on the
premises, which have led to
some very relaxed conversations.

Quite a few Briars have built their businesses around their own personal concept of fun. For example, the Down Depot is a family business that centers around one of the family's favorite hobbies: camping. The business was set up to clean parkas and sleeping bags (a whole new industry) and also to sell sporting accessories. The father has another major interest -- theatre -- so he has expanded the business to include that interest too. He picks up costumes from the theaters at night after the plays are over and delivers them, cleaned, the next day. The New Games Foundation, another Briarpatch organization, has developed (as its name suggests) new games; these are noncompetitive and encourage everyone's personal development. Briarpatch members participate in New Games tournaments, which spreads the fun.

The Pickle Family Circus is entirely in the fun business. A small traveling circus with clowns, musicians, trapeze artists, and so forth, the group works closely with its audiences and puts on performances cooperatively with community groups. It is a joy to have them in the Briarpatch.

When two Briar businesses get together to have some fun, the result can be marvelous. one such happy combination involved F.R.A.P., which makes acoustical pickups (the kind used on guitars so you don't need a microphone) which can pick up an enormous range of frequencies; and Music Works, a publication that contains music-related articles, cartoons, and listings of musical jobs and teachers in the Bay Area. The first cover of Music Works showed a picture of a Venusian (that is, a resident of Venus) "playing" the Golden Gate Bridge as though it were a harp. Inspired by this cover and using a device from F.R.A.P., a group of Briars went out to the Bridge at 2 o'clock one morning and connected pickups to the Bridge's cables. They then pounded on the cables and played them like harpstrings. The tape that resulted from this venture has been played on local radio stations and has received publicity that benefited both businesses.

Throughout the Patch, the businesses generally try to keep a light tone. Often this is reflected in their names: Raskinflakkers (an ice creamery); Sacred Grounds Coffee Home; Jersey Devil (architects who build unusual houses); Family Light Music School; C.O.Y.O.T.E. (a prostitutes' organization whose name is an acronym for "Call Off Your Old Tired Ethics" --all kinds of outcasts are part of the Briarpatch).

The Briarpatch Network itself reflects this light tone. There are no formal meetings and few serious events--almost all network get-togethers are parties, which are held on Mardi Gras, Halloween, Father's Day, and other occasions of celebration and joy. Even at Network-sponsored classes there is likely to be some Sufi dancing or other form of lighthearted play.

In the Briarpatch, business and learning about business can be full of excitement and pleasure. It is possible to work, create, produce, and enjoy yourself at the same time.

I was very interested to read in your latest issue about the personal book ordering service. I, too, have decided to go, in a very small and somewhat different way, into the bookselling business. Here's the story:

A friend of mine told me that in October he searched hard through both New York and Los Angeles trying to find a copy of my latest book, Instead of Education. No luck. The manager of one bookstore, on hearing that the book had come out about six months earlier, said with some surprise that, except for a few runaway best-sellers, they would never stock a book that old. So there it is. Publishers bring out, two or three times a year, a huge list of books. They dump them in the stores and wait to see which ones will turn up lucky. These, they push hard; their salesmen plug them, they give them follow-up advertising, make publicity efforts for them. The others, they let go. If by good luck they have been able to sell the paperback rights, as was the case with my book, they figure that they have gotten their money out of the book and don't need to worry about it. If they have not sold the paperback rights, they figure that there is no use throwing good money after bad, and let the book go. In neither case do they ever pay it any further attention.

For someone who has made it, and wants to continue to make it, his chief work to write serious books, this is very discouraging news. But I think something can be done about it. In any case, I am going to try to do something about it, following Ivan Illich's maxim that if an institution stops working for you, you should not waste time trying to make it into something very different, but think about doing without it.

More specifically, I have decided to try to sell my own books - and, along with them, the books of a few other people. My plan is to make this known, not only in letters, conversations, and in my lectures, but also with a number of very small and selected advertisements in exactly the kind of out-of-the way publications that people are likely to read who might be interested in my books, and that the big publishers would never think of advertising in. I can get the books at a discount from my publishers, and will sell them at something under list price, so that people can get them cheaper from me than they could in the stores, even if they could find them in the stores. Along with my own books, I would like to try to sell a very small number of books by other people, some of them about children, learning, schools, education, some about other topics, but all books that I feel strongly about, and that do not seem to me to be getting enough exposure. In this way I hope to make good books better known and available to more people, to keep at least some of them alive when they might otherwise have died.

If people want to find out what other books they can get from me, they can do so my sending me a self-addressed envelope.

John Holt
308 Boylston St.
Boston, Mass. 02116

We are a group of people in Mendocino County, California, forming a birth center where mothers and fathers will have the opportunity of giving birth to their children with competent medical care and in a manner that is harmonious with their understandings and lifestyles. We need a doctor to associate with us. We have the facility, energy, and love, and there are now many among us who are pregnantly waiting for a doctor to complete the whole in our birth center. If you are an interested doctor, or can put us in touch with one, please write us.

Esther Post
Birth Center
P. O. Box 547
Ukiah, CA 95482

The Fall, 1976, issue just arrived and I'm wondering a few things as I digest it.

First off, I approve totally of the idea of the Briarpatch and networking and sharing and letting us all in on how it's being done and who's doing it.

That brings me to Wonder #1 - maybe I've been in the woods too long (two years) but I wonder why a man with two kids needs $20,000-$25,000 per year and with that kind of income is he a Briar? How can the basics cost that much - and isn't the rest going to support this idiotic consumer monster we're all supposed to be wanting to get rid of?

Wonder #2 - How can the good
doctor justify his $60 per hour
fee? Are his books open so I
can see why he should charge
that much? Does a homeopathic
doctor need the fancy office
and medical layout a regular
MD does? Who can afford him -
only wage slaves who are kill-
ing themselves getting money
to pay fees like that - and
where's that at?
        My idea of a good Briar-
patch enterprise is "Rain" in
Portland (2270 N.W. Irving,
97210). And all Briars should
read Tom Bender's "Living
Lightly" (get it from "Rain,"
$1.50) and his "Sharing
Smaller Pies," $1.50, from
"Rain."

Marjorie C. Posner
Route 3, Box 49
Alsea, OR 97324

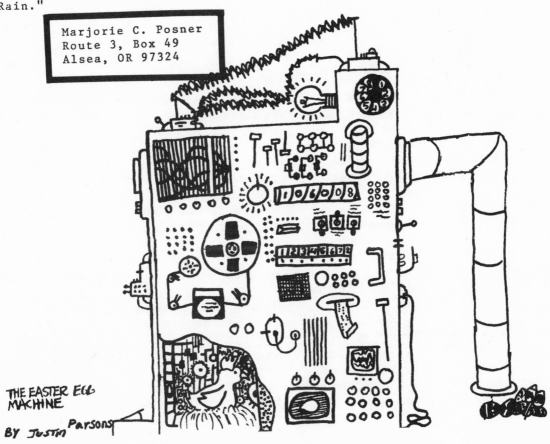

THE EASTER EGG
MACHINE

BY JUSTIN PARSONS

By Marc, Linda, Mitch, and Sully

NOTICE

THE THIRD NEW ENGLAND RIGHT LIVELIHOOD BUSINESS NETWORK CONFERENCE

April 15, 16, 17, 1977

Business is commerce; it is the flow of material energies between people. Business is an external symbol of the flow of emotional and spiritual energies of a society. Business is stewardship of the resources of earth. Business and money are a means of working with the energy of earth to make a transformation from the old ways of working for greater and greater profit-productivity, to the new ways of working for more ecologically sane products and more humane work process. This transformation occurs thru the values we seek to cultivate: honesty, fairness, compassion, and understanding. The more we enhance these values in ourselves, the more these energies grow in our business and the world.

Hello--This is a call to people who are involved in business to come together to meet each other, to learn how to do business as a service and as spiritual growth, and to have a good time and to develop a network of businesses in New England.

Our approach to the business network is through right livelihood. Right livelihood is a way of living which sees work as: 1) a process of refining oneself thru the discipline of creative labor; 2) a way of transcending one's own ego thru participating in a work greater than one's own self; and 3) a service to family, community, society, and planet--a manifestation of love in action.

Right livelihood sees this process of refining oneself and of manifesting love in service as going hand in hand with supporting one's own needs in the material world. We say needs here, not unlimited desire, because we are interested in simple living. Simple in the sense of balance and harmony with our natural environment, with our social-political environment, and with ourselves.

We see that business is a process of learning about ourselves and the world. Business brings us into touch with many varied peoples and this teaches us about the many parts of the one body which is human.

270

What is Right Livelihood:

Small groups on, What is right livelihood? What is a spiritual/political perspective on business? What are the values/definitions we are striving toward?

These workshops are the foundation of the conference. To give the schedule fullness and vitality, we ask you to lead a workshop on some aspect of business you would like to share. If you'd like to offer a workshop or other activity, write us a title and a short description on the registration form.

Another whole section of the conference will be devoted to developing a New England network of right livelihood businesses. We see this network as a community of people with common values...a community which extends over spacial boundaries. The network is a new form of social organization which gives each individual within it the gift of autonomy and responsibility, and a sense of being connected to a human evolution larger than just yourself.

The format of the gathering will be two days of workshops, shared meals, spring walks in open air, volleyball, and generally relaxing and getting to know each other. We will also be working on developing a business network strategy for New England

This is a third in a series of quarterly business conferences to develop this network. At previous conferences we have established the following purposes for our network:

1) To continue organizing the New England Regional Right Livelihood Conferences.
2) To develop networks in local areas throughout New England and New York State.
3) To develop an access journal for products, services, and jobs in New England which coincide with our values, and to develop this listing into an access catalog, which will then be distributed to the general public.
4) To develop analyses and visions to stimulate growth of the New England Right Livelihood Network.
5) To support each other in striving for honesty and fairness and wholeness as people-- to aid each other in general values clarification.
6) To trade services of accounting, financial planning, creative problem solving, group process, etc.
7) To encourage people to get into business and to help them in doing it.
8) To develop an educational outreach about right livelihood and our growth, to do this through media work, speaking, and direct teaching.
9) To develop a credit union.
10) To develop health care plans

which involve wholistic approaches to medicine.

11) To form arts cooperatives, building cooperatives, crafts cooperatives, etc.

12) To get together a travelling bus-fair-conference, to spread the word.

13) To connect up with other networks throughout New England such as the Community Network, the Social Healing Network, the Alternative Education Network, the Appropriate Technology and Alternative Energy Network.

14) To connect up with other networks nationally such as the Briarpatch Network (another business network) in California.

Our priorities for the immediate future are the first five on the list. Write us your ideas on these...

This gathering is being focalized through the energies of four friends: Marc from Another Place, Linda from Another Place and American Friends Service Committee, Mitch from an Amherst print works, and Sully from Earth Architecture in Amherst. Our intention is to involve all of our talents and skills in a synergy.

The cost of the gathering is based on a sliding scale of $20-60.

The breakdown of this fee is: 2/3 to Another Place for maintenance of the center, 1/6 for conference organizing costs, 1/6 for food. There will be a limited number of scholarships.

The gathering is being held at Another Place in Greenville, New Hampshire. Another Place is a center for growing networks to meet together, a center for quiet time and retreat, and a place for people being together in a clear open space. One of the goals of Another Place is to develop commonunity within groups and between them. The center is a non-profit business run by cooperative principles. The main shelter of the center is a big old farmhouse, set on 70 acres of land on top of a hill. There is space for 50 people in the house.

The gathering will begin Friday evening and run until Sunday afternoon. There will be dinner Friday evening for those of you who can make it early enough...See you then.

Thankyou

Marc, Linda, Mitch and Sully, and the rest of the family... c/o Another Place, Route 123, Greenville, New Hampshire 03048 (603) 878-1510, (603) 878-9883.

This issue of the Briarpatch Review was put together by Briars playing together. Some were Briars who are in the graphics field, others were apprenticing. We all had lots of fun. If you are a Briar who has always wanted to play in graphics, or a graphic artist looking for a busman's holiday, contact us and join in on the next issue. We can use you and you can use us.

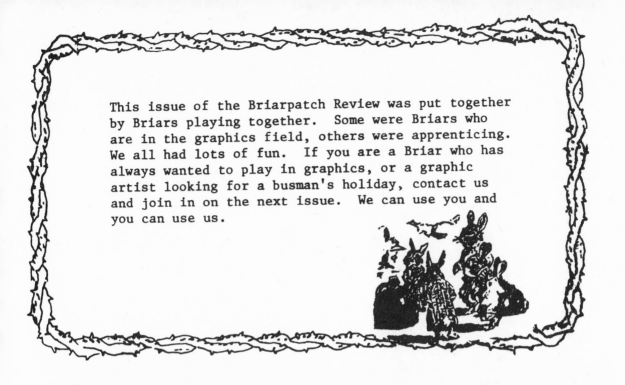

Distribution

Our distributors in the Bay Area are Serendipity Couriers and the Whole Earth Access Company. Bahaudin drops off copies of the Review when he visits Briarpatch stores in the Bay Area, and other Briars distribute copies in likely places.

Stores in other parts of the country order ten or more copies at our standard discount of 50%. If you know stores you think would be interested, we'd be glad to send you postage paid, ten or more copies for 50¢ each. Send payment with orders to: Briarpatch Review, 330 Ellis Street, San Francisco 94102, or call (415) 928-3960.

Costs

2,300 copies printed

Printing and production:	$ 570.01
Mailing:	66.98
Office expenses:	49.65
Miscellaneous:	40.00
	$ 726.64

Income since Fall issue:	$ 815.39

All labor donated.

BRIARPATCH REVIEW

What Is The Briarpatch   Carole Rae   Sisisote
Toy Go Round   You Start With A Vision
Notes From The Network

Table of Contents

This issue was put together by Aryea Coopersmith, Tom Hargadon, Greg Hastings, Deon Kaner, Diane Keenan, Phil Flotow, Chris Popp, Beverly Muir.

Art and Photo Credits by:

Cover drawing by Laverne Bowie of Sisisote.
Drawings by Greg Hastings, Kathleen Roberts, Amara and Deon Kaner, Justin Parsons, Michael Phillips, Carole Rae and Others.

The Briarpatch Review is a journal of the Briarpatch Network: a group of people interested in simple living, openness, sharing, and learning how the world works through business. It is published every three months at 330 Ellis Street, San Francisco, CA 94102; Tel. (415) 928-3960. Subscription rates are $5 per year (add $2 outside U.S.); supporting membership $25. Single issues and back copies are $1.25 postpaid. We welcome feedback and stories about your own Briarpatch.

You Start With A Vision

by Kristin Anundsen

In 1968, on an airplane returning to California from a distant land (Japan), Marion Saltman had a vision of her future in the world of work. She had spent a lot of time at Esalen Institute, so Esalen was the setting of her vision. "I saw a group of 30 or 40 people with various group leaders doing their processes. I thought, if I were called on to lead something, what would I do? Then I saw all these people in an early-education childhood setting; I saw them with blocks, finger paints, dress-up clothes, clay, rhythm instruments, bubbles and streamers."

That vision led her to a career in play therapy for adults. She had already done play therapy and exercises with children while running a parent cooperative pre-school and she had learned a great deal about play from having grown up with her two daughters (she's not a grandmother). She is firmly convinced that play is as important as any other kind of developmental process--and that when it is ignored, development becomes unbalanced.

"Our culture has deliberately emphasized the left hemisphere of the brain--the rational part--and has dismissed the right-hemisphere functions like creativity, daydreaming, and socialization as irrelevant," says Marion. "The Three R's are basic and necessary but when you focus only on these you become almost 'braindamaged.'"

The vision of a program to help "balance" those adults whose right hemispheres have been neglected was the first step. What remained was to actualize the vision. "That's what the Briarpatch is all about," says Marion--"giving form to your visions." During the last several years she has learned some basic ingredients for vision transformation, which she wants to share with fellow Briars.

FUN ON THE FERRYBOAT

She has also done play therapy in hospitals and run groups in her home. That home itself epitomizes Marion's own playfulness. It's an old ferryboat-converted-into-houseboat in Sausalito--the boat where Alan Watts and the artist Varda used to live. The first thing you see when you walk in the door is a swing hanging from the ceiling, and more often than not, Marion is swinging on it. The houseboat is full of toys and play-

things. It's hard to resist playing with them, but then you don't have to resist because Marion is more than willing to share her play experiences. She's a perfect illustration of the Briarpatch concept of fun as an integral part of work and life.

The first thing you need, she says, is will. "You must be both willing and determined to do it. That means you have to be willing to give up certain things that would get in your way--to lighten your pack."

The second ingredient is imagination. "Let the vision manifest itself. See the whole thing happening, with yourself in the picture. My experience on the plane involved a picture like that. You can make a conscious effort to see what you really want to do and how to do it."

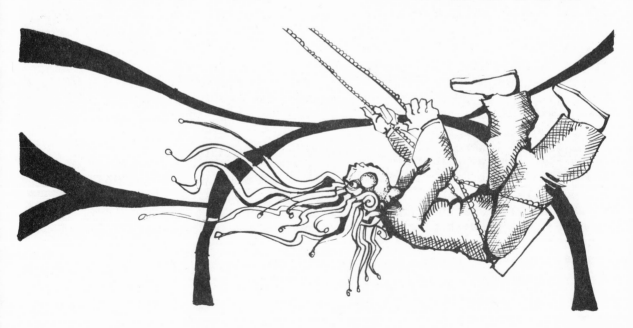

Third, you need <u>faith</u>, which Marion says is a sort of connection between the vision and the self-and-universe. "Faith is something that tells you there's no doubt that this thing is going to happen. It becomes a guiding force as well as your connection with your inner self, your source. You have to allow this faith to be your guide--to get out of the way of yourself. This involves taking some risks."

Finally, Marion says, you need a "<u>flair for secrecy</u>." She doesn't mean the kind of secrecy practiced by governments and the shadier segments of big business. "Just shut up and do it," she explains. "You can get lost talking to a lot of people about your plans, and finally the vision is gone. Everyone will have their two cents to put in or they'll tell you why it can't be done. When I used to try to explain what I wanted to do, people would say, 'Oh well, that's all very nice, but <u>practically speaking</u> it isn't possible.' It becomes irritating to have to defend your vision, so it's better to just go ahead quietly."

<u>DOING IT</u>

Armed with will, imagination, and faith, and working on developing a flair for secrecy, Marion set out to <u>do it</u>.

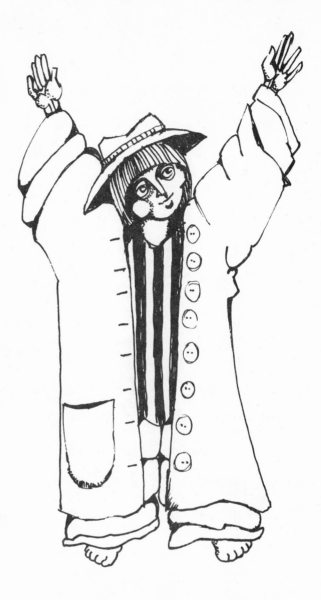

The first thing she needed, she decided, was blocks, so she looked in the phone book for "Playskool," a company that makes blocks for children. On the way to the "Playskool" listing, she came upon "Play-Mates Cooperative." "This was the same name as the

cooperative preschool I had been running in Los Angeles, so I thought 'This is cosmic.' I called the school and spoke to one of the teachers. When I explained that I wanted blocks so that grownups could play with them, she said, 'That sounds interesting-- why don't you come over?' I went right over and we hit it off. She said she'd let me use the preschool building for my work."

Next Marion needed people to participate in her program. She asked one of her daughter's teachers at San Francisco State

if his class would parti-
cipate. He invited her to
come and talk to the class,
which she did; she ended up
teaching a six-week, three-
hour-per-session class for
college students in a pre-
school setting.

She is still teaching in
the recreation department of
San Francisco State. "One
thing I always wanted to do
was teach in a university,"
she says. "I think it's interesting that it's the Department of Recreation--
Re-creation."

Doing it has involved
putting together a paper on
the concept of play therapy.
"No one understood what I
was talking about before but
the paper explained it, and it
was good for me to go through
the process of doing that
paper," she says. She uses
her contacts at San Francisco
State and various professional
organizations to bring her
more of the work she loves,
and she also gathers in
friends and colleagues who
help her out of love for her
and for fun--"This is not
a one-woman show." In 1971,
she founded the Lila Center
for Creative Play, to which
her friends Michael Shane,
Kathleen Roberts and Paul Rich
now contribute their talents.
Their newest venture is Sun-
Ray Camp in Mendocino County,
where adults (and children--
but primarily adults, singly

or in groups) can recapture
the joy of summer playtime.

The vision is operating
on schedule now...except for
the money part. "The trouble
is that play therapy is light
and beautiful and easy, and
people like to pay for things
that are painful and difficult,"
Marion explains ruefully. "I
must admit that I'm tired of
being hungry doing this.
Right livelihood should include
making a livelihood. That's
the part that needs to come
together now."

What she hopes to do soon
is get funding for an education
project--a "Method" or plan
(corresponding to the Dewey or
Montessori Method) for schools.
"I've come full circle--back
to education for children."
Her Method will emphasize the
balance between the left and
right brain hemispheres. With
the funding she will set up
a teaching program for teachers,
parents, and kids--incorporating
casettes, video materials, and
manuals. She is already filling
in the outlines of this new
vision in her mind.

282

Toy Go Round

by Andora Freeman and Joy Ernst

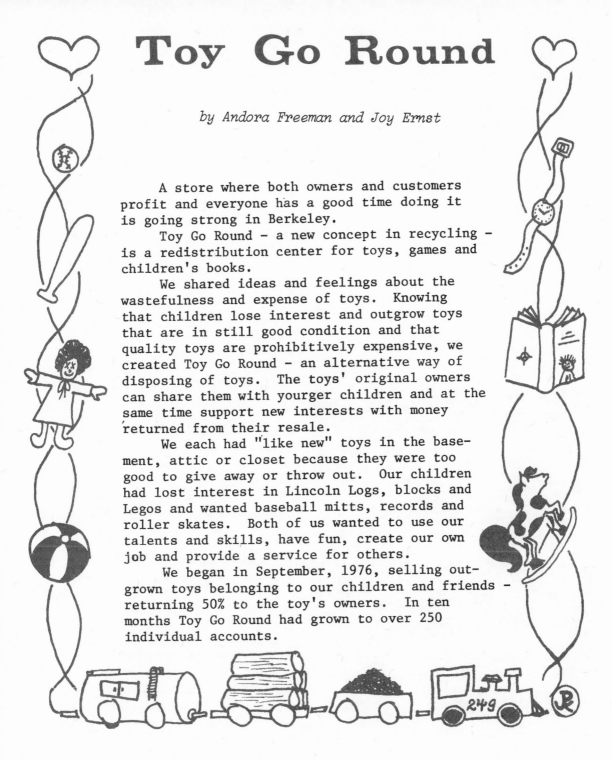

A store where both owners and customers profit and everyone has a good time doing it is going strong in Berkeley.

Toy Go Round - a new concept in recycling - is a redistribution center for toys, games and children's books.

We shared ideas and feelings about the wastefulness and expense of toys. Knowing that children lose interest and outgrow toys that are in still good condition and that quality toys are prohibitively expensive, we created Toy Go Round - an alternative way of disposing of toys. The toys' original owners can share them with yourger children and at the same time support new interests with money returned from their resale.

We each had "like new" toys in the basement, attic or closet because they were too good to give away or throw out. Our children had lost interest in Lincoln Logs, blocks and Legos and wanted baseball mitts, records and roller skates. Both of us wanted to use our talents and skills, have fun, create our own job and provide a service for others.

We began in September, 1976, selling outgrown toys belonging to our children and friends - returning 50% to the toy's owners. In ten months Toy Go Round had grown to over 250 individual accounts.

People bring in out-grown toys, books and games on consignment and receive 50% share upon their sale. Checks are available the first of each month for all items sold the previous month.

Everyone really seems to enjoy coming in to shop and visit because they know everything bolongs to someone and this creates a real feeling of sharing.

Children with their own accounts often return to make a purchase and to see what they have sold and what toys with their code number remains on the shelves for someone else to buy and enjoy.

We have done much research on prices and pricing, quality and availability. If a toy comes in "like new", we check to see what a reasonably priced store is selling the new one for, then we automatically discount it 30%. We have many catalogs and price lists to use as guides. One of our goals is to create an outlet for unwanted or out-grown toys and a place to buy toys at greatly reduced prices. We estimate our prices on toys to be sold by their condition and play value. For example, a cobblers bench might be nicked and dented and appear "well loved" but if the pegs and hammer are intact, it still has good play value.

Our ideas and skills are very compatible; we scrub, repair, improvise many - a tail, ear or wheel, make missing pieces to wooden puzzles with a jig saw and "try" to give others advice with their "problem" or "sick" toys.

When games arrive with missing pieces, we code them, set them aside to wait for another to arrive. Then we combine pieces, and both accounts receive credit. We match up toys to make complete sets. Some of our toys have returned for a second and third round.

Grandparents are frequent shoppers for "visiting"

grandchildren. They pur-
chase items for the duration
of the visit, then recycle
those same toys and others!

Toy Go Round assists in
fund-raising for schools,
nursery schools and play-
groups. They collect and
bring in toys in the group's
name and receive the 50% upon
their sale. They are able to
also buy toys and supplies
from us economically. By
working together, high quality
outgrown toys are available
to all children at lower
prices.

Our bulletin board, one
whole wall, is overflowing
with wanteds, for sales, play-
groups, schools and community
activities for children.

Both of us, as parents
and teachers, have looked for
places to purchase unique and
inexpensive arts and crafts
materials. We have assembled
an "arts and crafts" corner.
It keeps growing as ideas and
materials come forth. Collage
materials, homemade playdough,
paint cakes for finger and
brush painting, colored
macaroni shapes for stringing
and gluing, and sidewalk chalk
for murals or games are available at all times. We have
woodscraps, large headed
pounding nails and scrap
craft paper of varied size,
color and texture. Burlap
and yarn for stitchery and
wire bundles for creating
sculptures are popular items.

Recycled computer paper and
cards are sold by the bundle
for 10¢ and 5¢. Unique craft
packs and new parent re-
sources for creative activities change with the seasons
and with the availability of
supplies.

Toy Go Round welcomes
handcrafted toys and games
giving 75% to the craft person.
Personalized birthday banners
are made upon request - an
alternative to the usual
birthday card.

Both of us feel that the responsibility for nurturing still falls primarily on the parent. Often we parents find ourselves settling for toys with limited play value, because quality toys are costly. And making a homemade toy or art activity can be expensive as well as time consuming when resources are scattered. We hope the Toy Go Round meets these needs for parents.

One of our major goals is to create the happy blend of providing a place for people to find a good value when shopping but to let the person leaving the items on consignment receive a fair share for their initial investment. This share can be used to provide an on going creative play environment for their own children.

Toy Go Round is geared to save money and resources and promote a climate of recycling. We want to save resources by sharing toys with today's and tomorrows' children.

You are always welcome to stop by for a visit. You'll find us at 1715-B Solano Avenue in Berkeley - Tuesday, Thursday, Saturday, 12:00 - 5:30.

286

SISISOTE

Sisisote* (see see so tā), a Kiswahili word meaning "all of us," connotes the real energy and spirit of this design collective specializing in hand-printed textiles. These designs tell stories, state feelings, and convey visual messages and pleasures. These designs reflect the creative spirits of those whose wells of inspiration are rooted in the vast beauty of Africa. The incredible magnitude of Black Art, as well as the sensitive and often serene enclaves of the naturalistic ecstacy of North America, also serve as moving forces in the expression of our work.

Through the visual translation of ideas and feelings, Sisisote seeks to communicate with all our senses. Each expression is a visual treat that oftentimes solves a riddle or creates a visual poem. Sisisote designs adorn book jackets and exhibit frequently at Bay Area museums, fairs and galleries. You may even see a Sisisote concept

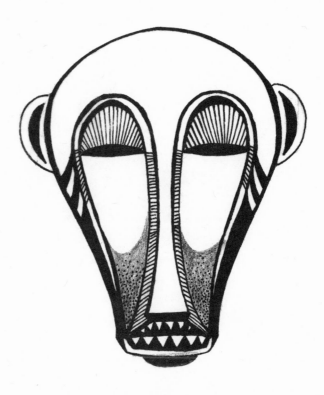

*Kiswahili is a language spoken in many of the eastern and some of the central regions in Africa.

287

regally worn, hanging on the wall of a tastefully deco- rated office, or serving as the linen compliment for a most divinely set table. Our designs can also be seen in scarves, dress-goods, draperies, bed linens and T-shirts. New concepts are always evolving from our creative realm.

Daphne P. Muse
Sisisote Screen Printing Service
4336 San Pablo Ave.
Emeryville, CA 94608
(415) 654-5283

"MOOD MASKS SERIES"

The mask is merely a reflection of whatever "one wants to see"--usually one will see himself...or an attribute thereof.

These three masks are part of a "MOOD SERIES" which are designed to remind you of the "old ones" while refreshing your vision for the "new ones".

As the designer, the circular, encompassing spheres and its serfaces are my personal passport to an "inner self."

"The Yin and Yang of my art form is the sun and moon of my soul."

Nadine Laws
"mood mask" c Sisisote 1977

290

WHAT IS THE BRIARPATCH ?

There's been increased public interest in the Briarpatch recently. Six Briars have offered to answer questions. Here's what they say:

Ann Styron
27 Cottage
Mill Valley, Ca. 94941
(415) 383-5961
Co-ordinator MINT,
Conservation Organization

The Briarpatch is a loose network of friends and businesses who rely on their own instincts and values in living and working. Usually, they choose to make less money instead of more, are honest, open, happy about the work they are involved in; and express themselves directly through their service to the community. Briars recommend each other knowing their values and standards are shared. They get together as a group and individually to share and have fun. They know that even though a business may seem the epitome of "Briarpatch" like a small solar energy research firm, if it is only concerned with making money, no matter what the original intent it is fundamentally no different than Exon. Briarpatch businesses may be small or large, but they all share similar values: openness, sharing, humor, simplicity and service.

For me, being a Briarpatch entrepeneur means expressing myself directly through my work, and I want to be proud of the results of what I do. Its what I enjoy doing the most, feel I'm good at, and gives me the opportunity to help other Briarpatch businesses succeed.

HOWARD

Howard Sutherland
P.O. Box 9061
Berkeley, Ca. 94709
(415) 843-1438
Makes bicycle repair
accessories

It's a loose organization of small businesses and several coordinators who exchange skills, goods, and workspaces.

The financial advice I've gotten from Michael Phillips has meant the difference between staying in business and going under. There were times when I felt I didn't have enough money to keep the business going. We went over the books together and discovered that there was a way to continue. That has meant an enormous amount to me.

I want to make bicycle shops work better. The better the service given by a bicycle shop, the more bikes will be used. The more bikes are used, the healthier people will be. Less pollution, too.

I've worked in several bicycle shops over the years and found they were all having the same daily problems - like what parts fit which bikes, and what length spokes to use when building a wheel, etc. So I put together a Handbook for Bicycle Mechanics. It's the only book that answers the questions shop mechanics and enthusiasts have. I also sell repair tags and other items. I feel I have made a big impact on the bicycle repair industry.

This is a small business, and I'm pretty much an idealist. I'm willing to live on less money in exchange for being able to have an impact on the world I care about.

ANN

Ann Price
1533 MacArthur
Oakland, Ca. 94602
(415) 531-3733
Candle Manufacturer
and Distributor

A method of communication
for people who are in-
terested in beginning a
business or who have been
in business yet have not
had an opportunity to meet
other people to discuss ideas
or innovations or to share
creations or the problems
they're coming up against in
business. I think it is also
an avenue for interconnectedness among people who have
common interests.

In the Briarpatch the common
interests are how we do business, and how we relate our
personal lives to our business.

So far, my relationship with
Briarpatch has been to support it. It's a network that
is beneficial for other small
businesses although, I have
only used the opportunity to
meet people. I'm very sym-
patico to this kind of organization and the effort
put forth by all the people
in the Briarpatch.

TOM

Tom Conlon
2398-4th St.
Berkeley, Ca. 94710
(415) 848-2710
Aeropower manufacturer
of wind generators

Briarpatch is a group of alternative businesses that
have formed a group where
they work with each other and
are inter-related with each
other, helping each other out,

with their experience and
with their contacts. They are
helping small businesses have
a chance at making it, towards
common goals: which are creating high quality products that
we can offer at very fair prices and while we live on modest incomes. We don't sell
something when it's not needed
and not required. We pay attention to how we are growing,
in other words we're trying to
operate as fairly and squarely
with everybody as we can.

We've formed the Briarpatch to
help all of us carry out these
goals. I've been helped quite
a bit by people in the Briarpatch who have given me a very
large degree of advice and as-

sistance in how to keep our
business growing and healthy
and avoiding the pitfalls that
many newcomers into the business world are not aware of
until after they've fallen into them. I've also had quite
a few people in the Briarpatch
contact us who needed our help
on the production of things,
wanting to know how to get
things manufactured/ where products can be obtained and the
kind of things that you ordinarily will find out about
after you'd had experience in
the shop work. (Aeropower
has helped create a whare-
house community made up of the
people who work with them so
that they can live together
and significantly lower the
cost of living for all of the
people involved.)

CAROLE

Carol Rae
151 Potrero
San Francisco, Ca. 94103
(415) 626-8903
Tapestry Weaver

Its a group of people who are
experiencing their own function in a business and also

294

we see ourselves. We learn complete new sets of rules.

As we go along we gradually define who we are as business people rather than switching off and on as we would have to do in a conventional job. The Briarpatch lets us hear other people who are also defining the same thing and we see how they grow; we all support each other in that growth.

LARRY

Larry Needleman
P.O. Box 881
San Rafael, Ca. 94901
(415) 456-7034
Makes Tofu Kits

how their lives function in relationship to that business. There is no separation between who we are and what our businesses are. We're all supporting each other in this process. I used to believe I had to change my creative perceptive attitudes to do business. That is a myth like the separation of your mind and your body; there's no such thing, there's no such separation. Business and personal reality are human growth and tuning into other people who, like ourselves are evolving; using their business as a vehicle. Its really important because

It is a network of people who realize that a lot of what is important in their lives is their relationship with other people who feel that what they do as their livelihood is important to them.

The Briarpatch is an exchange of skills among people with different personalities and experience; as a result, its very valuable to each of us

Why Lower Income?

Michael Phillips

I recently made a statement that completely surprised me. The surprise is that no one to my knowledge had said it before. The statement is: "the most effective thing each of us can do for conservation is to reduce our own income." This statement is a simple truth, a fundamental fact that no one seems to have discussed before.

Briars have been living on "less" for a long time, as many people; and ecology has been a widely discussed subject for six years. Now the fact that the two fit together is emerging. The cartoon on the next page shows in fairly simple terms the economic reality that changing consumption patterns or reducing spending is not a very effective form of conservation. When a person changes their consumption habits, using fewer material goods and more of other peoples services, very little benefit actually happens; the dollar that the person spends on services is spent again more than five times by other people. The first person who earns the dollar and spends it on ser-

because it fills in the gaps when we're trying to do something on our own.

For example, when I was confused and ignorant of certain financial matters I was able to go to Michael Phillips to ask about what was really happening in my business. It's also wonderful to feel that some of the skills that I have developed can help other people who are trying to develop them too. Being used in this way makes me feel as though some of the things that I did in the past weren't done for nothing.

****

vices is only having a small impact because the next five people spend their part of the dollar the way they want. If a person keeps the same income but spends less, which means saving more, then the effect can actually be negative. The reason is that the savings are used by banks, savings and loans etc. to invest in economic growth, then someday the savings are withdrawn, the savings are defferred income which will be used up later (or passed on to heirs to spend.) Reducing income in the first place is the only effective form of conservation.

On the last page is a chart that shows in graphic terms the relationship between income and destruction of the environment. As income goes up more trees are used, more rivers are damed, more asbestos is released in the air; as income goes down more resources are saved.

There are many personal benefits to living on less, and it turns out the environmental benefits are great too. **

THE FIRST YEAR OF ECOLOGY I CHANGED MY SPENDING. MORE SERVICES AND LESS PRODUCTS; I GOT ROLFED, SAW A PSYCHIATRIST AND HIRED A GARDENER.

THE ROLFER, THE PSYCHIATRIST AND THE GARDENER THEN BOUGHT SUMMER HOMES AT LAKE TAHOE

THE SECOND YEAR I SAVED MY MONEY AT CITZENS SAVINGS

THEN I FOUND OUT CITZENS IS THE BIGGEST LENDER ON CONDOMINIUMS AT LAKE TAHOE

THE THIRD YEAR I GAVE THE MONEY I DIDN'T SPEND TO MY CHURCH.

NOW THEY'RE BUILDING A RETIRE-MENT HOME AT LAKE TAHOE

I KNOW WHAT TO DO NOW!

I'M REDUCING MY INCOME

M. Phillyp

The following table shows the relationship between income and the consumption of natural resources. Some of the figures may seem high, but it should be remembered that the average household may only use 300 gallons of water in their home a day, they use water at school where they work, and eight times as much is used to irrigate the food that they eat. This table was prepared by Mint, a conservation organization dedicated to the concept of lower income. Ann Styron is the coordinator and Mint can be contacted at 330 Ellis, San Francisco 94102

CONSERVATION THRU LOWER INCOME

ESTIMATED USAGE OF RESOURCES
PER HOUSEHOLD IN THE UNITED STATES

	Usage per Household at $10,000	Usage per Household at $20,000
Electricity	2,170 Kilowatts per month	4,025 Kilowatts
Petroleum	300 gallons per month	475 gallons
Timber	6 Trees per year	8 Trees
Water (incl. irrigation)	3,300 gallons a day	4,000 gallons
Fertilizer	106 pounds per month	135 pounds
Crab	4.4 pounds per year	5.5 pounds
Shrimp	5.8 pounds per year	8.0
Outboard Motors	One for every Nine households	One for every Five households
Asbestos	4 pounds per year	8½ pounds
Lead	18 pounds	33 pounds

-Based on 1970 U.S. Census.
-Calculations are based on 30 years of data from the U.S. Statistical Abstract.
 In a regression of Y=a+bX where Y is GNP in constant dollars and X is quantities of physical resources "b" is assumed to be the "income effect" for each resource. Each "b" is used as a multiplier in the table of $20,000 households shown above. Table by Michael Phillips June 1977.

Carole Rae

There is a handwoven trail
between the setting moon
and my range of high and
diverse mountains.

Weaving is the thread trail.
It is pulled and tied in knots,
untangled, cut dyed sold,
given away, manipulated,
loved mirrored married
demistified, untied.

Simultaneously, I watch my progress on the trail
through levels of the tapestry; I am also the
eyes observing the boundries and limits I've created;
and the creator capable of manifesting a total
scene change with vast ranges of color and
form. The totality of this vision allows my
conscious progression through each stage.
Weaving is my fundamental center. The tapestry a map of who I am.

When I take time to refill my creative spring I am taken care of with sales and satisfaction. When I am impatient and contracted creativity stops. When I stick my neck out and try new ideas my perception expands on a variety of levels. My Fiber Center business, my art, my daily process is all a continuous weaving.

The principles of right livlihood have been an important centering place as I revolve on spirals of growth and exploration. There is little fear once you realize those principles work wherever you are. The following excerpts from my journals illustrate personal principles of right livlihood and how they have evolved.

California College of Arts & Crafts - 1967

<u>Insist on following immediate creative instincts</u>

My first rug was ripped in critique. "Whats

that bursting sun on the end when classic rugs have straight beginnings and endings?" Me "after beginning to duplicate the sampler an explosive feeling came over me and I had to weave it into the rug." I'm learning to protect my creative process and breathing during criticism. Fall 1968 <u>Take time to gain personal union with your work</u> My marriage today is a choice of lifestyle. Moving to the redwoods will solidify my rythm, dicipline and personal style. "When the voice of the wilderness was in us we were able to hear the voice of ourselves" R. Yelland Spring 1969 <u>All levels of your progression are equally important</u> Death & rebirth-as the flower of the week blooms everywhere and disappears. I am the firecracker lilly spinning on river deck reeling in this weeks yarn orders. Self sufficiency is measured in piles of snow peas to trade with the community we are creating.

Winter 1971 <u>Dicipline</u> of <u>Daily Practice Creates Strength</u> Weaving sixty pillows in nine days pushes me beyond all preconceptions of colors and design. My sense of duty and dicipline in this rain forest is my own moral test. Survival of body – preservation of spirit is my reality.

Spring 1973 <u>Gracefully let go as growth ceases believing your skills will recreate the next stage</u> message from bird: And furthermore take this dictation from the new wing that encircles you. I'm flying through you not stopping at point where your blue vision ends, but continuing to spiral and lead you beyond this perception. Weave wings fly out of your homespun Wilderness Road to tapestry weaver in the city.

Fall 1974 I dropped last names of husband & father. Carole Rae weaver, mother, self directing super female just sold half of my first tapestry show at two hour opening. My sense of isolation right in the middle of the city is overwhelming.

August 1975 **Frustration is the beginning of rebirth.** My arms are full of disease preventative shots for escape to India and I can't escape. I need a transformation to create self value and sense of secure home right here right now!

October 1975 **Jump in. Whats important is the depth of your personal experience.** I want to interact, and serve people who respond to my work. It took three days to visualize the space where this interaction is possible. The Design Center will build me a showroom, collect a percentage, and I'll learn to do business. Vulnerability and ecstasy are closely connected.

Right now learn to balance serve & soar

Retaining my creative vitality and functioning as director of Fiber Center is a continual dance of balance. I need challenges and security simultaneously. I'm learning that self responsibility means respecting my limitations and being protective of my human rights. I have to sift through my responsibilities and devote time to those parts most valuable to the life I enjoy. Interaction with clients and weavers, experimentation with my work, and the sense of service are worth cultivating. Believing that the passion of this work will nourish me in all ways keeps the process alive. My next change is to let parts of Fiber Center go and experience a greater creative freedom.

Notes From The Network

by Charles Albert and Baha-uddin

Brer Rabbit gets lots of invitations for conferences and workshops. Most of the time s/he prefers to stay in his burrow. However, on the weekend of June 3-5, s/he attended a conference at the S.F. Zen Center's Green Gulch Farm (Briarpatch Members) in Muir Beach, entitled "Business and Right Livelihood" and attended by thirty invitees from around the States and Canada. During the three days and nights, a great deal of networking occurred amongst the entrepeneurs and social scientists there. Here's some of what we learned from each of the participants.

<u>Gar Alpervotiz</u> (Exploratory Project for Economic Alternatives, Washington, D.C.) The sky is falling and we are going up an escalator that is moving down faster than we're progressing.

<u>Marsha Angus</u> (Therapist) Therapists <u>do</u> get out of their heads and into their hearts.

<u>Richard Baker Roshi</u> (Zen Abbot) Right Livelihood's part in the Eight Fold Path of right speech, right attitude, etc.

<u>Tom Bender & Lane deMoll</u> (Rain Magazine) How a national magazine can come out of the back woods of Oregon.

<u>John Biersdorf</u> (Institute for Advanced Pastoral Studies, Michigan) How a clergyman can enter the growth movement and maintain a religious perspective.

<u>Porter Briggs</u> (Consultant to trade Associations, Little Rock, Arkansas) How a person can serve his community through real estate, experience right livelihood and make a lot of money.

<u>Scott Burns</u> (syndicated columnist, Massachusetts) The labor intensive street-merchant versus traditional department store business and the increased efficiency per sq. foot being 10 - 50 times greater.

Harriet Coffin (Ground-work, Sausalito) How to grace-
fully put on a conference and not lose ones sanity entirely.

Paul Winter & David Darling (Paul Winter Consort, Conn.)
The experience of "Big Mind" (Zen term) in music.

Phillip Harvey (Population Services International, N.Y.C.)
The importance of population control in socio-economic
terms.

Carter Henderson (Princeton Center for Alternative
Futures, New Jersey) How a "mom & pop -think tank" can
generate right livelihood for the ex-speech writer for
the Chairman of I.B.M.

Norrie Huddle (Project America, Pennsylvania) The Sea-
brook anti-nuclear demonstration/internment; the purchase
of the Japanese whaling fleet for an international ecological peace corps and automatic/meditative writing of
a book.

Paul Hivoschinsky (Callanish Fund, Menlo Park) High risk
venture capital investing in new age technology and climbing Mount Everst.

Michael Maccoby (Institute for Policy Studies, Washington,
D.C.) Humanizing the work-place in worker-owned businesses.
Ibn Khaldun, a 14th century Islamic economist and his
involvement with right livelihood. How to have a #6 book
on the best seller list and a huge heart.

Eleanor McCallier (Earthworks, S.F.) The task of educating the consumer about food distribution and experiencing
right livelihood in so doing.

Michael Phillips (Briarpatch Consultant, S.F.) How reducing ones income, not only reducing ones consumption,
is part of simple living.

Mark Sarkady (Another Place, New Hampshire) A communal
conference center experimenting with a group right livelihood.

Bob Schwartz (Tarrytown Conference Center, New York)
The clown prince of entrepeneurship; a West Coast course
for new age entrepeneurs in the Fall.

306

Letters

Dear Rabbits,

Enclosed is a five-spot for a year's subscription. Also a little about what I've done and the directions I'm headed. It's my hope some of these ideas might strike a responsive chord with other rabbits, hopefully leading to an exchange of info and concepts.

For the past three years I've supported myself with my own landscaping, gardening, maintenance venture. I work organically and attempt to keep my fees below "industry" standards even though I work for the wealthy of Marin. My experience, beyond landscaping per se, includes: playgrounds, patios, stone and brick masonry, greywater systems, edible foods site plans, greenhouses and drip irrigation.

Tangent to this, but also inter-twined is my desire to grow more and more food and varieties of food; while exploring the most efficient (whole systems efficiencies), productive, and nutritious methods of gardening. The current state of my thinking involves two concents:

1. Perennial food crops lend themselves to high yields with the least impact on other systems - water, energy, and labor.

2. The most important task facing "agriculture", perhaps more aptly spoken of as horticulture or gardening, is to distribute the knowledge, skills, and means of home-based self-sufficient food production to all stratas of the social structure; whether it be urban, semi-urban or rural.

I wish to meet people interested in actualizing intensive/backyard perennial food production for the people with the greatest need, the poor and near poor. Maximum nutrition is bital to the health and well-being of the so called poorer folks of our culture. I have many thoughts on this subject, too many for a short letter, but wish to hear and meet people with new or different ideas along these lines. Contact me at 488-9017 or PO 236, Lagunitas, CA 94938.

Thanks,
Robert Kowik

ear Rabbits,
    Enclosed is a
check for one year's
subscription to the
Briarpatch Review.
Please send me the next
issue (or the current
issue).
    I read about you
briefly in the last
CQ (Co-evolution
Quarterly) issue. I
have heard "VS"*
referred to by many
names and i am inter-
ested in some of your
ideas.
    I'll pass along
this quote from an old
Paul Muni movie (The
Life of Emil Zola).
Paul Cezanne says this
to EZ when EZ has made
it big and is asking
PC to stay with him
in Paris. "The artist
must remain poor or
his art, like his
stomach, becomes fat
and stuffy." I am
certain that artist can
be translated into a
category of persons
not usually thought
of as artists. I am
a teacher and carpenter
and i keep my wages
down to a level that
reflects some sanity,
namely - my needs are
covered, i live simply
and i earn enough to
cover my expenses plus
something in the nest-
egg. Much of my "wealth"
is salvaged from the
trashman and recycled.

    Anyway, i am look-
ing forward to reading
your magazine.

*Voluntary simplicity

Thank you,
Serving the People,
Stephen Armstrong
24409 Neece
Torrance, CA. 90505

    We are getting
lots of letters from
Briars in Wisconsin,
Minnesotta and state
of Washington, who
would like to know if
there are other Briars
out there. We would also
appreciate articles from
any Briarpatch businesses,
especially outside of the
Bay Area.

    Editors

Dear Rabbits,
    Please put me on
your mailing list.
Read about you in CQ
(Co-evolution Quarter-
ly). Are there any
Briarpatch businesses
in Minnesotta??

Sincerely,
Bill Hagen
1317 Kenwood Ave.
Duluth, Minn. 55811

Dear People,
    Thank you for what
you are doing. I've fol-
lowed your progress for
several years, having
lived in the Bay Area
all my life. The free-
dom for our spirit and
the natural gifts of our
spirit to be fully ex-
pressed only happens
when we can align all
our endeavors with the
expression of this
freedom - including our
livelihood. Your efforts
in this area are right on.
    I have just returned
to America after a year
in the Findhorn Commu-
nity in Scotland. Com-
munity finances was my
major area of respon-
sibility. I feel I am
being asked to initiate
a Briarpatch network
in this area of So. east
Connecticut. I am also
interested in bringing
the philosophy and prac-
ticality of community
economics to the atten-
tion of anyone who will
listen. A primary goal
is to bring new vita-
lity into home econo-
mics (food production
and consumption, skills
exchange, technology in
the home, home as an
income-producing unit).
Can you help me with
any information or
contacts relevant to
these ideas?

Also, I would like
to know how to obtain a
copy of Michael Phillips'
The Seven Laws of Money.
    Thank you for any
help you can provide.

With Love & Good Wishes,
Bill Raap
29 Grimes Rd.
Old Greenwich, Conn. 06870

There will be a conference this fall for people who want to take a short breather to step back from their work, relax in a beautiful country setting, evaluate their work and careers, and come out with focus, energy and clarity to strengthen the practice of right livelihood in their lives.

THE NEXT BEGINNING: A Career Transitions Conference Focused on Right Livelihood will be held twice this fall, one weekend in October and one in November, at the Westerbeke Ranch in Sonoma County. Job Effectiveness Training, a right livelihood counseling and consulting agency started by members of the Black Bart Center, is organizing the conference. The program features counselors and consultants associated with the Briarpatch Network. For more information contact: Job Effectiveness Training, 1152 Sanchez, San Francisco, CA 94114; phone: 285-8112

Aryae Coopersmith

HOW TO START YOUR OWN SMALL BUSINESS

Bernard Karoroff, author of the book, "Small Time Operator: How to Start Your Own Small Business,' (Briarpatch Review, Fall, 1976, Spring, 1977) will be teaching a special one-day seminar on How to Start and Operate Your Own Small Business. The class will be given Saturday October 15 and Saturday November 26 in San Francisco, and Saturday January 21, in Davis.

The class will cover all aspects of small business including basics of getting started, types and forms of business, financing, permits and licensing, insurance, bookkeeping, hiring help, taxes and more. A full question-and-answer session will follow the class.

The San Francisco classes are sponsored by the Open Education Exchange. They will be held at the Holistic Life University, 1601 Tenth Avenue (corner of Tenth and Lawton). Class fee is $22. You may preregister with the Open Education Exchange, 6526 Telegraph Avenue, Oakland, Telephone (415) 655-6791. Or you may register the morning of the class, space permitting.

The Davis class is sponsored by University of California Extension and pre-registration is required. For full information, you should contact University Extension, Room 4445, Chemistry Addition, U.C. Davis Campus, Telephone (916) 752-0880.

<u>Alice Tepper Martin</u> (Council on Economic Priorities, N.Y.)
How ranking corporations on other than profit criteria
(i.e., pollution control, military contracts, affirmative
action) can bring about positive competition.

<u>Eric Utne</u> (<u>New Age</u> Magazine, Massachusetts) Raising money
through networking.

<u>Jean Boudreau</u> (Public Interest Communications Associates,
Ottawa, CAnada) Transfer of management to the workers in
a printing business.

PHEW! When it was all over, Brer Rabbit went back to his
burrow and didn't listen to anybody for three days!!